VISIT OUR WEBSITE:
www.drivei95.com
for more info and links
for I-95

INTERSTATE

Drive I-95

Exit by Exit Info, Maps, History and Trivia

by Stan Posner and Sandra Phillips-Posner

You can buy more copies of Drive I-95 at:

 Chain and independant book stores in the US and Canada
by Title, Author or by number: ISBN 1-894979-81-8

 Our web site www.drivei95.com – credit cards accepted

 Toll free 888-GUIDE95 (888-484-3395) – credit cards accepted

 Internet book stores

 Mail order coupon on the last page of this book – credit cards accepted

---

Please feel free to contact us at:

TRAVELSMART
P.O. Box 3, Roxboro, Quebec, Canada H8Y 3E8
info@drivei95.com • ☎ 514-684-4020 • Fax: 514-684-6938

2nd EDITION 2004
Copyright © 2004 by Stan Posner and Sandra Phillips-Posner

QUANTITY DISCOUNTS AVAILABLE FOR FUND-RAISING AND VOLUME PURCHASES

Copyright First Printing 2003
Second Printing 2004
Third Printing (2nd Edition) 2004

Cataloguing in Publication Data
Posner, Stan, 1947-
Drive I-95 : exit by exit info, maps, history, and trivia / Stan Posner, Sandra Phillips-Posner.
(Interstate drive series)
ISBN 1-894979-78-8
1. Interstate 95—Guidebooks.
2. Automobile travel—Atlantic States—Guidebooks.
3. Atlantic States—Guidebooks.
I. Phillips-Posner, Sandra, 1949-   II. Title. III. Series.
F106.P68 2003   917.504'44   C2003-903712-6

Cover Design by David Leblanc, Studio Oneonone
Maps designed by Albert Albala Infographie (spin@colba.net) and drawn by Albert Albala and a team consisting of: Stan Posner, Brandon Posner, Natalie Joseph, Julie Howick, Georgette Haddad and Khalil Atiyeh
Cover Photos: Alexandria, Virginia; Stan Posner; Daytona Beach, Florida
Photos taken by Stan Posner, Sandra Phillips-Posner and, as noted, provided by: Abingdon Manor (W. Benton Henry), Ava Gardner Museum, Elk Forge B & B, Open Gates B & B, Six Flags, Simply ___ B & B, The Garden Kitchen
___ **hy** by Josiane Trépanier, Compographe
___ and **Photo Editing** by Brandon Posner

Table of Contents

This book is dedicated to Dave Hunter, best-selling author of *Along Interstate I-75, Local Knowledge and Insider Information*. Dave was most generous, never refusing to give of his vast knowledge and experience with travel guides. It is rare in this world to come across such a giving person whose only goal was to make others as successful as he is and to revel in their success. Dave, we thank you.

Hi fellow travelers,

We were overwhelmed by the excitement generated by the first edition of this book. Each time someone looked at it, they said the same four words, "I need that book!".

The guidebook was written with the hope that everyone can be comfortable and secure enough to get on the road. If you know ahead of time what exits are coming up, how far it is till you find the food you're in the mood for, or where you can stop when you're tired, you can travel stress-free and enjoy your trip.

Each Fall when the new edition comes out, we add more stories and useful features. This year we were saddened to see so many gas station bays unfortunately turning into mini marts, so we made sure to stop at every real live mechanic we found and created a chart of auto repair shops for you.

We salute those independent types who still manage to run their own motels or restaurants. There is a new listing of all the unaffiliated motels if you prefer their hominess to more cookie-cutter chains. For instance, at the Simply Divine B & B, the hostess is as charming as the Inn, and she even irons the sheets each day!

Of the 130 new stories we've added, we came across everything from a free National Park with the Oxon Hill Zoo to the USS Nautilus, the first nuclear powered submersible which you can board, or the Tobacco Life Museum, a quaint slice of old America. Long-lasting local eateries, where everyone knows your name, can make your trip so much more enjoyable. Nick's Luncheonette in CT or Summerton Diner in SC fit the bill, and we liked the food so much we've talked them into sharing one of their recipes.

A new trend we discovered are amusement arcades in MA, Fredricksburg VA and Florence SC. These tempt youngsters and oldsters to get out, stretch, and play pinball machines, go on go-karts, bumper boats, play miniature golf, bat in cages or even climb up walls.

So much of the history of the United States happened on I-95: John Wilkes Booth ran from the law after shooting Abraham Lincoln, "Yankee Doodle Dandy" was created on it, slaves escaped along the Underground Railroad on I-95 and Washington rode in triumph after being elected.

We've added amusing trivia, including: the last four Presidents went to Yale, how cranberry sauce was invented, and what the color of George Washington's hair and eyes were.

Try to walk around one of the small towns. We've drawn a few little maps for you. This time, perhaps try Northeast MD, with gift shops, antiques and a tea parlor for a lovely snack.

Hopefully some of these hors d'oeuvres will entice you to not only read the stories for enjoyment but to get out and discover someplace new.

Let us be your tour guides to the I-95,

Stan   Sandra

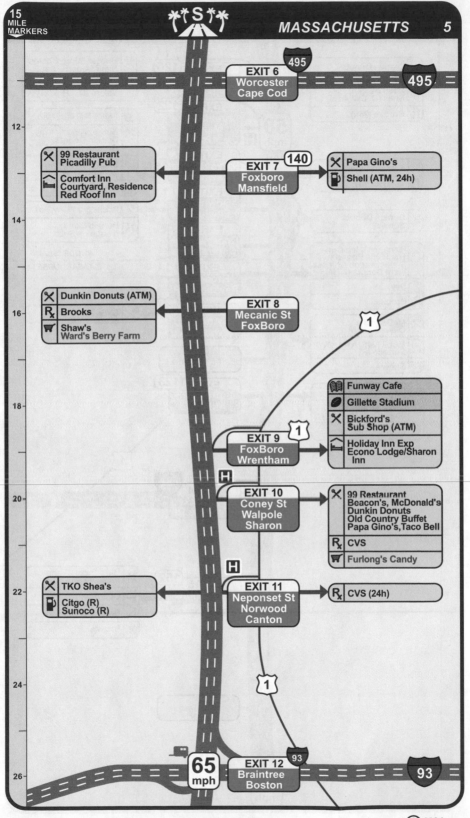

EXIT 6 495
Worcester
Cape Cod

495

99 Restaurant
Picadilly Pub

Comfort Inn
Courtyard, Residence
Red Roof Inn

EXIT 7 140
Foxboro
Mansfield

Papa Gino's

Shell (ATM, 24h)

Dunkin Donuts (ATM)

Brooks

Shaw's
Ward's Berry Farm

EXIT 8
Mecanic St
FoxBoro

1

Funway Cafe

Gillette Stadium

Bickford's
Sub Shop (ATM)

Holiday Inn Exp
Econo Lodge/Sharon
Inn

EXIT 9 1
FoxBoro
Wrentham

H

EXIT 10
Coney St
Walpole
Sharon

99 Restaurant
Beacon's, McDonald's
Dunkin Donuts
Old Country Buffet
Papa Gino's, Taco Bell

CVS

Furlong's Candy

H

TKO Shea's

Citgo (R)
Sunoco (R)

EXIT 11
Neponset St
Norwood
Canton

CVS (24h)

1

65 mph

EXIT 12 93
Braintree
Boston

93

© 2004

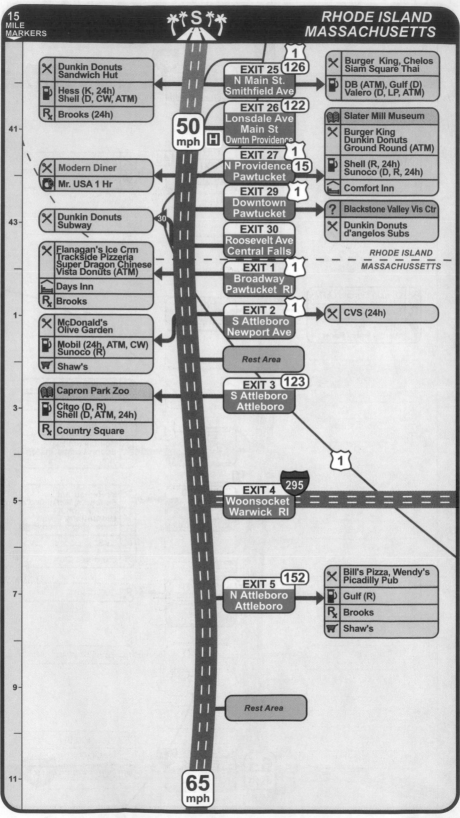

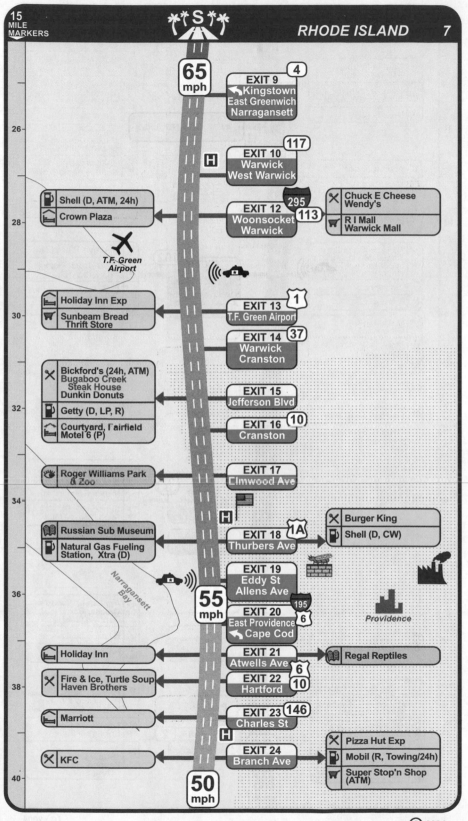

S

65 mph

EXIT 9 [4]
↖ Kingstown
East Greenwich
Narragansett

26

EXIT 10 [117]
H Warwick
West Warwick

⛽ Shell (D, ATM, 24h)
🏨 Crown Plaza

EXIT 12 [295] [113]
Woonsocket
Warwick

✕ Chuck E Cheese
Wendy's
🛒 R I Mall
Warwick Mall

28

✈ T.F. Green Airport

🏨 Holiday Inn Exp
🛒 Sunbeam Bread
Thrift Store

EXIT 13 [1]
T.F. Green Airport

30

EXIT 14 [37]
Warwick
Cranston

✕ Bickford's (24h, ATM)
Bugaboo Creek
Steak House
Dunkin Donuts

EXIT 15
Jefferson Blvd

⛽ Getty (D, LP, R)

EXIT 16 [10]
Cranston

🏨 Courtyard, Fairfield
Motel 6 (P)

32

👐 Roger Williams Park
& Zoo

EXIT 17
Elmwood Ave

34

H

📖 Russian Sub Museum
⛽ Natural Gas Fueling
Station, Xtra (D)

EXIT 18 [1A]
Thurbers Ave

✕ Burger King
⛽ Shell (D, CW)

EXIT 19
Eddy St
Allens Ave

Narragansett Bay

55 mph

36

EXIT 20 [195] [6]
East Providence
↖ Cape Cod

Providence

🏨 Holiday Inn

EXIT 21
Atwells Ave

📖 Regal Reptiles

✕ Fire & Ice, Turtle Soup
Haven Brothers

EXIT 22 [6] [10]
Hartford

38

🏨 Marriott

EXIT 23 [146]
Charles St

H

✕ KFC

EXIT 24
Branch Ave

✕ Pizza Hut Exp
⛽ Mobil (R, Towing/24h)
🛒 Super Stop'n Shop
(ATM)

40

50 mph

© 2004

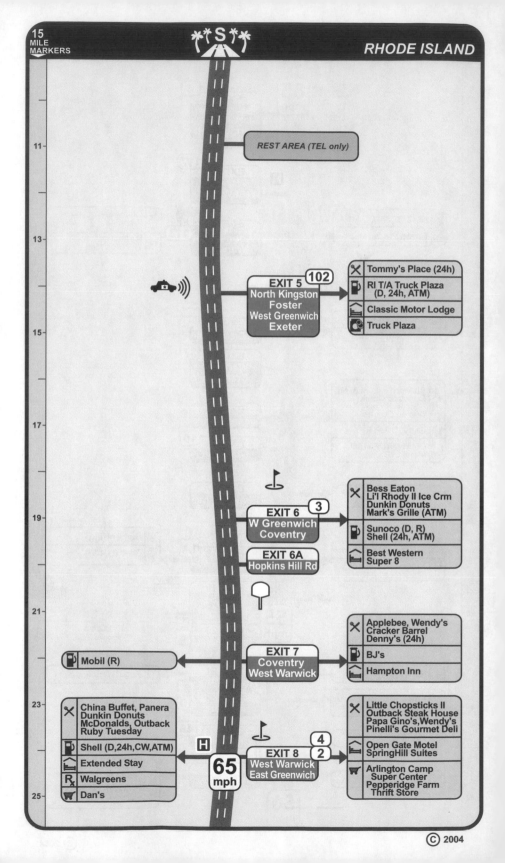

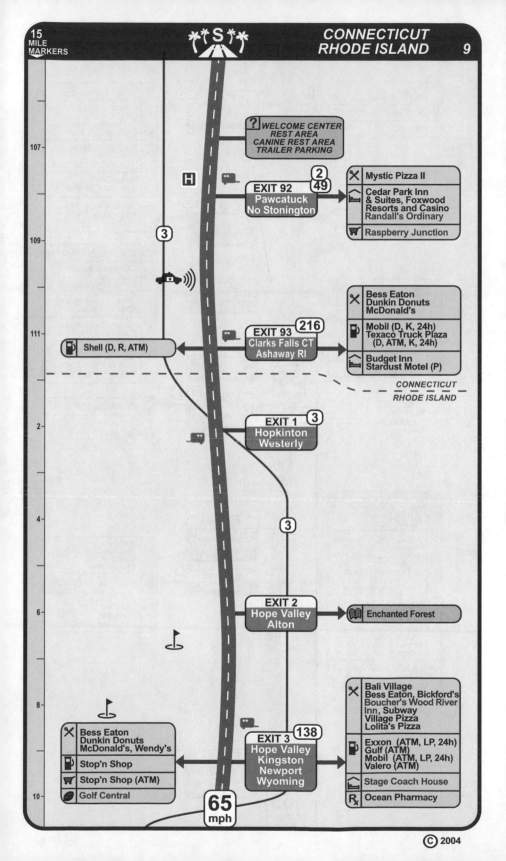

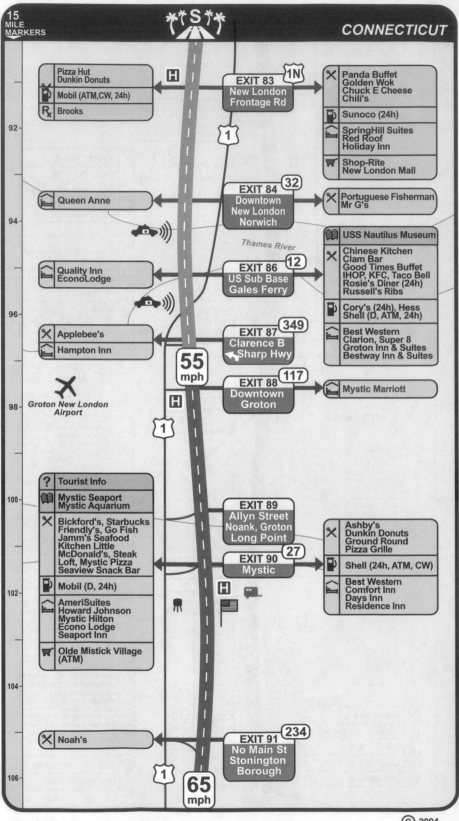

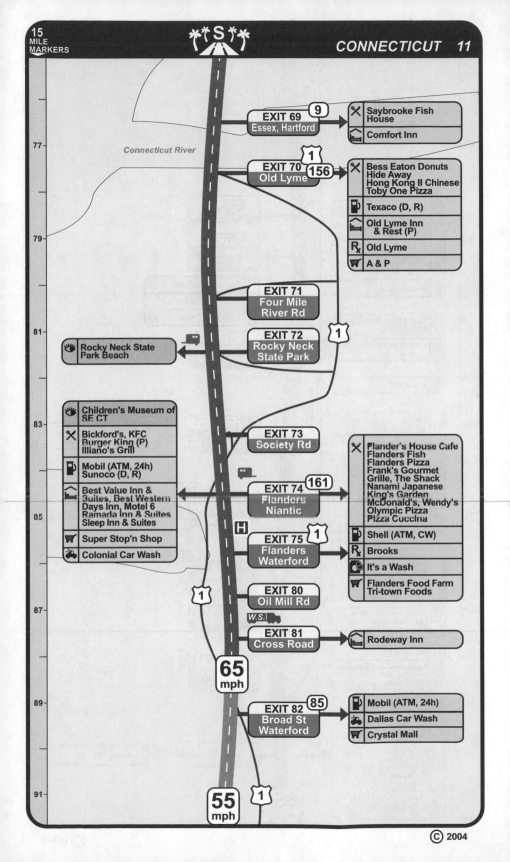

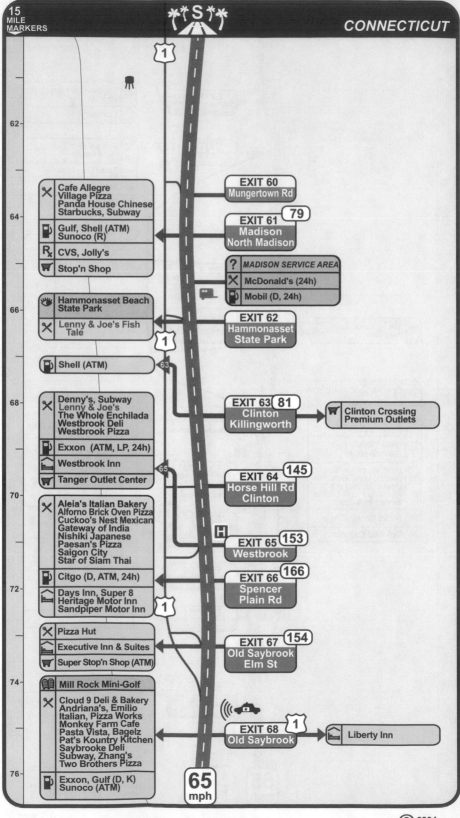

15 MILE MARKERS

CONNECTICUT

1

62

64
- ✕ Cafe Allegre
  Village Pizza
  Panda House Chinese
  Starbucks, Subway
- ⛽ Gulf, Shell (ATM)
  Sunoco (R)
- ℞ CVS, Jolly's
- 🛒 Stop'n Shop

EXIT 60
Mungertown Rd

EXIT 61 [79]
Madison
North Madison

MADISON SERVICE AREA
- ?
- ✕ McDonald's (24h)
- ⛽ Mobil (D, 24h)

66
- 🌳 Hammonasset Beach
  State Park
- ✕ Lenny & Joe's Fish
  Tale

EXIT 62
Hammonasset
State Park

1

- ⛽ Shell (ATM) 63

68
- ✕ Denny's, Subway
  Lenny & Joe's
  The Whole Enchilada
  Westbrook Deli
  Westbrook Pizza
- ⛽ Exxon (ATM, LP, 24h)
- 🛏 Westbrook Inn
- 🛒 Tanger Outlet Center

EXIT 63 [81]
Clinton
Killingworth

🛒 Clinton Crossing
Premium Outlets

65

70
- ✕ Aleia's Italian Bakery
  Alforno Brick Oven Pizza
  Cuckoo's Nest Mexican
  Gateway of India
  Nishiki Japanese
  Paesan's Pizza
  Saigon City
  Star of Siam Thai

EXIT 64 [145]
Horse Hill Rd
Clinton

H
EXIT 65 [153]
Westbrook

- ⛽ Citgo (D, ATM, 24h)

EXIT 66 [166]
Spencer
Plain Rd

72
- 🛏 Days Inn, Super 8
  Heritage Motor Inn
  Sandpiper Motor Inn

1

- ✕ Pizza Hut
- 🛏 Executive Inn & Suites
- 🛒 Super Stop'n Shop (ATM)

EXIT 67 [154]
Old Saybrook
Elm St

74
- 📖 Mill Rock Mini-Golf
- ✕ Cloud 9 Deli & Bakery
  Andriana's, Emilio
  Italian, Pizza Works
  Monkey Farm Cafe
  Pasta Vista, Bagelz
  Pat's Kountry Kitchen
  Saybrooke Deli
  Subway, Zhang's
  Two Brothers Pizza

EXIT 68 [1]
Old Saybrook

🛏 Liberty Inn

76
- ⛽ Exxon, Gulf (D, K)
  Sunoco (ATM)

65
mph

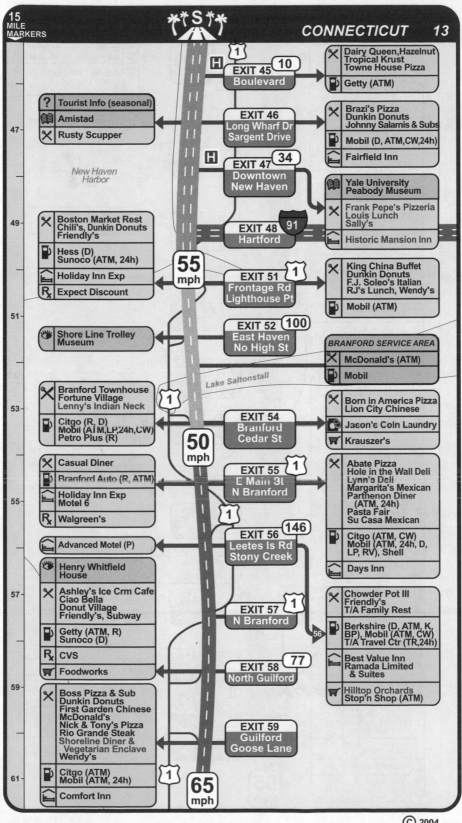

EXIT 45 (1) 10 — Boulevard
- ✕ Dairy Queen, Hazelnut Tropical Krust, Towne House Pizza
- ⛽ Getty (ATM)

EXIT 46 — Long Wharf Dr / Sargent Drive
- ? Tourist Info (seasonal)
- 📖 Amistad
- ✕ Rusty Scupper
- ✕ Brazi's Pizza, Dunkin Donuts, Johnny Salamis & Subs
- ⛽ Mobil (D, ATM, CW, 24h)
- 🏨 Fairfield Inn

New Haven Harbor

EXIT 47 (34) — Downtown New Haven
- 📖 Yale University Peabody Museum
- ✕ Frank Pepe's Pizzeria, Louis Lunch, Sally's

EXIT 48 (91) — Hartford
- 🏨 Historic Mansion Inn

- ✕ Boston Market Rest, Chili's, Dunkin Donuts, Friendly's
- ⛽ Hess (D), Sunoco (ATM, 24h)
- 🏨 Holiday Inn Exp
- ℞ Expect Discount

55 mph

EXIT 51 (1) — Frontage Rd / Lighthouse Pt
- ✕ King China Buffet, Dunkin Donuts, F.J. Soleo's Italian, RJ's Lunch, Wendy's
- ⛽ Mobil (ATM)

EXIT 52 (100) — East Haven / No High St
- 👋 Shore Line Trolley Museum

BRANFORD SERVICE AREA
- ✕ McDonald's (ATM)
- ⛽ Mobil

Lake Saltonstall

- ✕ Branford Townhouse, Fortune Village, Lenny's Indian Neck
- ⛽ Citgo (R, D), Mobil (ATM, LP, 24h, CW), Petro Plus (R)

EXIT 54 — Branford / Cedar St
- ✕ Born in America Pizza, Lion City Chinese
- 🧺 Jason's Coin Laundry
- 🛒 Krauszer's

50 mph

EXIT 55 (1) — E Main St / N Branford
- ✕ Casual Diner
- ⛽ Branford Auto (R, ATM)
- 🏨 Holiday Inn Exp, Motel 6
- ℞ Walgreen's
- ✕ Abate Pizza, Hole in the Wall Deli, Lynn's Deli, Margarita's Mexican, Parthenon Diner (ATM, 24h), Pasta Fair, Su Casa Mexican
- ⛽ Citgo (ATM, CW), Mobil (ATM, 24h, D, LP, RV), Shell
- 🏨 Days Inn

EXIT 56 (146) — Leetes Is Rd / Stony Creek
- 🏨 Advanced Motel (P)

EXIT 57 (1) — N Branford
- 👋 Henry Whitfield House
- ✕ Ashley's Ice Crm Cafe, Ciao Bella, Donut Village, Friendly's, Subway
- ⛽ Getty (ATM, R), Sunoco (D)
- ℞ CVS
- 🛒 Foodworks
- ✕ Chowder Pot III, Friendly's, T/A Family Rest
- ⛽ Berkshire (D, ATM, K, BP), Mobil (ATM, CW), T/A Travel Ctr (TR, 24h) — 56

EXIT 58 (77) — North Guilford
- ✕ Boss Pizza & Sub, Dunkin Donuts, First Garden Chinese, McDonald's, Nick & Tony's Pizza, Rio Grande Steak, Shoreline Diner & Vegetarian Enclave, Wendy's
- 🏨 Best Value Inn, Ramada Limited & Suites
- 🛒 Hilltop Orchards, Stop'n Shop (ATM)

EXIT 59 — Guilford / Goose Lane
- ⛽ Citgo (ATM), Mobil (ATM, 24h)
- 🏨 Comfort Inn

65 mph

© 2004

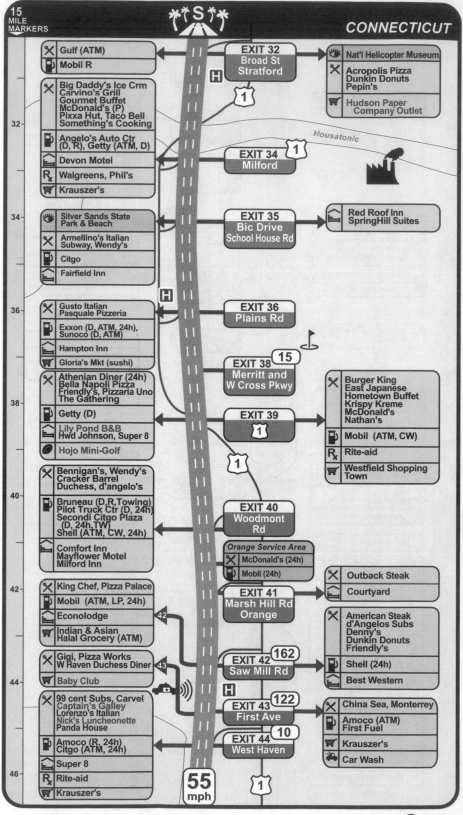

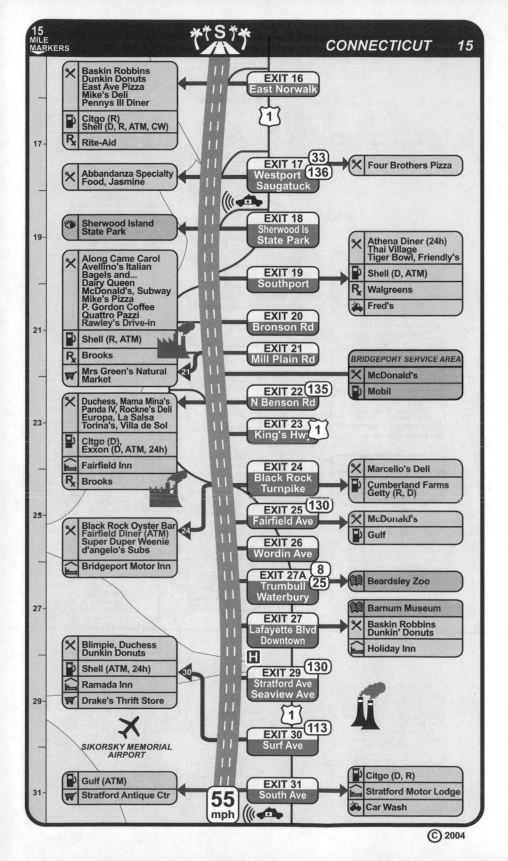

EXIT 16
East Norwalk
1

- ✕ Baskin Robbins
  Dunkin Donuts
  East Ave Pizza
  Mike's Deli
  Pennys III Diner
- ⛽ Citgo (R)
  Shell (D, R, ATM, CW)
- ℞ Rite-Aid

17

EXIT 17 33 136
Westport
Saugatuck

✕ Four Brothers Pizza

- ✕ Abbandanza Specialty
  Food, Jasmine

EXIT 18
Sherwood Is
State Park

- ✋ Sherwood Island
  State Park

19

- ✕ Athena Diner (24h)
  Thai Village
  Tiger Bowl, Friendly's
- ⛽ Shell (D, ATM)
- ℞ Walgreens
- 🚗 Fred's

EXIT 19
Southport

- ✕ Along Came Carol
  Avellino's Italian
  Bagels and...
  Dairy Queen
  McDonald's, Subway
  Mike's Pizza
  P. Gordon Coffee
  Quattro Pazzi
  Rawley's Drive-in

EXIT 20
Bronson Rd

21

- ⛽ Shell (R, ATM)
- ℞ Brooks

EXIT 21
Mill Plain Rd

- 🛒 Mrs Green's Natural
  Market

21

BRIDGEPORT SERVICE AREA

- ✕ McDonald's
- ⛽ Mobil

EXIT 22 135
N Benson Rd

- ✕ Duchess, Mama Mina's
  Panda IV, Rockne's Deli
  Europa, La Salsa
  Torina's, Villa de Sol

23

EXIT 23
King's Hwy 1

- ⛽ Citgo (D),
  Exxon (D, ATM, 24h)
- 🛏 Fairfield Inn
- ℞ Brooks

EXIT 24
Black Rock
Turnpike

- ✕ Marcello's Deli
- ⛽ Cumberland Farms
  Getty (R, D)

EXIT 25 130
Fairfield Ave

- ✕ McDonald's
- ⛽ Gulf

25

- ✕ Black Rock Oyster Bar
  Fairfield Diner (ATM)
  Super Duper Weenie
  d'angelo's Subs

24

- 🛏 Bridgeport Motor Inn

EXIT 26
Wordin Ave

EXIT 27A 8 25
Trumbull
Waterbury

- 📖 Beardsley Zoo

27

EXIT 27
Lafayette Blvd
Downtown

- 📖 Barnum Museum
- ✕ Baskin Robbins
  Dunkin' Donuts
- 🛏 Holiday Inn

- ✕ Blimpie, Duchess
  Dunkin Donuts
- ⛽ Shell (ATM, 24h)
- 🛏 Ramada Inn
- 🛒 Drake's Thrift Store

30

H
EXIT 29 130
Stratford Ave
Seaview Ave

1

29

✈ SIKORSKY MEMORIAL
AIRPORT

EXIT 30 113
Surf Ave

- ⛽ Gulf (ATM)
- 🛒 Stratford Antique Ctr

31

55
mph

EXIT 31
South Ave

- ⛽ Citgo (D, R)
- 🛏 Stratford Motor Lodge
- 🚗 Car Wash

© 2004

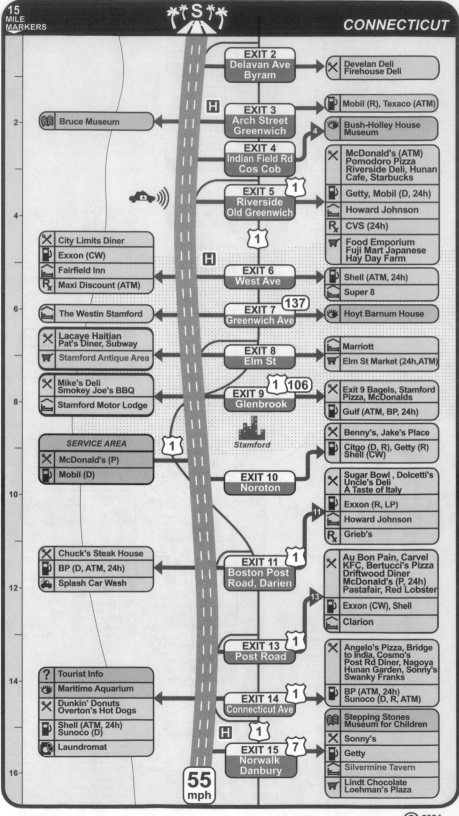

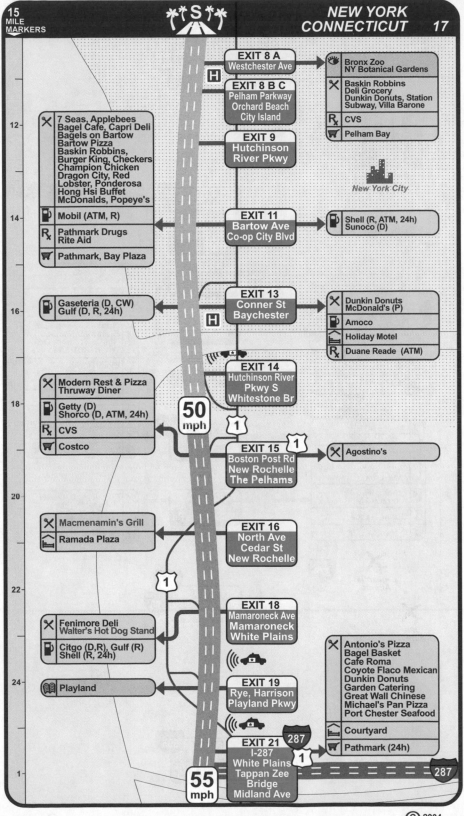

EXIT 8 A
Westchester Ave

H

Bronx Zoo
NY Botanical Gardens

Baskin Robbins
Deli Grocery
Dunkin Donuts, Station
Subway, Villa Barone

CVS

Pelham Bay

EXIT 8 B C
Pelham Parkway
Orchard Beach
City Island

7 Seas, Applebees
Bagel Cafe, Capri Deli
Bagels on Bartow
Bartow Pizza
Baskin Robbins,
Burger King, Checkers
Champion Chicken
Dragon City, Red
Lobster, Ponderosa
Hong Hsi Buffet
McDonalds, Popeye's

EXIT 9
Hutchinson
River Pkwy

New York City

Mobil (ATM, R)

Pathmark Drugs
Rite Aid

Pathmark, Bay Plaza

EXIT 11
Bartow Ave
Co-op City Blvd

Shell (R, ATM, 24h)
Sunoco (D)

Gaseteria (D, CW)
Gulf (D, R, 24h)

EXIT 13
Conner St
Baychester

H

Dunkin Donuts
McDonald's (P)

Amoco

Holiday Motel

Duane Reade (ATM)

EXIT 14
Hutchinson River
Pkwy S
Whitestone Br

Modern Rest & Pizza
Thruway Diner

Getty (D)
Shorco (D, ATM, 24h)

CVS

Costco

50 mph

1

EXIT 15
Boston Post Rd
New Rochelle
The Pelhams

1

Agostino's

Macmenamin's Grill

Ramada Plaza

EXIT 16
North Ave
Cedar St
New Rochelle

1

EXIT 18
Mamaroneck Ave
Mamaroneck
White Plains

Fenimore Deli
Walter's Hot Dog Stand

Citgo (D,R), Gulf (R)
Shell (R, 24h)

Antonio's Pizza
Bagel Basket
Cafe Roma
Coyote Flaco Mexican
Dunkin Donuts
Garden Catering
Great Wall Chinese
Michael's Pan Pizza
Port Chester Seafood

Playland

EXIT 19
Rye, Harrison
Playland Pkwy

Courtyard

Pathmark (24h)

EXIT 21
I-287
White Plains
Tappan Zee
Bridge
Midland Ave

287

1

287

55 mph

© 2004

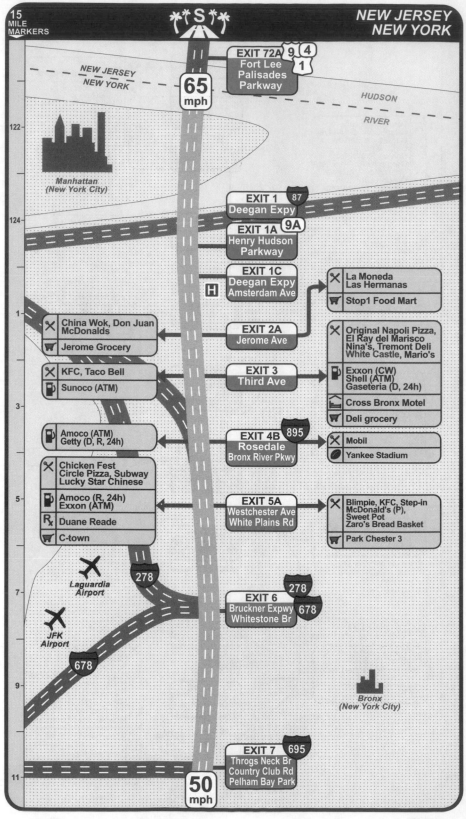

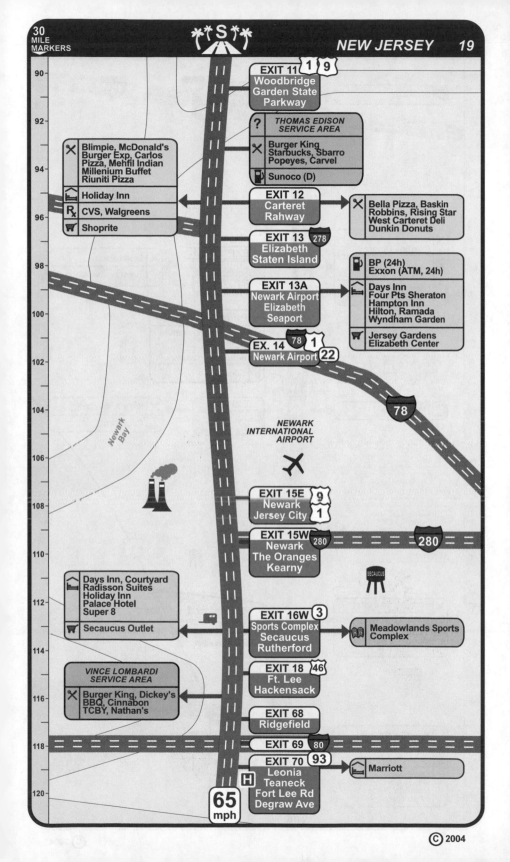

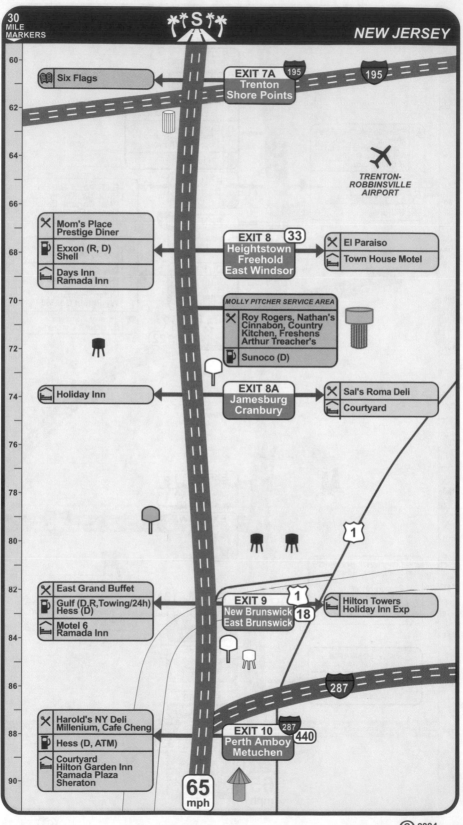

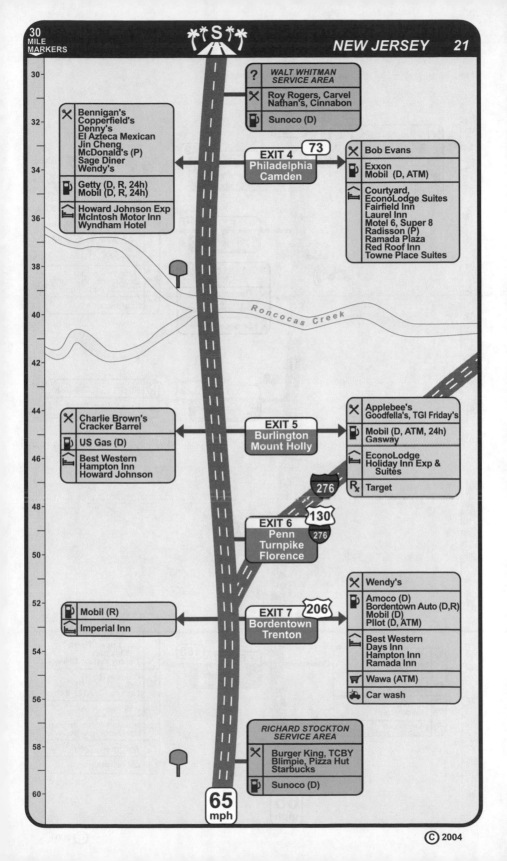

WALT WHITMAN SERVICE AREA
- ?
- Roy Rogers, Carvel Nathan's, Cinnabon
- Sunoco (D)

Bennigan's
Copperfield's
Denny's
El Azteca Mexican
Jin Cheng
McDonald's (P)
Sage Diner
Wendy's

Getty (D, R, 24h)
Mobil (D, R, 24h)

Howard Johnson Exp
McIntosh Motor Inn
Wyndham Hotel

EXIT 4 73
Philadelphia
Camden

Bob Evans

Exxon
Mobil (D, ATM)

Courtyard,
EconoLodge Suites
Fairfield Inn
Laurel Inn
Motel 6, Super 8
Radisson (P)
Ramada Plaza
Red Roof Inn
Towne Place Suites

Roncocas Creek

Charlie Brown's
Cracker Barrel

US Gas (D)

Best Western
Hampton Inn
Howard Johnson

EXIT 5
Burlington
Mount Holly

Applebee's
Goodfella's, TGI Friday's

Mobil (D, ATM, 24h)
Gasway

EconoLodge
Holiday Inn Exp &
Suites

276

Rx Target

EXIT 6 130
Penn
Turnpike
Florence

276

Mobil (R)
Imperial Inn

EXIT 7 206
Bordentown
Trenton

Wendy's

Amoco (D)
Bordentown Auto (D,R)
Mobil (D)
Pilot (D, ATM)

Best Western
Days Inn
Hampton Inn
Ramada Inn

Wawa (ATM)

Car wash

RICHARD STOCKTON SERVICE AREA
- Burger King, TCBY Blimpie, Pizza Hut Starbucks
- Sunoco (D)

65 mph

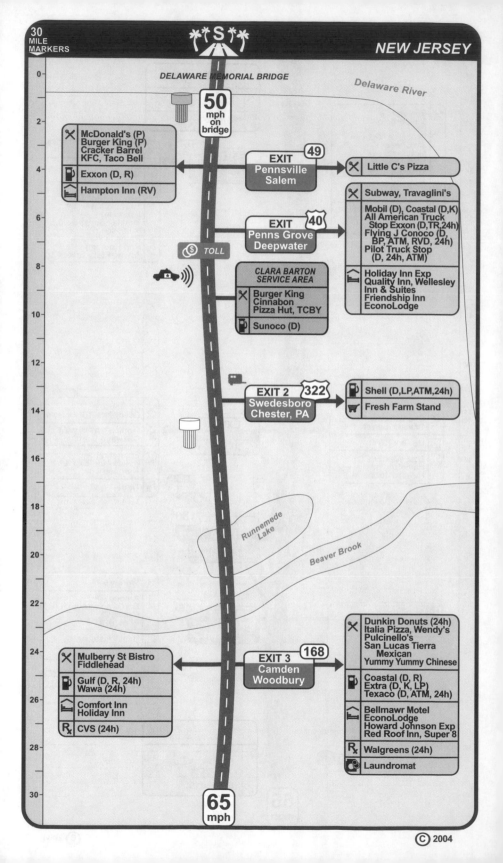

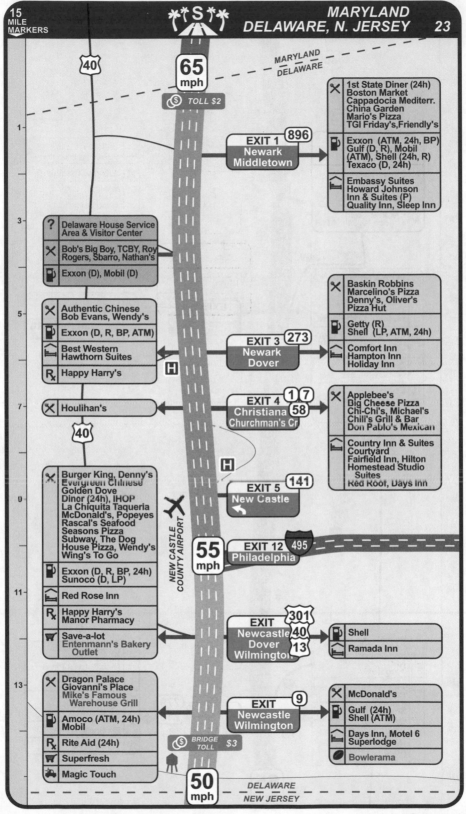

40

65 mph

💲 **TOLL $2**

MARYLAND
DELAWARE

EXIT 1 (896)
Newark
Middletown

✕	1st State Diner (24h) Boston Market Cappadocia Mediterr. China Garden Mario's Pizza TGI Friday's, Friendly's
⛽	Exxon (ATM, 24h, BP) Gulf (D, R), Mobil (ATM), Shell (24h, R) Texaco (D, 24h)
🏨	Embassy Suites Howard Johnson Inn & Suites (P) Quality Inn, Sleep Inn

?	Delaware House Service Area & Visitor Center
✕	Bob's Big Boy, TCBY, Roy Rogers, Sbarro, Nathan's
⛽	Exxon (D), Mobil (D)

✕	Authentic Chinese Bob Evans, Wendy's
⛽	Exxon (D, R, BP, ATM)
🏨	Best Western Hawthorn Suites
℞	Happy Harry's

H

EXIT 3 (273)
Newark
Dover

✕	Baskin Robbins Marcelino's Pizza Denny's, Oliver's Pizza Hut
⛽	Getty (R) Shell (LP, ATM, 24h)
🏨	Comfort Inn Hampton Inn Holiday Inn

✕	Houlihan's

40

EXIT 4 (1)(7)(58)
Christiana
Churchman's Cr

H

✕	Applebee's Big Cheese Pizza Chi-Chi's, Michael's Chili's Grill & Bar Don Pablo's Mexican
🏨	Country Inn & Suites Courtyard Fairfield Inn, Hilton Homestead Studio Suites Red Roof, Days Inn

✕	Burger King, Denny's Evergreen Chinese Golden Dove Diner (24h), IHOP La Chiquita Taqueria McDonald's, Popeyes Rascal's Seafood Seasons Pizza Subway, The Dog House Pizza, Wendy's Wing's To Go
⛽	Exxon (D, R, BP, 24h) Sunoco (D, LP)
🏨	Red Rose Inn
℞	Happy Harry's Manor Pharmacy
🛒	Save-a-lot Entenmann's Bakery Outlet

EXIT 5 (141)
New Castle

✈ **NEW CASTLE COUNTY AIRPORT**

55 mph

EXIT 12 (495)
Philadelphia

EXIT
Newcastle
Dover
Wilmington **(301)(40)(13)**

⛽	Shell
🏨	Ramada Inn

✕	Dragon Palace Giovanni's Place Mike's Famous Warehouse Grill
⛽	Amoco (ATM, 24h) Mobil
℞	Rite Aid (24h)
🛒	Superfresh
🚜	Magic Touch

EXIT (9)
Newcastle
Wilmington

💲 **BRIDGE TOLL $3**

✕	McDonald's
⛽	Gulf (24h) Shell (ATM)
🏨	Days Inn, Motel 6 Superlodge
🎳	Bowlerama

50 mph

DELAWARE
NEW JERSEY

© 2004

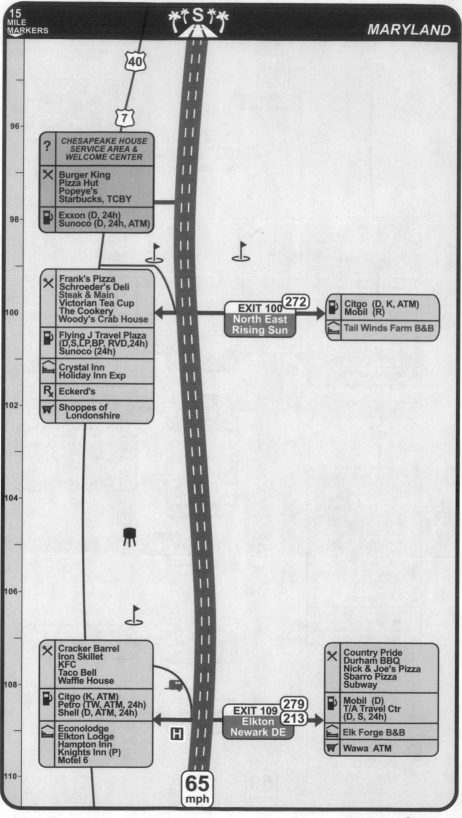

15 MILE MARKERS

MARYLAND

S

40

7

96

? CHESAPEAKE HOUSE SERVICE AREA & WELCOME CENTER

✕ Burger King
Pizza Hut
Popeye's
Starbucks, TCBY

⛽ Exxon (D, 24h)
Sunoco (D, 24h, ATM)

98

✕ Frank's Pizza
Schroeder's Deli
Steak & Main
Victorian Tea Cup
The Cookery
Woody's Crab House

EXIT 100 272
**North East
Rising Sun**

⛽ Citgo (D, K, ATM)
Mobil (R)

🛏 Tail Winds Farm B&B

100

⛽ Flying J Travel Plaza
(D,S,LP,BP, RVD,24h)
Sunoco (24h)

🛏 Crystal Inn
Holiday Inn Exp

℞ Eckerd's

🛒 Shoppes of
Londonshire

102

104

106

✕ Cracker Barrel
Iron Skillet
KFC
Taco Bell
Waffle House

✕ Country Pride
Durham BBQ
Nick & Joe's Pizza
Sbarro Pizza
Subway

108

⛽ Citgo (K, ATM)
Petro (TW, ATM, 24h)
Shell (D, ATM, 24h)

EXIT 109 279
213
**Elkton
Newark DE**

⛽ Mobil (D)
T/A Travel Ctr
(D, S, 24h)

🛏 Econolodge
Elkton Lodge
Hampton Inn
Knights Inn (P)
Motel 6

H

🛏 Elk Forge B&B

🛒 Wawa ATM

110

65 mph

© 2004

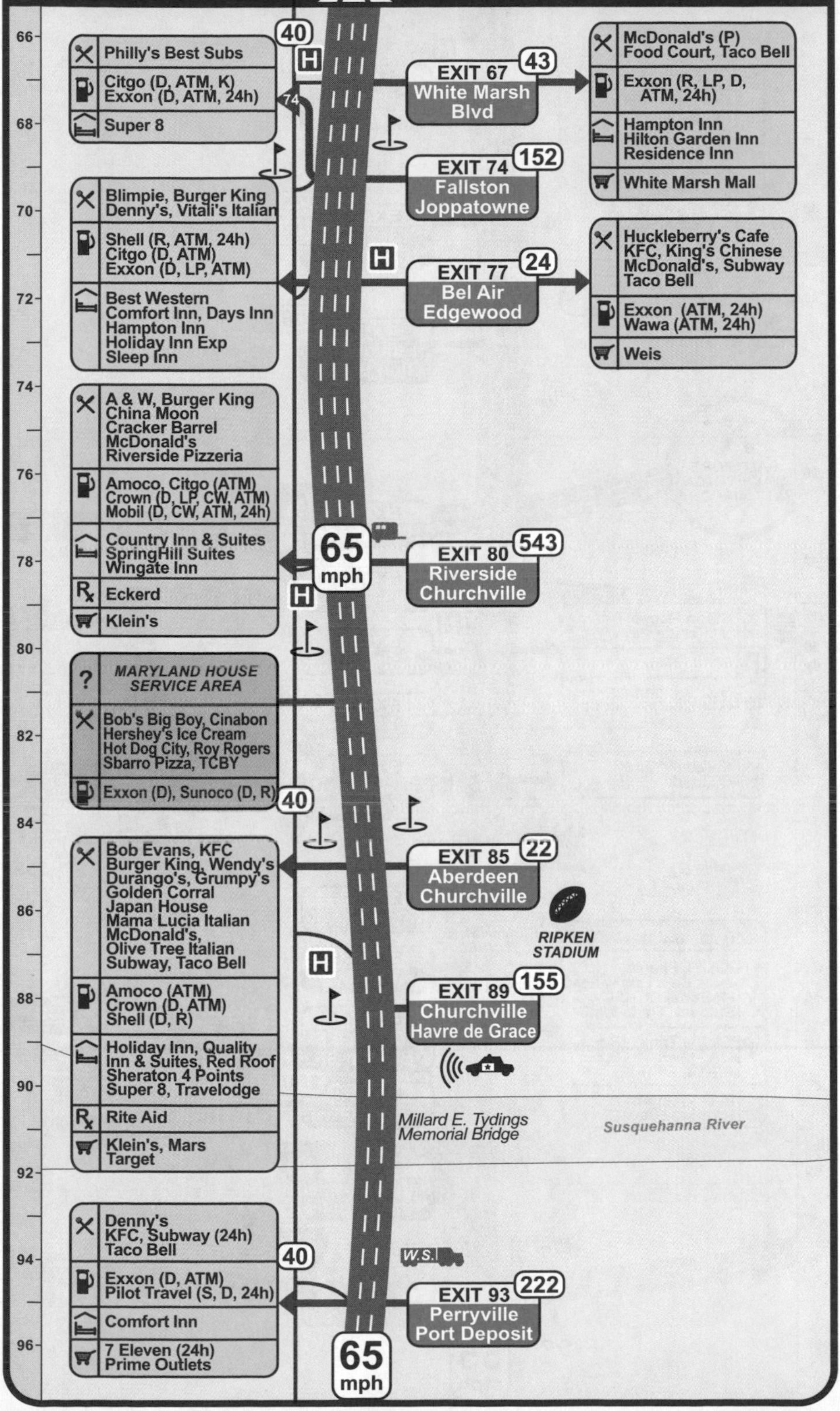

Mile		
66		
68		
70		
72		
74		
76		
78		
80		
82		
84		
86		
88		
90		
92		
94		
96		

S

40
H
74

Left side (West)

Philly's Best Subs
Citgo (D, ATM, K)
Exxon (D, ATM, 24h)
Super 8

Blimpie, Burger King
Denny's, Vitali's Italian
Shell (R, ATM, 24h)
Citgo (D, ATM)
Exxon (D, LP, ATM)
Best Western
Comfort Inn, Days Inn
Hampton Inn
Holiday Inn Exp
Sleep Inn

A & W, Burger King
China Moon
Cracker Barrel
McDonald's
Riverside Pizzeria
Amoco, Citgo (ATM)
Crown (D, LP, CW, ATM)
Mobil (D, CW, ATM, 24h)
Country Inn & Suites
SpringHill Suites
Wingate Inn
Rₓ Eckerd
Klein's

? MARYLAND HOUSE SERVICE AREA
Bob's Big Boy, Cinabon
Hershey's Ice Cream
Hot Dog City, Roy Rogers
Sbarro Pizza, TCBY
Exxon (D), Sunoco (D, R) **40**

Bob Evans, KFC
Burger King, Wendy's
Durango's, Grumpy's
Golden Corral
Japan House
Mama Lucia Italian
McDonald's,
Olive Tree Italian
Subway, Taco Bell
Amoco (ATM)
Crown (D, ATM)
Shell (D, R)
Holiday Inn, Quality
Inn & Suites, Red Roof
Sheraton 4 Points
Super 8, Travelodge
Rₓ Rite Aid
Klein's, Mars
Target

Denny's
KFC, Subway (24h)
Taco Bell
Exxon (D, ATM)
Pilot Travel (S, D, 24h)
Comfort Inn
7 Eleven (24h)
Prime Outlets

Exits (center/right)

EXIT 67 (43)
White Marsh Blvd

EXIT 74 (152)
Fallston
Joppatowne

H

EXIT 77 (24)
Bel Air
Edgewood

65 mph
H

EXIT 80 (543)
Riverside
Churchville

40

EXIT 85 (22)
Aberdeen
Churchville

RIPKEN STADIUM

H

EXIT 89 (155)
Churchville
Havre de Grace

Millard E. Tydings Memorial Bridge

Susquehanna River

W.S.

EXIT 93 (222)
Perryville
Port Deposit

65 mph

Right side (East)

McDonald's (P)
Food Court, Taco Bell
Exxon (R, LP, D, ATM, 24h)
Hampton Inn
Hilton Garden Inn
Residence Inn
White Marsh Mall

Huckleberry's Cafe
KFC, King's Chinese
McDonald's, Subway
Taco Bell
Exxon (ATM, 24h)
Wawa (ATM, 24h)
Weis

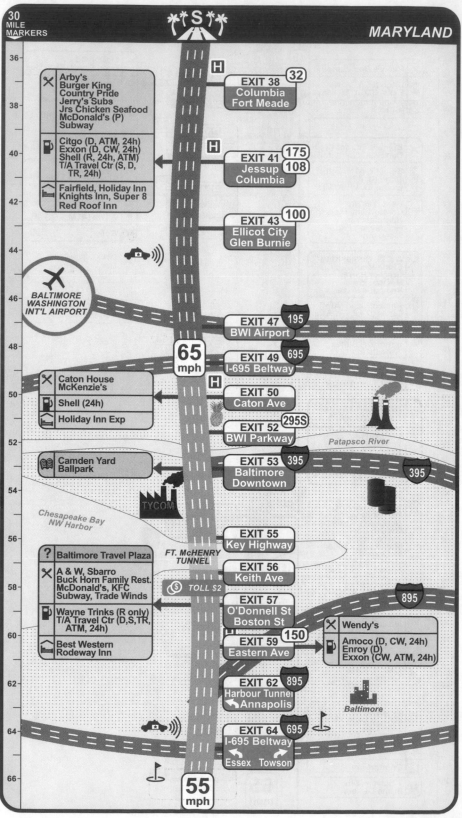

30 MILE MARKERS

MARYLAND

36 —

H EXIT 38 [32]
Columbia
Fort Meade

38 —

Arby's
Burger King
Country Pride
Jerry's Subs
Jrs Chicken Seafood
McDonald's (P)
Subway

Citgo (D, ATM, 24h)
Exxon (D, CW, 24h)
Shell (R, 24h, ATM)
T/A Travel Ctr (S, D, TR, 24h)

40 —

H EXIT 41 [175] [108]
Jessup
Columbia

Fairfield, Holiday Inn
Knights Inn, Super 8
Red Roof Inn

42 —

EXIT 43 [100]
Ellicot City
Glen Burnie

44 —

BALTIMORE
WASHINGTON
INT'L AIRPORT

46 —

EXIT 47 [195]
BWI Airport

48 —

65 mph

EXIT 49 [695]
I-695 Beltway

Caton House
McKenzie's

Shell (24h)

Holiday Inn Exp

H EXIT 50
Caton Ave

50 —

EXIT 52 [295S]
BWI Parkway

Patapsco River

52 —

Camden Yard
Ballpark

EXIT 53 [395]
Baltimore
Downtown

[395]

54 —

Chesapeake Bay NW Harbor

TYCOM

56 —

FT. McHENRY TUNNEL

EXIT 55
Key Highway

? Baltimore Travel Plaza

A & W, Sbarro
Buck Horn Family Rest.
McDonald's, KFC
Subway, Trade Winds

Wayne Trinks (R only)
T/A Travel Ctr (D,S,TR, ATM, 24h)

Best Western
Rodeway Inn

EXIT 56
Keith Ave

58 —

$ TOLL $2

EXIT 57
O'Donnell St
Boston St

[895]

Wendy's

Amoco (D, CW, 24h)
Enroy (D)
Exxon (CW, ATM, 24h)

60 —

EXIT 59 [150]
Eastern Ave

62 —

EXIT 62 [895]
Harbour Tunnel
Annapolis

Baltimore

64 —

EXIT 64 [695]
I-695 Beltway
Essex   Towson

66 —

55 mph

© 2004

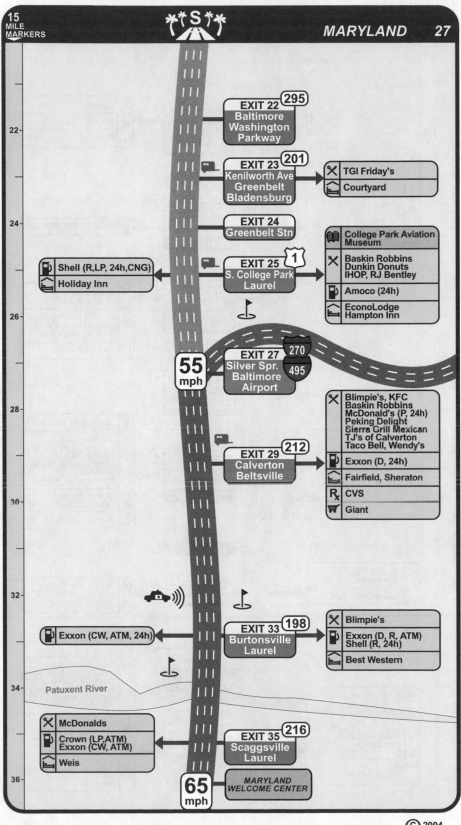

EXIT 22 295
Baltimore
Washington
Parkway

EXIT 23 201
Kenilworth Ave
Greenbelt
Bladensburg

✕ TGI Friday's
🛏 Courtyard

EXIT 24
Greenbelt Stn

📖 College Park Aviation Museum
✕ Baskin Robbins
Dunkin Donuts
IHOP, RJ Bentley
⛽ Amoco (24h)
🛏 EconoLodge
Hampton Inn

⛽ Shell (R,LP, 24h,CNG)
🛏 Holiday Inn

EXIT 25 1
S. College Park
Laurel

55 mph

EXIT 27 270 495
Silver Spr.
Baltimore
Airport

✕ Blimpie's, KFC
Baskin Robbins
McDonald's (P, 24h)
Peking Delight
Sierra Grill Mexican
TJ's of Calverton
Taco Bell, Wendy's
⛽ Exxon (D, 24h)
🛏 Fairfield, Sheraton
℞ CVS
🛒 Giant

EXIT 29 212
Calverton
Beltsville

EXIT 33 198
Burtonsville
Laurel

⛽ Exxon (CW, ATM, 24h)

✕ Blimpie's
⛽ Exxon (D, R, ATM)
Shell (R, 24h)
🛏 Best Western

Patuxent River

✕ McDonalds
⛽ Crown (LP,ATM)
Exxon (CW, ATM)
🛏 Weis

EXIT 35 216
Scaggsville
Laurel

65 mph

MARYLAND
WELCOME CENTER

© 2004

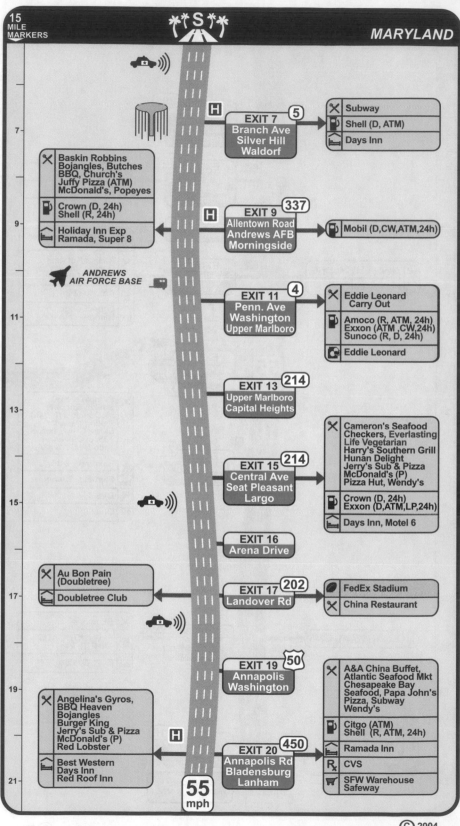

15
MILE
MARKERS

MARYLAND

EXIT 7 (5)
Branch Ave
Silver Hill
Waldorf
- ✕ Subway
- ⛽ Shell (D, ATM)
- 🛏 Days Inn

- ✕ Baskin Robbins
  Bojangles, Butches
  BBQ, Church's
  Juffy Pizza (ATM)
  McDonald's, Popeyes
- ⛽ Crown (D, 24h)
  Shell (R, 24h)
- 🛏 Holiday Inn Exp
  Ramada, Super 8

EXIT 9 (337)
Allentown Road
Andrews AFB
Morningside
- ⛽ Mobil (D,CW,ATM,24h)

🛩 ANDREWS
AIR FORCE BASE

EXIT 11 (4)
Penn. Ave
Washington
Upper Marlboro
- ✕ Eddie Leonard
  Carry Out
- ⛽ Amoco (R, ATM, 24h)
  Exxon (ATM ,CW,24h)
  Sunoco (R, D, 24h)
- 🛏 Eddie Leonard

EXIT 13 (214)
Upper Marlboro
Capital Heights

EXIT 15 (214)
Central Ave
Seat Pleasant
Largo
- ✕ Cameron's Seafood
  Checkers, Everlasting
  Life Vegetarian
  Harry's Southern Grill
  Hunan Delight
  Jerry's Sub & Pizza
  McDonald's (P)
  Pizza Hut, Wendy's
- ⛽ Crown (D, 24h)
  Exxon (D,ATM,LP,24h)
- 🛏 Days Inn, Motel 6

EXIT 16
Arena Drive

- ✕ Au Bon Pain
  (Doubletree)
- 🛏 Doubletree Club

EXIT 17 (202)
Landover Rd
- 🏟 FedEx Stadium
- ✕ China Restaurant

EXIT 19 (50)
Annapolis
Washington
- ✕ A&A China Buffet,
  Atlantic Seafood Mkt
  Chesapeake Bay
  Seafood, Papa John's
  Pizza, Subway
  Wendy's
- ⛽ Citgo (ATM)
  Shell (R, ATM, 24h)
- 🛏 Ramada Inn
- ℞ CVS
- 🛒 SFW Warehouse
  Safeway

- ✕ Angelina's Gyros,
  BBQ Heaven
  Bojangles
  Burger King
  Jerry's Sub & Pizza
  McDonald's (P)
  Red Lobster
- 🛏 Best Western
  Days Inn
  Red Roof Inn

EXIT 20 (450)
Annapolis Rd
Bladensburg
Lanham

55 mph

© 2004

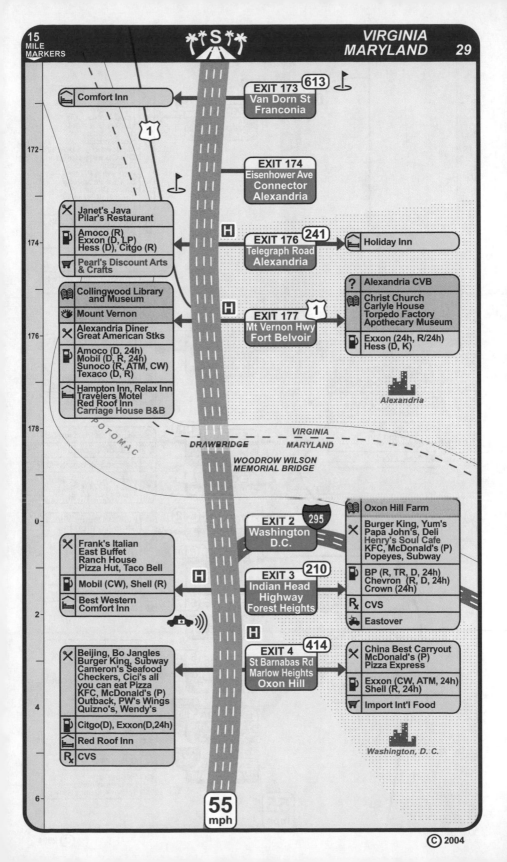

Comfort Inn

EXIT 173 613
Van Dorn St
Franconia

1

EXIT 174
Eisenhower Ave
Connector
Alexandria

Janet's Java
Pilar's Restaurant

Amoco (R)
Exxon (D, LP)
Hess (D), Citgo (R)

Pearl's Discount Arts
& Crafts

H **EXIT 176** 241 Holiday Inn
Telegraph Road
Alexandria

Collingwood Library
and Museum

Mount Vernon

Alexandria Diner
Great American Stks

Amoco (D, 24h)
Mobil (D, R, 24h)
Sunoco (R, ATM, CW)
Texaco (D, R)

Hampton Inn, Relax Inn
Travelers Motel
Red Roof Inn
Carriage House B&B

? Alexandria CVB

Christ Church
Carlyle House
Torpedo Factory
Apothecary Museum

Exxon (24h, R/24h)
Hess (D, K)

H **EXIT 177** 1
Mt Vernon Hwy
Fort Belvoir

Alexandria

POTOMAC

DRAWBRIDGE

VIRGINIA MARYLAND

WOODROW WILSON
MEMORIAL BRIDGE

EXIT 2 295
Washington
D.C.

Oxon Hill Farm

Burger King, Yum's
Papa John's, Deli
Henry's Soul Cafe
KFC, McDonald's (P)
Popeyes, Subway

Frank's Italian
East Buffet
Ranch House
Pizza Hut, Taco Bell

Mobil (CW), Shell (R)

Best Western
Comfort Inn

H **EXIT 3** 210
Indian Head
Highway
Forest Heights

BP (R, TR, D, 24h)
Chevron (R, D, 24h)
Crown (24h)

CVS

Eastover

Beijing, Bo Jangles
Burger King, Subway
Cameron's Seafood
Checkers, Cici's all
you can eat Pizza
KFC, McDonald's (P)
Outback, PW's Wings
Quizno's, Wendy's

Citgo(D), Exxon(D,24h)

Red Roof Inn

CVS

H **EXIT 4** 414
St Barnabas Rd
Marlow Heights
Oxon Hill

China Best Carryout
McDonald's (P)
Pizza Express

Exxon (CW, ATM, 24h)
Shell (R, 24h)

Import Int'l Food

Washington, D.C.

55 mph

© 2004

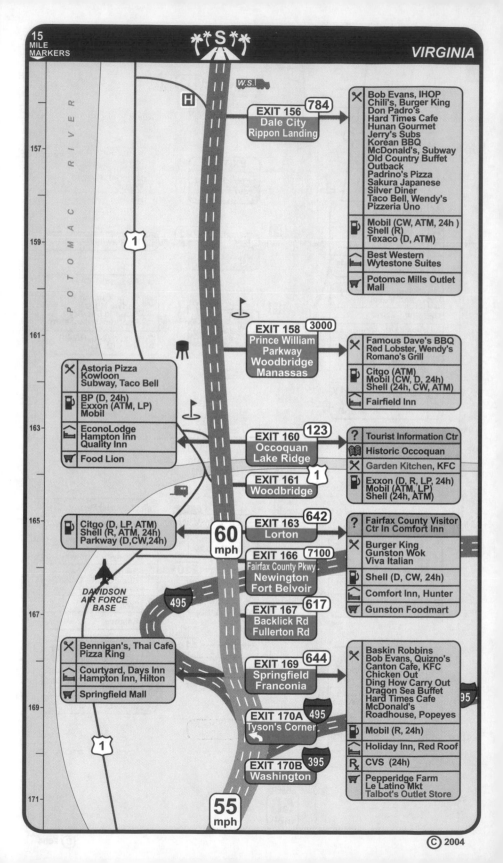

15 MILE MARKERS

VIRGINIA

EXIT 156 784
Dale City
Rippon Landing

- Bob Evans, IHOP
Chili's, Burger King
Don Padro's
Hard Times Cafe
Hunan Gourmet
Jerry's Subs
Korean BBQ
McDonald's, Subway
Old Country Buffet
Outback
Padrino's Pizza
Sakura Japanese
Silver Diner
Taco Bell, Wendy's
Pizzeria Uno
- Mobil (CW, ATM, 24h)
Shell (R)
Texaco (D, ATM)
- Best Western
Wytestone Suites
- Potomac Mills Outlet
Mall

EXIT 158 3000
Prince William
Parkway
Woodbridge
Manassas

- Famous Dave's BBQ
Red Lobster, Wendy's
Romano's Grill
- Citgo (ATM)
Mobil (CW, D, 24h)
Shell (24h, CW, ATM)
- Fairfield Inn

- Astoria Pizza
Kowloon
Subway, Taco Bell
- BP (D, 24h)
Exxon (ATM, LP)
Mobil
- EconoLodge
Hampton Inn
Quality Inn
- Food Lion

EXIT 160 123
Occoquan
Lake Ridge

- ? Tourist Information Ctr
- Historic Occoquan
- Garden Kitchen, KFC
- Exxon (D, R, LP, 24h)
Mobil (ATM, LP)
Shell (24h, ATM)

EXIT 161 1
Woodbridge

EXIT 163 642
Lorton

- ? Fairfax County Visitor
Ctr In Comfort Inn
- Burger King
Gunston Wok
Viva Italian
- Shell (D, CW, 24h)
- Comfort Inn, Hunter
- Gunston Foodmart

- Citgo (D, LP, ATM)
Shell (R, ATM, 24h)
Parkway (D,CW,24h)

60 mph

EXIT 166 7100
Fairfax County Pkwy
Newington
Fort Belvoir

EXIT 167 617
Backlick Rd
Fullerton Rd

DAVIDSON
AIR FORCE
BASE

495

- Bennigan's, Thai Cafe
Pizza King
- Courtyard, Days Inn
Hampton Inn, Hilton
- Springfield Mall

EXIT 169 644
Springfield
Franconia

- Baskin Robbins
Bob Evans, Quizno's
Canton Cafe, KFC
Chicken Out
Ding How Carry Out
Dragon Sea Buffet
Hard Times Cafe
McDonald's
Roadhouse, Popeyes
95

EXIT 170A 495
Tyson's Corner

- Mobil (R, 24h)
- Holiday Inn, Red Roof
- Rx CVS (24h)

EXIT 170B 395
Washington

- Pepperidge Farm
Le Latino Mkt
Talbot's Outlet Store

1

55 mph

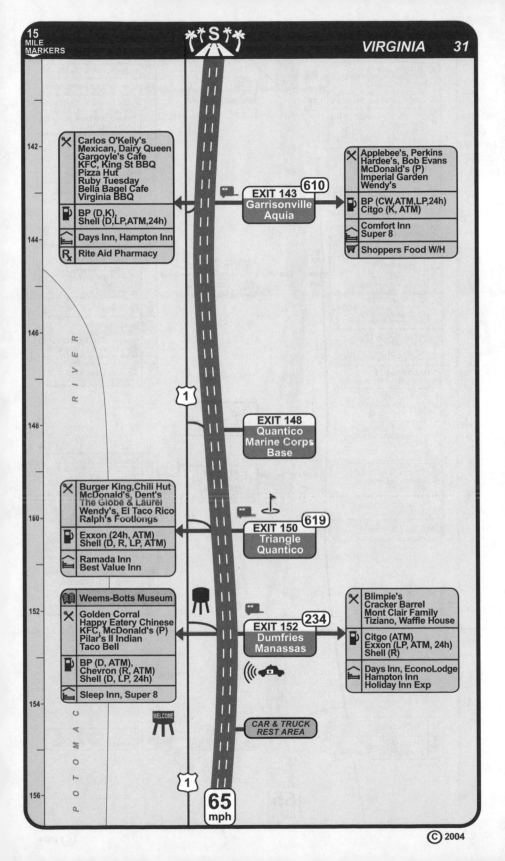

EXIT 143 610
Garrisonville
Aquia

Carlos O'Kelly's
Mexican, Dairy Queen
Gargoyle's Cafe
KFC, King St BBQ
Pizza Hut
Ruby Tuesday
Bella Bagel Cafe
Virginia BBQ

BP (D,K),
Shell (D,LP,ATM,24h)

Days Inn, Hampton Inn

Rite Aid Pharmacy

Applebee's, Perkins
Hardee's, Bob Evans
McDonald's (P)
Imperial Garden
Wendy's

BP (CW,ATM,LP,24h)
Citgo (K, ATM)

Comfort Inn
Super 8

Shoppers Food W/H

EXIT 148
Quantico
Marine Corps
Base

Burger King,Chili Hut
McDonald's, Dent's
The Globe & Laurel
Wendy's, El Taco Rico
Ralph's Footlongs

Exxon (24h, ATM)
Shell (D, R, LP, ATM)

Ramada Inn
Best Value Inn

EXIT 150 619
Triangle
Quantico

Weems-Botts Museum

Golden Corral
Happy Eatery Chinese
KFC, McDonald's (P)
Pilar's II Indian
Taco Bell

BP (D, ATM),
Chevron (R, ATM)
Shell (D, LP, 24h)

Sleep Inn, Super 8

EXIT 152 234
Dumfries
Manassas

Blimpie's
Cracker Barrel
Mont Clair Family
Tiziano, Waffle House

Citgo (ATM)
Exxon (LP, ATM, 24h)
Shell (R)

Days Inn, EconoLodge
Hampton Inn
Holiday Inn Exp

WELCOME

CAR & TRUCK REST AREA

65 mph

© 2004

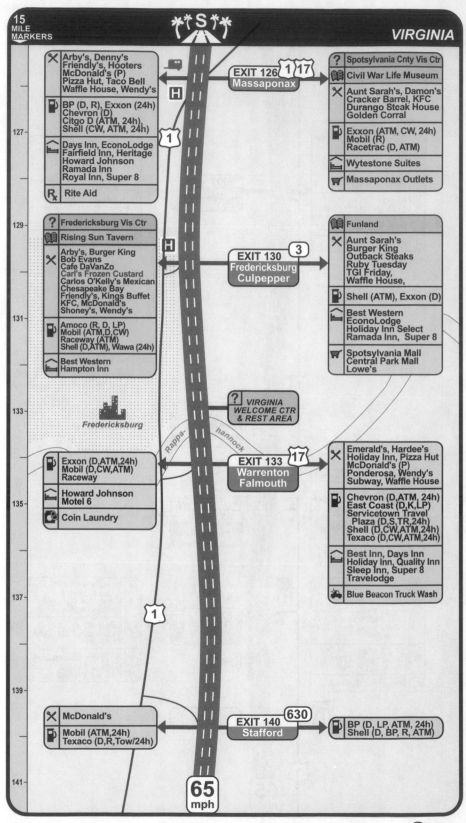

15 MILE MARKERS

VIRGINIA

EXIT 126 1 17
Massaponax

✗ Arby's, Denny's Friendly's, Hooters McDonald's (P) Pizza Hut, Taco Bell Waffle House, Wendy's

⛽ BP (D, R), Exxon (24h) Chevron (D) Citgo D (ATM, 24h) Shell (CW, ATM, 24h)

🛏 Days Inn, EconoLodge Fairfield Inn, Heritage Howard Johnson Ramada Inn Royal Inn, Super 8

Rx Rite Aid

? Spotsylvania Cnty Vis Ctr

🏛 Civil War Life Museum

✗ Aunt Sarah's, Damon's Cracker Barrel, KFC Durango Steak House Golden Corral

⛽ Exxon (ATM, CW, 24h) Mobil (R) Racetrac (D, ATM)

🛏 Wytestone Suites

🛒 Massaponax Outlets

? Fredericksburg Vis Ctr

🏛 Rising Sun Tavern

✗ Arby's, Burger King Bob Evans Cafe DaVanZo Carl's Frozen Custard Carlos O'Kelly's Mexican Chesapeake Bay Friendly's, Kings Buffet KFC, McDonald's Shoney's, Wendy's

⛽ Amoco (R, D, LP) Mobil (ATM,D,CW) Raceway (ATM) Shell (D,ATM), Wawa (24h)

🛏 Best Western Hampton Inn

EXIT 130 3
Fredericksburg
Culpepper

🏛 Funland

✗ Aunt Sarah's Burger King Outback Steaks Ruby Tuesday TGI Friday, Waffle House,

⛽ Shell (ATM), Exxon (D)

🛏 Best Western EconoLodge Holiday Inn Select Ramada Inn, Super 8

🛒 Spotsylvania Mall Central Park Mall Lowe's

Fredericksburg

? VIRGINIA WELCOME CTR & REST AREA

Rappa-hannock

EXIT 133 17
Warrenton
Falmouth

⛽ Exxon (D,ATM,24h) Mobil (D,CW,ATM) Raceway

🛏 Howard Johnson Motel 6

🧺 Coin Laundry

✗ Emerald's, Hardee's Holiday Inn, Pizza Hut McDonald's (P) Ponderosa, Wendy's Subway, Waffle House

⛽ Chevron (D,ATM, 24h) East Coast (D,K,LP) Servicetown Travel Plaza (D,S,TR,24h) Shell (D,CW,ATM,24h) Texaco (D,CW,ATM,24h)

🛏 Best Inn, Days Inn Holiday Inn, Quality Inn Sleep Inn, Super 8 Travelodge

🚜 Blue Beacon Truck Wash

EXIT 140 630
Stafford

✗ McDonald's

⛽ Mobil (ATM,24h) Texaco (D,R,Tow/24h)

⛽ BP (D, LP, ATM, 24h) Shell (D, BP, R, ATM)

65 mph

© 2004

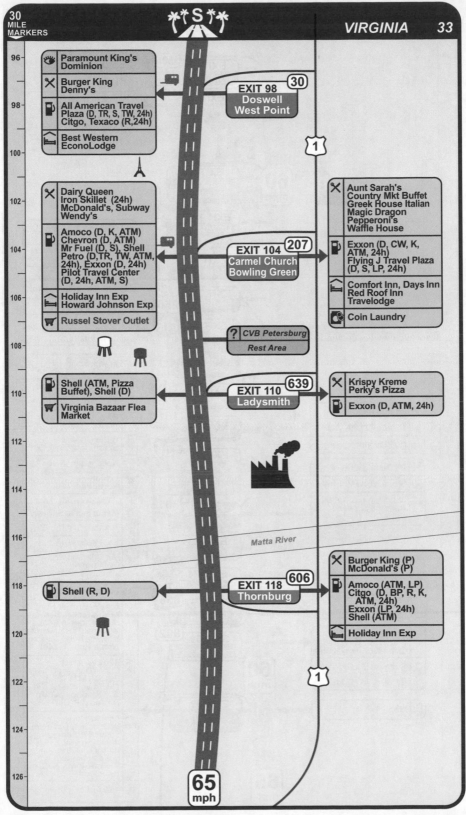

Mile		
96		Paramount King's Dominion
		Burger King / Denny's
98	**EXIT 98** (30) Doswell / West Point	All American Travel Plaza (D, TR, S, TW, 24h) Citgo, Texaco (R,24h)
100		Best Western / EconoLodge
102		Dairy Queen / Iron Skillet (24h) / McDonald's, Subway / Wendy's	Aunt Sarah's / Country Mkt Buffet / Greek House Italian / Magic Dragon / Pepperoni's / Waffle House
104	**EXIT 104** (207) Carmel Church / Bowling Green	Amoco (D, K, ATM) / Chevron (D, ATM) / Mr Fuel (D, S), Shell Petro (D,TR, TW, ATM, 24h), Exxon (D, 24h) / Pilot Travel Center (D, 24h, ATM, S)	Exxon (D, CW, K, ATM, 24h) / Flying J Travel Plaza (D, S, LP, 24h)
106		Holiday Inn Exp / Howard Johnson Exp	Comfort Inn, Days Inn / Red Roof Inn / Travelodge
		Russel Stover Outlet	Coin Laundry
108	? CVB Petersburg / Rest Area		
110	**EXIT 110** (639) Ladysmith	Shell (ATM, Pizza Buffet), Shell (D)	Krispy Kreme / Perky's Pizza
		Virginia Bazaar Flea Market	Exxon (D, ATM, 24h)
112			
114			
116	*Matta River*		
118	**EXIT 118** (606) Thornburg	Shell (R, D)	Burger King (P) / McDonald's (P)
			Amoco (ATM, LP) / Citgo (D, BP, R, K, ATM, 24h) / Exxon (LP, 24h) / Shell (ATM)
120			Holiday Inn Exp
122			
124			
126	**65** mph		

1 (US Route 1)

© 2004

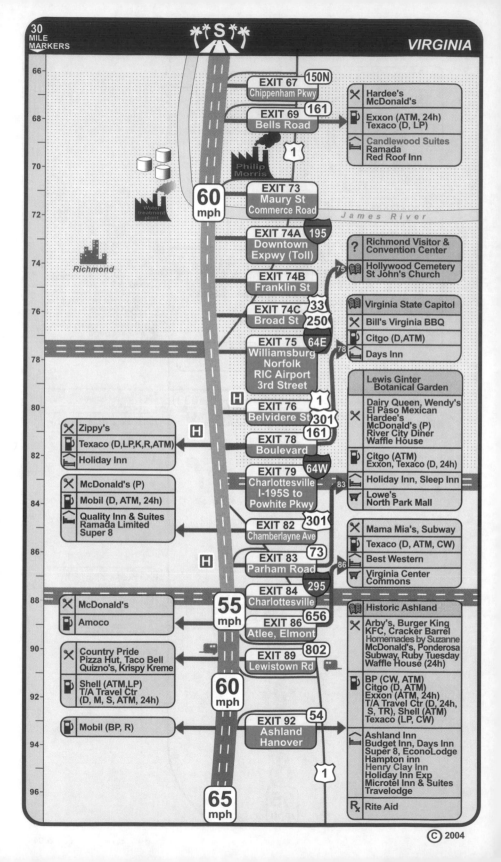

S

EXIT 51 85 85
Durham 460
Atlanta

Petersburg

- 📖 Petersburg Nat'l Battlefield
- ✖ Jade Garden
- ⛽ Crown (D, LP) / Exxon (LP, D, ATM)
- 🛏 Economy Inn / Royal Inn, Best Value / King Motel, Super 8

H **EXIT 52** 301
Dntn Petersburg
Washington St
Wythe St

🛏 Quality Inn / Radisson

- ✖ Burger King (P) / Padow's Hams & Deli / Pizza Hut, Subway / Taco Bell
- ⛽ Citgo (CW,ATM,LP,24h) / Exxon (LP, CW, ATM)
- 🛏 Comfort Suites

EXIT 53
Southpark Blvd

Appomattox River

- ✖ Applebee's / McDonald's (P) / Golden Corral / Lone Star Steaks / Old Country Buffet / Piccadilly Cafeteria / Ruby Tuesday
- ⛽ BP (D, LP)
- 🛒 Southpark Mall

55 mph

EXIT 54 144
Temple Ave

- ✖ Hardee's
- ⛽ Texaco (D, CW, ATM, LP, 24h)

🛏 Chester Inn

EXIT 58 620 746
Woods Edge Rd
Ruffin Mill Rd

- ✖ Godfather's / McDonalds / Subway
- ⛽ Exxon (D, ATM, CW, LP)
- 🛏 Days Inn / Interstate Inns

1 301

- ✖ Burger King / Cracker Barrel / Denny's (24h) / Friendly's, Hooters / Shoney's, Wendy's / Waffle House (24h)

- ✖ George's Steakhouse / Hardee's / Mai Ling Chinese
- ⛽ Race Trac (24h)
- 🛏 Comfort Inn / Courtyard / Hampton Inn / Holiday Inn Exp / Quality Inn

H **EXIT 61** 10
Hopewell
Chester

- ⛽ Citgo (D, LP, CW, ATM) / Crown (D, LP, CW, ATM, 24h), / Exxon (D, LP, ATM) / Sunoco (R ONLY)
- 🛏 Days Inn / Fairfield Inn / Clarion Inn, Super 8
- ℞ Rite Aid
- 🛒 Ukrops

EXIT 62 288
Chesterfield to
Powhite Pkwy

✈ *Chesterfield County Airport*

- ✖ Waffle House
- ⛽ Shell (R)
- 🛏 EconoLodge

EXIT 64 613
Willis Road

- ✖ Allman's BBQ / Bridgette's / Burger King P / McDonald's P
- ⛽ Chevron (ATM) / Mobil (ATM, D) / Shell (D, LP, ATM, 24h)
- 🛏 Country Inn & Suites / Sleep Inn, Super 8 / VIP Inn

1 301

60 mph

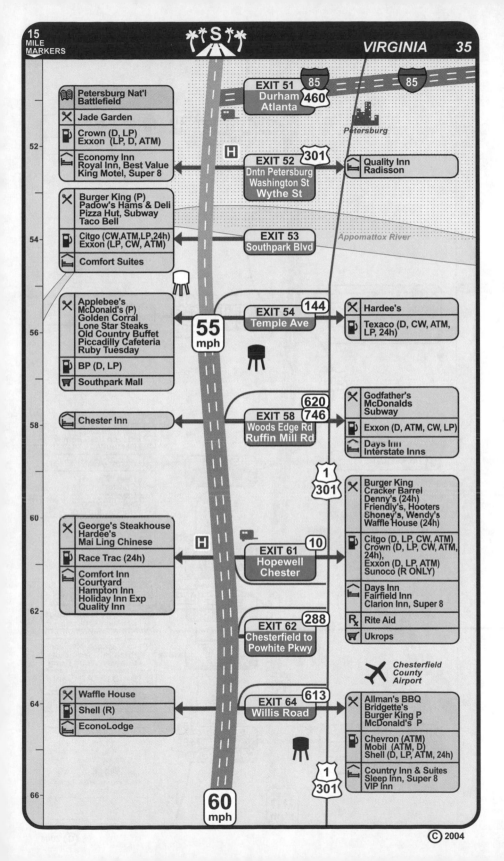

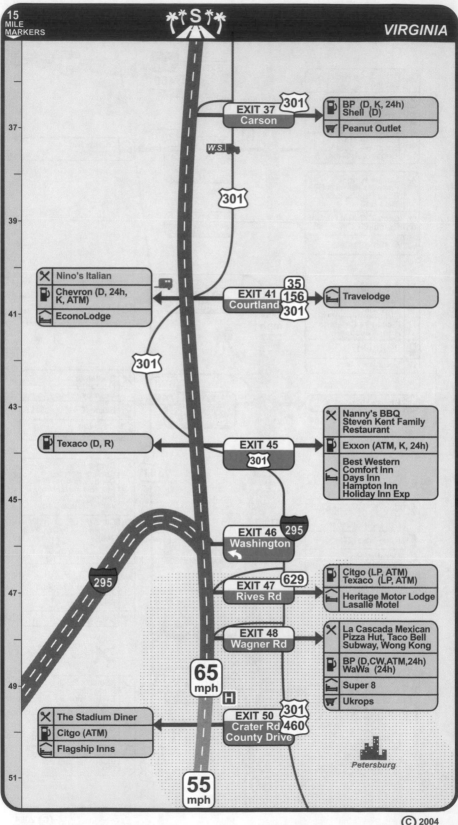

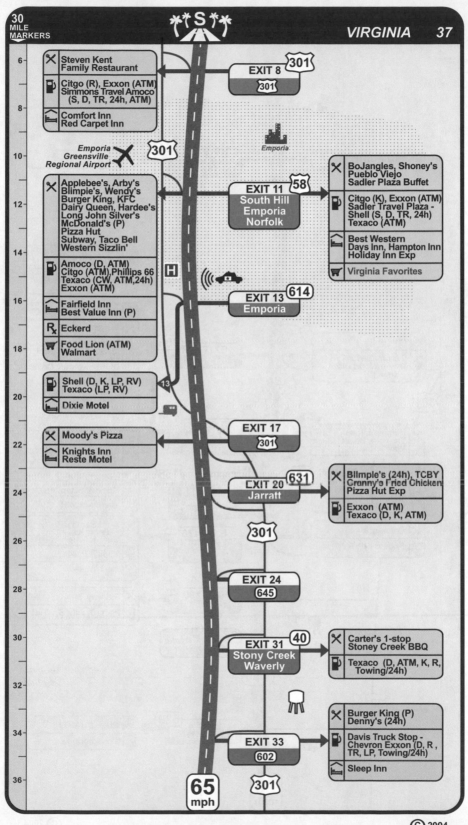

Mile	Exit	Services

EXIT 8 — 301 / 301

- ✕ Steven Kent Family Restaurant
- ⛽ Citgo (R), Exxon (ATM) Simmons Travel Amoco (S, D, TR, 24h, ATM)
- 🛏 Comfort Inn / Red Carpet Inn

Emporia Greensville Regional Airport ✈ 301

EXIT 11 — 58 — South Hill / Emporia / Norfolk

- ✕ Applebee's, Arby's, Blimpie's, Wendy's, Burger King, KFC, Dairy Queen, Hardee's, Long John Silver's, McDonald's (P), Pizza Hut, Subway, Taco Bell, Western Sizzlin'
- ⛽ Amoco (D, ATM) Citgo (ATM), Phillips 66 Texaco (CW, ATM, 24h) Exxon (ATM)
- 🛏 Fairfield Inn / Best Value Inn (P)
- Rx Eckerd
- 🛒 Food Lion (ATM) / Walmart

Right side of EXIT 11:
- ✕ BoJangles, Shoney's, Pueblo Viejo, Sadler Plaza Buffet
- ⛽ Citgo (K), Exxon (ATM) Sadler Travel Plaza - Shell (S, D, TR, 24h) Texaco (ATM)
- 🛏 Best Western, Days Inn, Hampton Inn, Holiday Inn Exp
- 🛒 Virginia Favorites

[H]

EXIT 13 — 614 — Emporia

- ⛽ Shell (D, K, LP, RV) Texaco (LP, RV)
- 🛏 Dixie Motel

EXIT 17 — 301

- ✕ Moody's Pizza
- 🛏 Knights Inn / Reste Motel

EXIT 20 — 631 — Jarratt

- ✕ Blimple's (24h), TCBY, Granny's Fried Chicken, Pizza Hut Exp
- ⛽ Exxon (ATM) Texaco (D, K, ATM)

301

EXIT 24 — 645

301

EXIT 31 — 40 — Stony Creek / Waverly

- ✕ Carter's 1-stop, Stoney Creek BBQ
- ⛽ Texaco (D, ATM, K, R, Towing/24h)

EXIT 33 — 602

- ✕ Burger King (P) / Denny's (24h)
- ⛽ Davis Truck Stop - Chevron Exxon (D, R, TR, LP, Towing/24h)
- 🛏 Sleep Inn

301

65 mph

© 2004

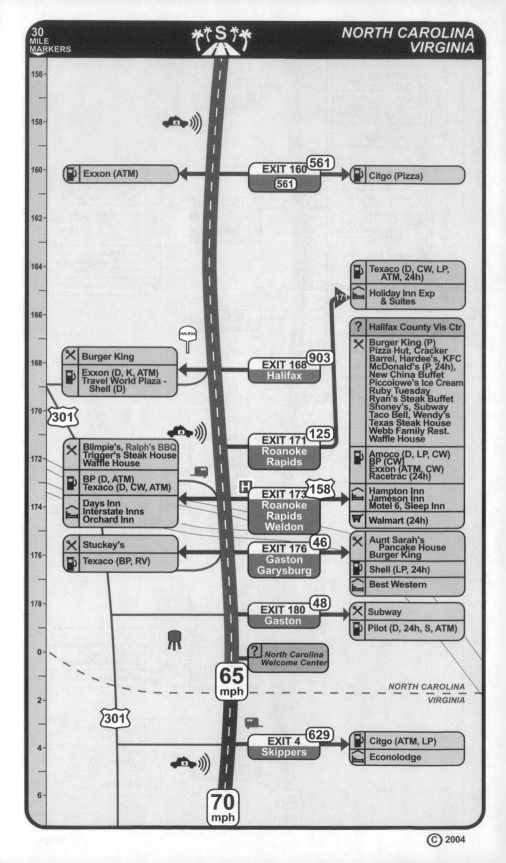

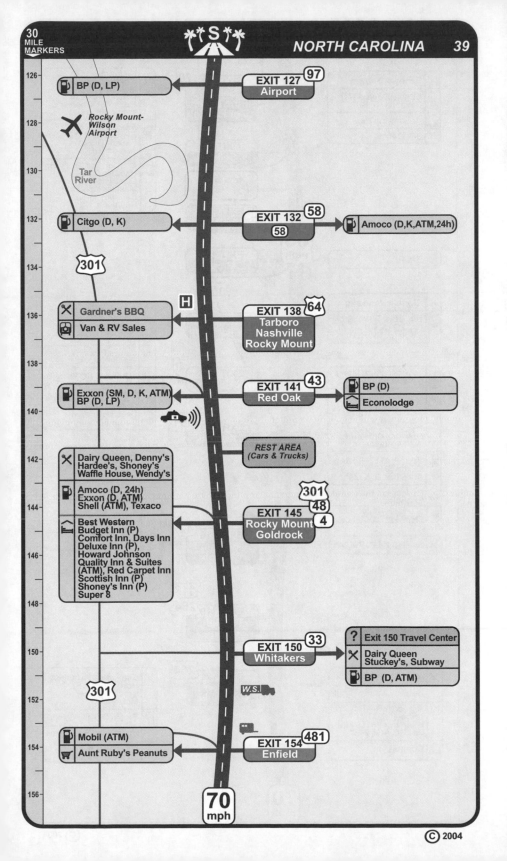

126

EXIT 127 [97]
Airport

BP (D, LP)

128

Rocky Mount-Wilson Airport

130

Tar River

132

Citgo (D, K)

EXIT 132 [58]
[58]

Amoco (D,K,ATM,24h)

134

301

136

[H]

Gardner's BBQ

Van & RV Sales

EXIT 138 [64]
Tarboro
Nashville
Rocky Mount

138

EXIT 141 [43]
Red Oak

Exxon (SM, D, K, ATM)
BP (D, LP)

BP (D)

Econolodge

140

142

Dairy Queen, Denny's
Hardee's, Shoney's
Waffle House, Wendy's

REST AREA
(Cars & Trucks)

144

Amoco (D, 24h)
Exxon (D, ATM)
Shell (ATM), Texaco

301
[48]

EXIT 145
Rocky Mount
Goldrock
[4]

Best Western
Budget Inn (P)
Comfort Inn, Days Inn
Deluxe Inn (P),
Howard Johnson
Quality Inn & Suites
(ATM), Red Carpet Inn
Scottish Inn (P)
Shoney's Inn (P)
Super 8

146

148

150

EXIT 150 [33]
Whitakers

? Exit 150 Travel Center

Dairy Queen
Stuckey's, Subway

BP (D, ATM)

301

152

W.S.

154

Mobil (ATM)

Aunt Ruby's Peanuts

EXIT 154 [481]
Enfield

156

70 mph

© 2004

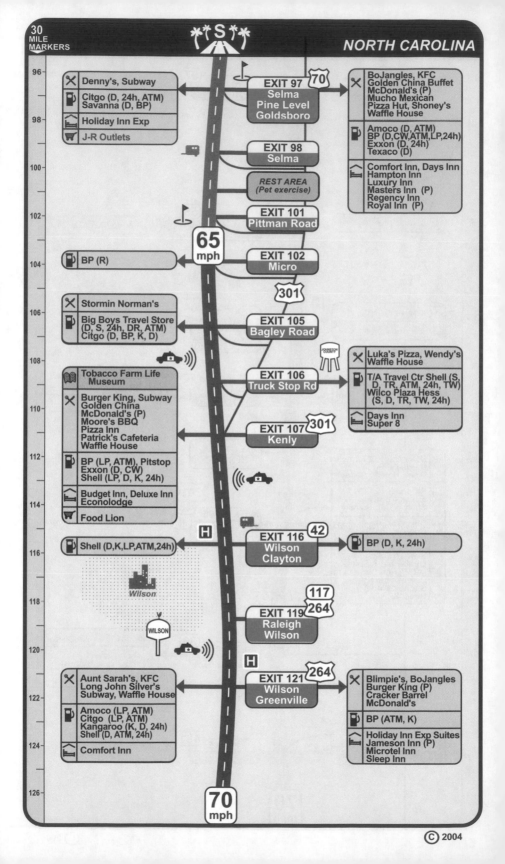

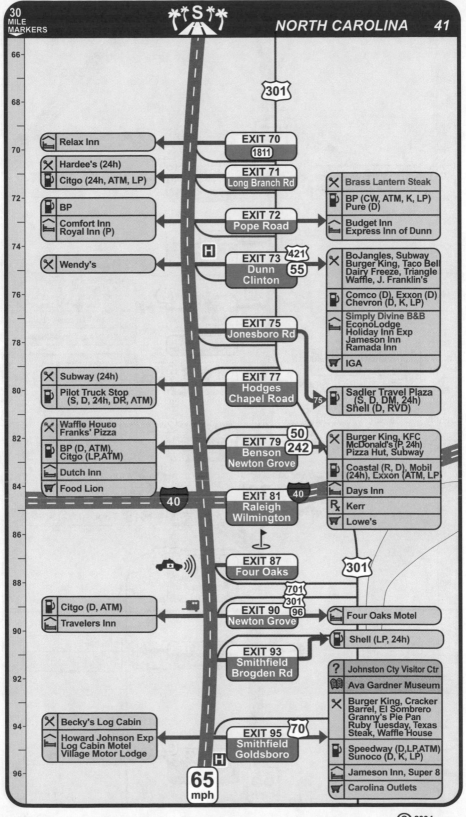

301

EXIT 70 1811	Relax Inn

| EXIT 71 Long Branch Rd | Hardee's (24h) / Citgo (24h, ATM, LP) | Brass Lantern Steak / BP (CW, ATM, K, LP) Pure (D) / Budget Inn Express Inn of Dunn |

| EXIT 72 Pope Road | BP / Comfort Inn Royal Inn (P) |

H

| EXIT 73 Dunn Clinton **421** **55** | Wendy's | BoJangles, Subway Burger King, Taco Bell Dairy Freeze, Triangle Waffle, J. Franklin's / Comco (D), Exxon (D) Chevron (D, K, LP) / Simply Divine B&B EconoLodge Holiday Inn Exp Jameson Inn Ramada Inn / IGA |

| EXIT 75 Jonesboro Rd |

| EXIT 77 Hodges Chapel Road 75 | Subway (24h) / Pilot Truck Stop (S, D, 24h, DR, ATM) | Sadler Travel Plaza (S, D, DM, 24h) Shell (D, RVD) |

| EXIT 79 Benson Newton Grove **50** **242** | Waffle House Franks' Pizza / BP (D, ATM), Citgo (LP,ATM) / Dutch Inn / Food Lion | Burger King, KFC McDonald's (P, 24h) Pizza Hut, Subway / Coastal (R, D), Mobil (24h), Exxon (ATM, LP) |

40

| EXIT 81 Raleigh Wilmington **40** | | Days Inn / Kerr / Lowe's |

| EXIT 87 Four Oaks | | **301** |

701 301 96

| EXIT 90 Newton Grove | Citgo (D, ATM) / Travelers Inn | Four Oaks Motel |

| EXIT 93 Smithfield Brogden Rd | | Shell (LP, 24h) / Johnston Cty Visitor Ctr / Ava Gardner Museum / Burger King, Cracker Barrel, El Sombrero Granny's Pie Pan Ruby Tuesday, Texas Steak, Waffle House |

| EXIT 95 Smithfield Goldsboro **70** | Becky's Log Cabin / Howard Johnson Exp Log Cabin Motel Village Motor Lodge | Speedway (D,LP,ATM) Sunoco (D, K, LP) / Jameson Inn, Super 8 / Carolina Outlets |

H

65 mph

© 2004

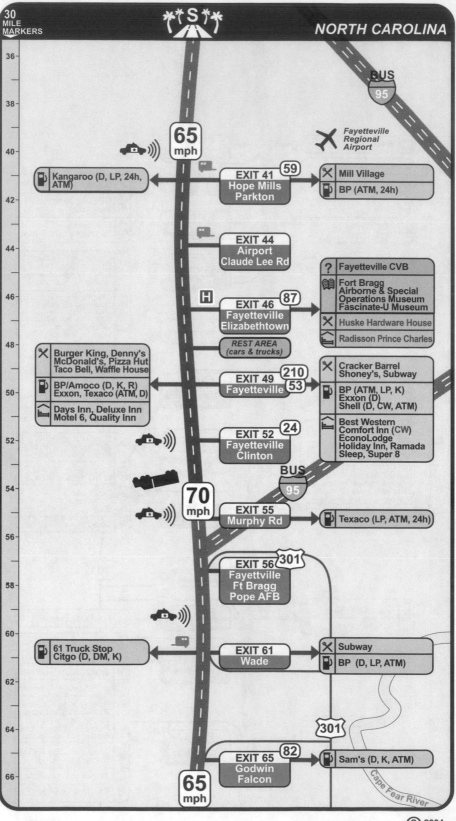

30 MILE MARKERS

NORTH CAROLINA

BUS 95

65 mph

Fayetteville Regional Airport

Kangaroo (D, LP, 24h, ATM)

EXIT 41 59
Hope Mills Parkton

Mill Village
BP (ATM, 24h)

EXIT 44
Airport Claude Lee Rd

H

EXIT 46 87
Fayetteville Elizabethtown

? Fayetteville CVB

Fort Bragg Airborne & Special Operations Museum Fascinate-U Museum

Huske Hardware House

Radisson Prince Charles

REST AREA (cars & trucks)

Burger King, Denny's McDonald's, Pizza Hut Taco Bell, Waffle House

BP/Amoco (D, K, R) Exxon, Texaco (ATM, D)

Days Inn, Deluxe Inn Motel 6, Quality Inn

EXIT 49 210 53
Fayetteville

Cracker Barrel Shoney's, Subway

BP (ATM, LP, K) Exxon (D) Shell (D, CW, ATM)

Best Western Comfort Inn (CW) EconoLodge Holiday Inn, Ramada Sleep, Super 8

EXIT 52 24
Fayetteville Clinton

BUS 95

70 mph

EXIT 55
Murphy Rd

Texaco (LP, ATM, 24h)

EXIT 56 301
Fayettville Ft Bragg Pope AFB

61 Truck Stop Citgo (D, DM, K)

EXIT 61
Wade

Subway
BP (D, LP, ATM)

301

EXIT 65 82
Godwin Falcon

Sam's (D, K, ATM)

Cape Fear River

65 mph

© 2004

S

Mile		Interstate Exits	

6 –

8 –

EXIT 7
McDonald
Raynham

S E Agricultural Farmers' Market — 14

EXIT 10 301
Fairmont → Hunts 301 (K)

Burger King, Hardee's Huddle House (24h) Little China, Stuckey's McDonald's (P) Subway, Wendy's Waffle House

10 –

EXIT 14 74
Maxton
Laurinburg → BP (D, LP, K, ATM)

BP (D, ATM), Texaco Exxon (ATM,D,24h,LP) Go Gas (D, K,24h) Mobil (R, 24h, D, ATM) Shell (ATM, CW, 24h)

12 –

Budget Inn, Fairfield

14 –

Rx CVS Drug

Food Lion

EXIT 17 711 72
Pembroke
Lumberton

16 –

Lumberton Municipal Airport
Lumberton

Taqueria Mexican

Exxon (CW, D) Texaco (K)

EXIT 19
Carthage Road

Mi Casita Restaurante

Knight's Inn Motel 6

18 –

Traveler's Inn

H

EXIT 20 211 41
Lumberton
Red Springs

? Lumberton CVB

BK, Little Caesar's New China, Subway McDonald's (P) Shoney's, Village Stn Waffle House

Cracker Barrel, Fullers BBQ, Lung Wah San Jose Mexican

20 –

Amoco (D,LP,ATM) Citgo (24h, LP) Exxon (D, ATM)

Texaco (D,ATM,K,24h)

22 –

Deluxe Inn, Quality Howard Johnson Exp

Country Inn & Suites Days Inn, EconoLodge Fairfield Inn, Comfort

Food Lion Merita Bakery Outlet

Tienda Carniceria

24 –

EXIT 22 301
Lumberton

Subway Uncle George's Italian

Burger King, China Wok, Dairy Queen Denny's, Hardee's Huddle House (24h) Outback, Quizno's Ruby Tuesday, Ryan's San Jose Mexican Smithfield's Chicken Texas Steak, Zaxby's Waffle House,

Sun-to (LP, D, ATM) Circle B (LP, 24h) Texaco (D)

26 –

W.S.

EXIT 25 301
Local Traffic

28 –

Exxon (CW, D, ATM) Shell (ATM, CW, 24h)

Best Western, Comfort Suites, Hampton Inn Holiday Inn, Super 8

30 –

Lowe's

BP (D, K, LP) — 25

32 –

EXIT 31 20
St. Pauls
Raeford → Citgo (K, ATM) Exxon (D, ATM)

Blimpie's, TCBY Burger King (P) Huddle House (24h) McDonald's (P)

34 –

Amoco (LP, 24h, ATM) BP (ATM), Shell (D) Mobil (LP, CW)

Days Inn

36 –

Amoco (D, 24h) ← **65 mph** **EXIT 33** 301
St. Pauls

© 2004

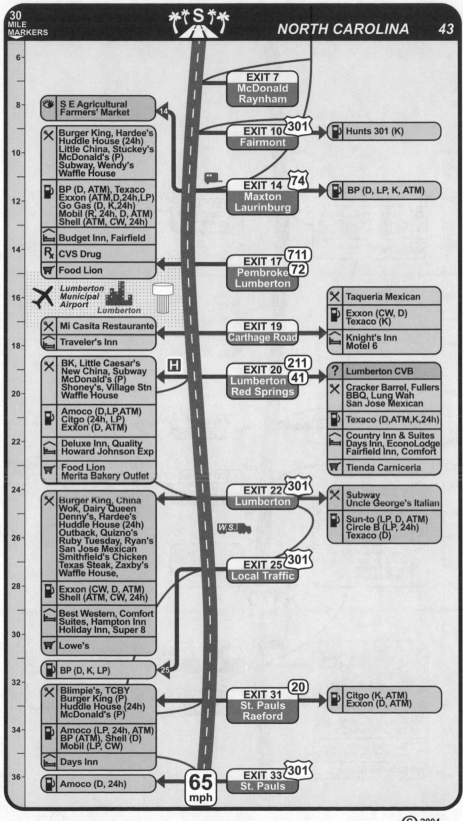

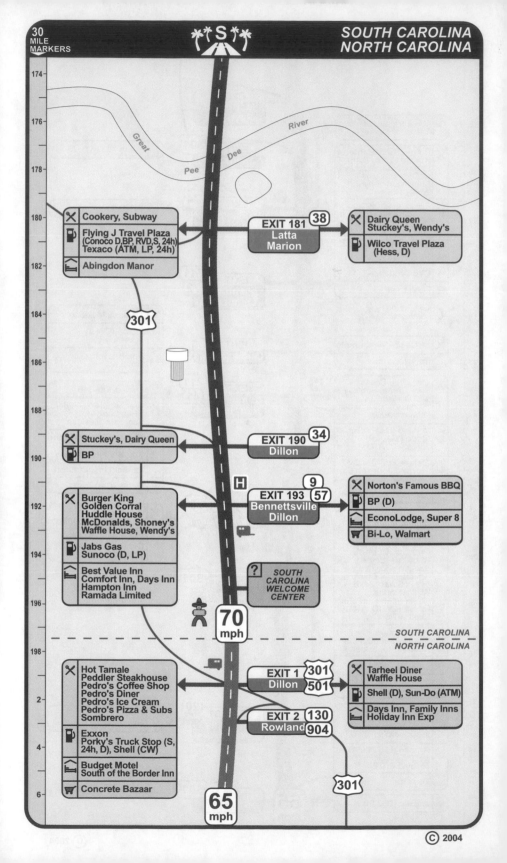

SOUTH CAROLINA
NORTH CAROLINA

30 MILE MARKERS

174

176

178

River

Great Pee Dee

180

Cookery, Subway

Flying J Travel Plaza (Conoco D,BP, RVD,S, 24h) Texaco (ATM, LP, 24h)

Abingdon Manor

EXIT 181 38
Latta
Marion

Dairy Queen Stuckey's, Wendy's

Wilco Travel Plaza (Hess, D)

182

184

301

186

188

190

Stuckey's, Dairy Queen

BP

EXIT 190 34
Dillon

192

H

Burger King Golden Corral Huddle House McDonalds, Shoney's Waffle House, Wendy's

Jabs Gas Sunoco (D, LP)

Best Value Inn Comfort Inn, Days Inn Hampton Inn Ramada Limited

EXIT 193 9 57
Bennettsville
Dillon

Norton's Famous BBQ

BP (D)

EconoLodge, Super 8

Bi-Lo, Walmart

194

? SOUTH CAROLINA WELCOME CENTER

196

70 mph

SOUTH CAROLINA
NORTH CAROLINA

198

Hot Tamale Peddler Steakhouse Pedro's Coffee Shop Pedro's Diner Pedro's Ice Cream Pedro's Pizza & Subs Sombrero

Exxon Porky's Truck Stop (S, 24h, D), Shell (CW)

Budget Motel South of the Border Inn

Concrete Bazaar

EXIT 1 301 501
Dillon

EXIT 2 130 904
Rowland

Tarheel Diner Waffle House

Shell (D), Sun-Do (ATM)

Days Inn, Family Inns Holiday Inn Exp

2

4

301

6

65 mph

EXIT 146
Lynchburg
Lake City — 341

🏨 Relax Inn

403

EXIT 150
Sardis — 403

🍴 Darrell's Diner
⛽ Exxon (D)

⛽ BP (D, 24h)
🏨 Budget Inn

🍴 McDonald's
Swamp Fox Diner
Waffle House

⛽ Amoco (R,LP,Tow/24h)
Exxon (ATM), Phillips 66
Texaco (D,LP,24h,ATM)

🏨 Days Inn
Howard Johnson Exp
& Suites, Swampfox
Inn, Villager Lodge

EXIT 153
Honda Way

76

70 mph

🏙️ *Florence*   H

EXIT 157
Timmonsville
Florence — 76

🍴 Carol's
Young's Plantation Inn
⛽ Sunoco
🏨 Tree Top Inn
Young's Plantation Inn

? Florence Visitor's Ctr.

🍴 Arby's, Baskin Robbins
Burger King (P)
Chick-Fil-A, Outback
Huddle House, IHOP
Percy & Willey's
Pizza Hut, Red Lobster
Redbone Alley
Ruby Tuesday
Shoney's, Waffle House
Western Sizzlin' Steak

⛽ Shell (D, ATM)

🏨 Courtyard, Fairfield
Hampton Inn & Suites
Holiday Inn Exp
Red Roof Inn
SpringHill Suites

H   **EXIT 160**
Columbia
Florence — 20

55 mph

🍴 Arby's, Bojangles
Burger King, Shoney's
Country Kitchen
Mainstreet Cafe
Subway (24h)
Taco Bell, Fatz Cafe

🍴 Baskin Robbins
Chicken Kitchen
Cracker Barrel, Pizza
Hut, Hardee's (24h)
McDonald's (P)
Quincy's Steak, Wendy's
Ruby Tuesday, Quizno's
Waffle House (24h)

⛽ Citgo (ATM, D, 24h)
Exxon (D,LP,ATM,CW)
Raceway (ATM)

🏨 Best Western, Comfort
EconoLodge
Hampton Inn
Holiday Inn & Suites(P)
Motel 6, Super 8
Suburban Extended

EXIT 164
Darlington
Florence — 52

⛽ Hess (ATM, D, 24h)
Pilot Travel Ctr (S, D, 24h)
William's Trav Ctr (D,S)

🏨 Days Inn, Wingate Inn
Guest House Inn (P)
Microtel Inn & Suites
Ramada, Sleep Inn
Thunderbird Inn

H   **EXIT 169**
TV Road
Quinby
Florence

🍴 Iron Skillet (24h)
⛽ Amoco, Shell (D, RVD,
CW, LP, 24h)
Petro (D, TR, TW, RVD,
24h, ATM)
🏨 Rodeway Inn

🍴 McDonalds (P), Wendy's
⛽ BP (ATM), Pilot (D, S)
🏨 Holiday Inn Exp Suites

EXIT 170
Florence — 327

✈️ *Florence
Regional
Airport*

*REST AREA
(TRUCKS)*

70 mph

© 2004

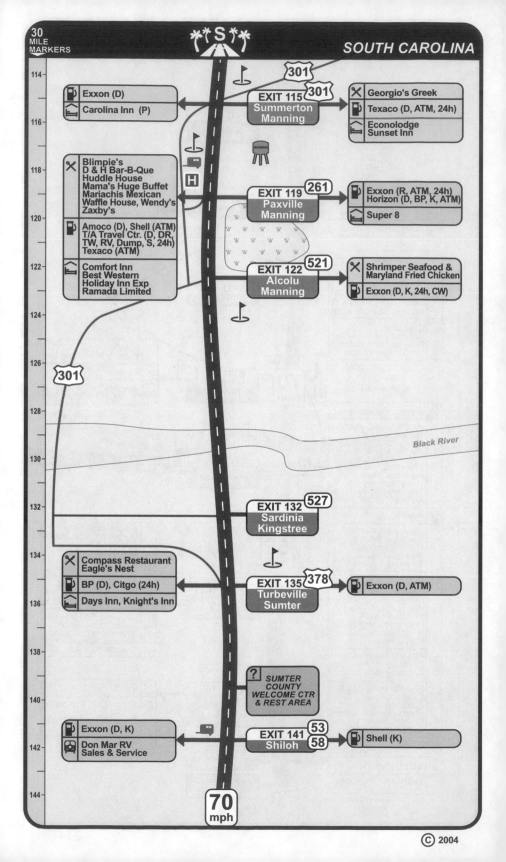

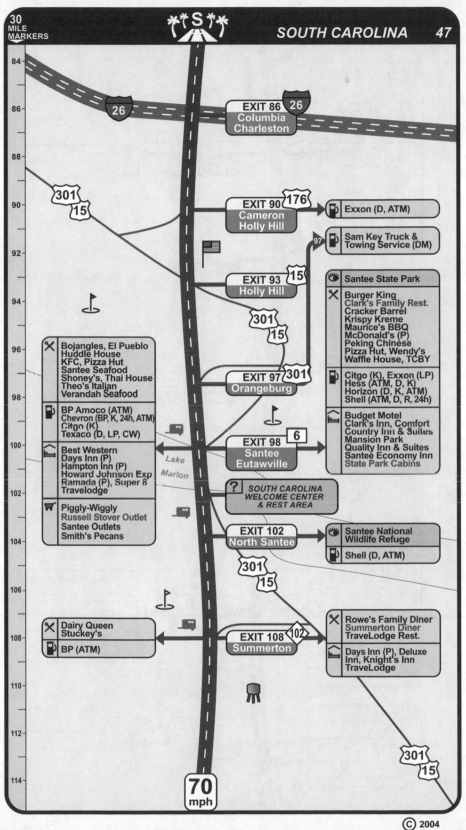

EXIT 86 26
Columbia
Charleston

EXIT 90 176
Cameron
Holly Hill
→ ⛽ Exxon (D, ATM)
⛽ Sam Key Truck & Towing Service (DM)

EXIT 93 15
Holly Hill

EXIT 97 301
Orangeburg

✊ Santee State Park

✕ Burger King
Clark's Family Rest.
Cracker Barrel
Krispy Kreme
Maurice's BBQ
McDonald's (P)
Peking Chinese
Pizza Hut, Wendy's
Waffle House, TCBY

⛽ Citgo (K), Exxon (LP)
Hess (ATM, D, K)
Horizon (D, K, ATM)
Shell (ATM, D, R, 24h)

🏠 Budget Motel
Clark's Inn, Comfort
Country Inn & Suites
Mansion Park
Quality Inn & Suites
Santee Economy Inn
State Park Cabins

✕ Bojangles, El Pueblo
Huddle House
KFC, Pizza Hut
Santee Seafood
Shoney's, Thai House
Theo's Italian
Verandah Seafood

⛽ BP Amoco (ATM)
Chevron (BP, K, 24h, ATM)
Citgo (K)
Texaco (D, LP, CW)

🏠 Best Western
Days Inn (P)
Hampton Inn (P)
Howard Johnson Exp
Ramada (P), Super 8
Travelodge

🛒 Piggly-Wiggly
Russell Stover Outlet
Santee Outlets
Smith's Pecans

EXIT 98 6
Santee
Eutawville

Lake Marion

? SOUTH CAROLINA
WELCOME CENTER
& REST AREA

EXIT 102
North Santee
→ ✊ Santee National Wildlife Refuge
⛽ Shell (D, ATM)

✕ Dairy Queen
Stuckey's
⛽ BP (ATM)

EXIT 108 102
Summerton

✕ Rowe's Family Diner
Summerton Diner
TraveLodge Rest.

🏠 Days Inn (P), Deluxe
Inn, Knight's Inn
TraveLodge

70 mph

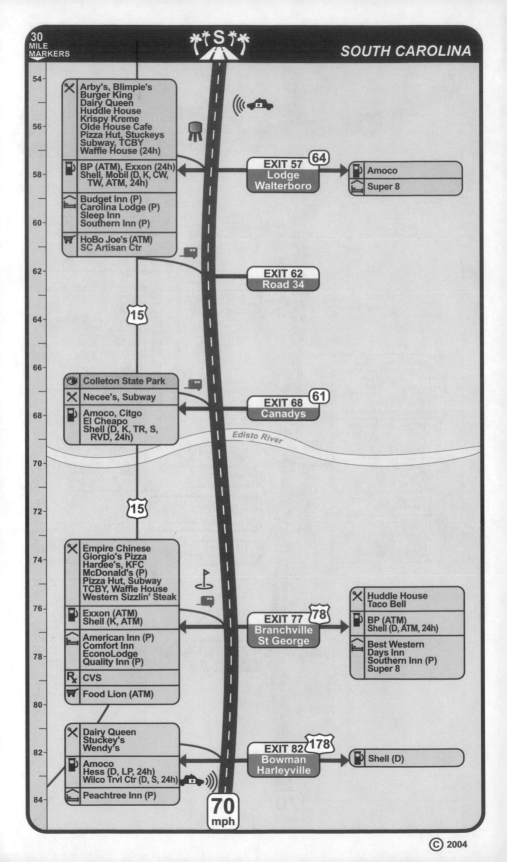

30 MILE MARKERS

SOUTH CAROLINA

EXIT 57
Lodge
Walterboro [64]

Arby's, Blimpie's
Burger King
Dairy Queen
Huddle House
Krispy Kreme
Olde House Cafe
Pizza Hut, Stuckeys
Subway, TCBY
Waffle House (24h)

BP (ATM), Exxon (24h)
Shell, Mobil (D, K, CW,
TW, ATM, 24h)

Budget Inn (P)
Carolina Lodge (P)
Sleep Inn
Southern Inn (P)

HoBo Joe's (ATM)
SC Artisan Ctr

Amoco
Super 8

EXIT 62
Road 34

15

EXIT 68
Canadys [61]

Colleton State Park

Necee's, Subway

Amoco, Citgo
El Cheapo
Shell (D, K, TR, S,
RVD, 24h)

Edisto River

15

Empire Chinese
Giorgio's Pizza
Hardee's, KFC
McDonald's (P)
Pizza Hut, Subway
TCBY, Waffle House
Western Sizzlin' Steak

Exxon (ATM)
Shell (K, ATM)

American Inn (P)
Comfort Inn
EconoLodge
Quality Inn (P)

Rx CVS

Food Lion (ATM)

EXIT 77
Branchville
St George [78]

Huddle House
Taco Bell

BP (ATM)
Shell (D, ATM, 24h)

Best Western
Days Inn
Southern Inn (P)
Super 8

Dairy Queen
Stuckey's
Wendy's

Amoco
Hess (D, LP, 24h)
Wilco Trvl Ctr (D, S, 24h)

Peachtree Inn (P)

EXIT 82
Bowman
Harleyville [178]

Shell (D)

70 mph

© 2004

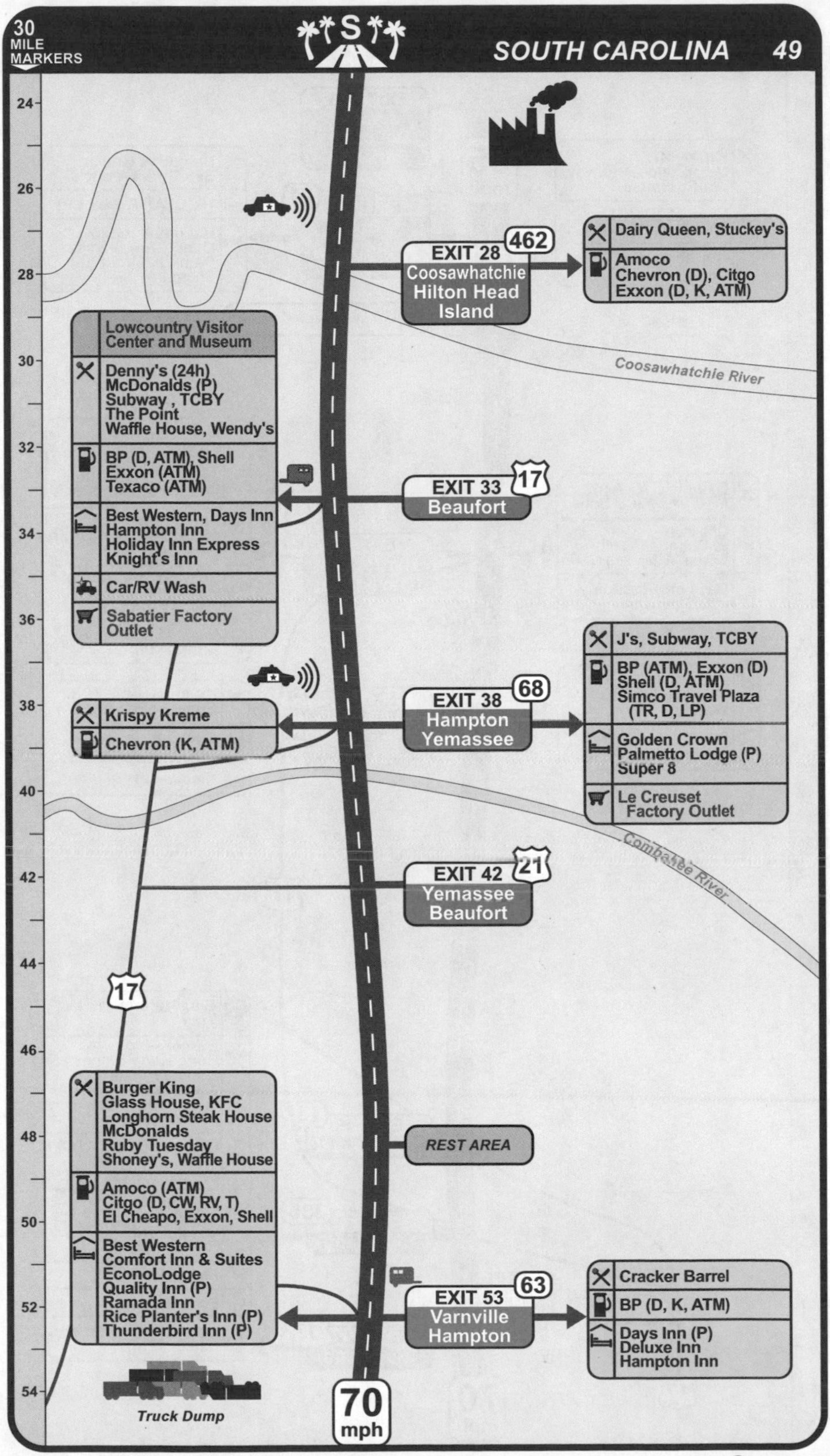

EXIT 28 **462**
Coosawhatchie
Hilton Head
Island

✕ Dairy Queen, Stuckey's
⛽ Amoco
Chevron (D), Citgo
Exxon (D, K, ATM)

Coosawhatchie River

Lowcountry Visitor Center and Museum

✕ Denny's (24h)
McDonalds (P)
Subway , TCBY
The Point
Waffle House, Wendy's

⛽ BP (D, ATM), Shell
Exxon (ATM)
Texaco (ATM)

🏨 Best Western, Days Inn
Hampton Inn
Holiday Inn Express
Knight's Inn

🚗 Car/RV Wash

🛒 Sabatier Factory Outlet

EXIT 33 **17**
Beaufort

✕ Krispy Kreme
⛽ Chevron (K, ATM)

EXIT 38 **68**
Hampton
Yemassee

✕ J's, Subway, TCBY
⛽ BP (ATM), Exxon (D)
Shell (D, ATM)
Simco Travel Plaza
(TR, D, LP)

🏨 Golden Crown
Palmetto Lodge (P)
Super 8

🛒 Le Creuset
Factory Outlet

Combahee River

EXIT 42 **21**
Yemassee
Beaufort

17

✕ Burger King
Glass House, KFC
Longhorn Steak House
McDonalds
Ruby Tuesday
Shoney's, Waffle House

⛽ Amoco (ATM)
Citgo (D, CW, RV, T)
El Cheapo, Exxon, Shell

🏨 Best Western
Comfort Inn & Suites
EconoLodge
Quality Inn (P)
Ramada Inn
Rice Planter's Inn (P)
Thunderbird Inn (P)

REST AREA

EXIT 53 **63**
Varnville
Hampton

✕ Cracker Barrel
⛽ BP (D, K, ATM)
🏨 Days Inn (P)
Deluxe Inn
Hampton Inn

Truck Dump

70 mph

© 2004

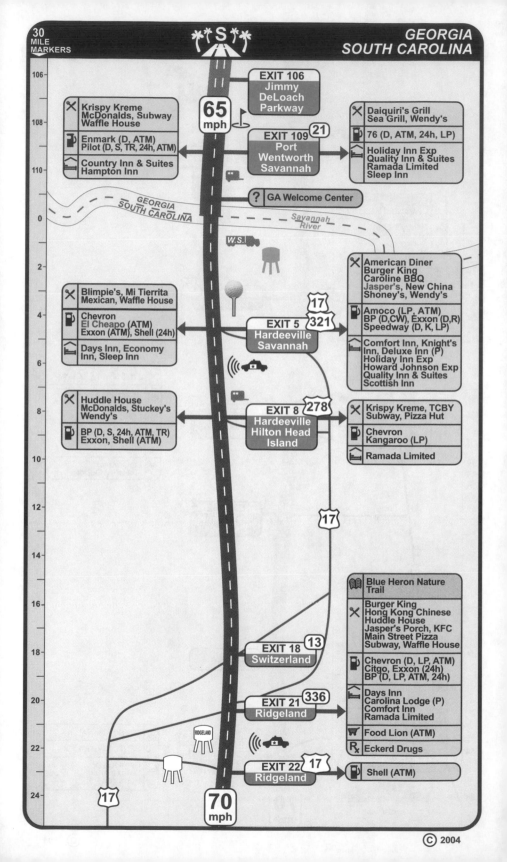

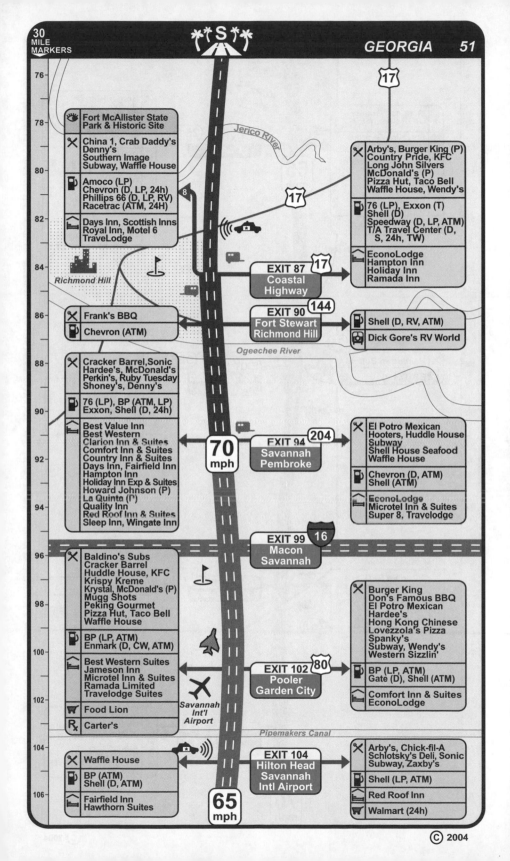

17

Jerico River

Fort McAllister State Park & Historic Site

China 1, Crab Daddy's
Denny's
Southern Image
Subway, Waffle House

Amoco (LP)
Chevron (D, LP, 24h)
Phillips 66 (D, LP, RV)
Racetrac (ATM, 24H)

Days Inn, Scottish Inns
Royal Inn, Motel 6
TraveLodge

8

17

Arby's, Burger King (P)
Country Pride, KFC
Long John Silvers
McDonald's (P)
Pizza Hut, Taco Bell
Waffle House, Wendy's

76 (LP), Exxon (T)
Shell (D)
Speedway (D, LP, ATM)
T/A Travel Center (D, S, 24h, TW)

EconoLodge
Hampton Inn
Holiday Inn
Ramada Inn

Richmond Hill

EXIT 87 〔17〕
Coastal Highway

Frank's BBQ

Chevron (ATM)

EXIT 90 〔144〕
Fort Stewart Richmond Hill

Shell (D, RV, ATM)

Dick Gore's RV World

Ogeechee River

Cracker Barrel, Sonic
Hardee's, McDonald's
Perkin's, Ruby Tuesday
Shoney's, Denny's

76 (LP), BP (ATM, LP)
Exxon, Shell (D, 24h)

Best Value Inn
Best Western
Clarion Inn & Suites
Comfort Inn & Suites
Country Inn & Suites
Days Inn, Fairfield Inn
Hampton Inn
Holiday Inn Exp & Suites
Howard Johnson (P)
La Quinta (P)
Quality Inn
Red Roof Inn & Suites
Sleep Inn, Wingate Inn

70 mph

EXIT 94 〔204〕
Savannah Pembroke

El Potro Mexican
Hooters, Huddle House
Subway
Shell House Seafood
Waffle House

Chevron (D, ATM)
Shell (ATM)

EconoLodge
Microtel Inn & Suites
Super 8, Travelodge

EXIT 99 〔16〕
Macon Savannah

Baldino's Subs
Cracker Barrel
Huddle House, KFC
Krispy Kreme
Krystal, McDonald's (P)
Mugg Shots
Peking Gourmet
Pizza Hut, Taco Bell
Waffle House

BP (LP, ATM)
Enmark (D, CW, ATM)

Best Western Suites
Jameson Inn
Microtel Inn & Suites
Ramada Limited
Travelodge Suites

Food Lion

Carter's

Savannah Int'l Airport

Burger King
Don's Famous BBQ
El Potro Mexican
Hardee's
Hong Kong Chinese
Lovezzola's Pizza
Spanky's
Subway, Wendy's
Western Sizzlin'

BP (LP, ATM)
Gate (D), Shell (ATM)

Comfort Inn & Suites
EconoLodge

EXIT 102 〔80〕
Pooler Garden City

Pipemakers Canal

Waffle House

BP (ATM)
Shell (D, ATM)

Fairfield Inn
Hawthorn Suites

EXIT 104
Hilton Head Savannah Intl Airport

Arby's, Chick-fil-A
Schlotsky's Deli, Sonic
Subway, Zaxby's

Shell (LP, ATM)

Red Roof Inn

Walmart (24h)

65 mph

© 2004

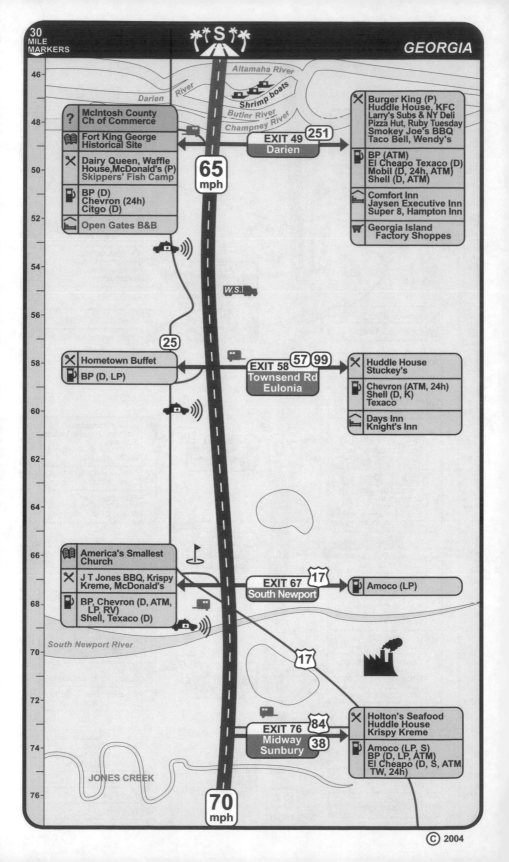

16
18
20
22
24
26
28
30
32
34
36
38
40
42
44
46

Satilla River

Marshes of Glynn

Turtle River

Glynco Jetport

EXIT 26
Dover Bluff Rd

17

17

EXIT 29
Brunswick
Waycross
S Ga Pkwy
17
82
520

EXIT 36
Jesup
Brunswick
341
25

EXIT 38
Brunswick
N Golden
Isles Pkwy
17
25

70 mph

? Golden Isles Welcome Ctr

REST AREA with RV Dump Pets welcome

EXIT 42
99

17

65 mph

Choo Choo BBQ
Mobil (D, ATM)

Church's Chicken
Huddle House
Krispie Kreme, Krystal
McDonalds, Steak &
Shake (24h), Subway
The GA Pig BBQ

Amoco (D, CW)
Mobil (D)
Phillips 66 (D)
Pilot Travel Center (S,
D, 24h, ATM, LP)
Texaco (LP, ATM)

Blue Beacon Truck Wash

Burger King (P), KFC
Cracker Barrel, IHOP
Krystal, McDonald's (P)
Pizza Hut, Quizno's
Shoney's, Wendy's
Taco Bell, Waffle House

Chevron (D, CW, LP)
Exxon (D, ATM, 24h)
Racetrac (ATM, 24h)
Texaco, (D, LP)

Days Inn, Hampton
Knight's Inn, Ramada
Red Roof Inn & Suites

Racetrac (ATM, 24h)

Cambridge Suites
Fairfield Inn
Microtel Inn & Suites

Hofwyl-Broadfield
Plantation

Country Market
Country Pride
Magic Dragon
Pepperoni's
Waffle House

Flying J Plaza Conoco
(D, BP, S, ATM, 24h)
Shell/El Cheapo (D,
ATM, 24h, S)
T/A Travel (D, TR, S, 24h)

Daystop Inn, Microtel
Super 8

Captain Joe's Seafood
China Lee, Denny's
Huddle House
Jay's Fish & Steak
Larry's Subs / NY Deli
Matteo's Italian
Minh-Sun Chinese
Mulligan's, Sonny's BBQ
Subway, Waffle House

Amoco (CW, ATM)
El Cheapo (D, ATM)
Mobil (D, ATM)

Best Western
Comfort Inn
Holiday Inn, Motel 6
Sleep Inn, Super 8

CVS

Winn Dixie

Sun Coast RV Center

China Town
Crackers Seafood
Huddle House
Manhattan Subs
Waffle House

Amoco (24h, ATM)
BP ATM 24h
Chevron (D, LP, ATM)
Flash (ATM, 24h)
Shell (D, LP, RV, T)

EconoLodge
Guest Cottage
Quality Inn

Food Lion

© 2004

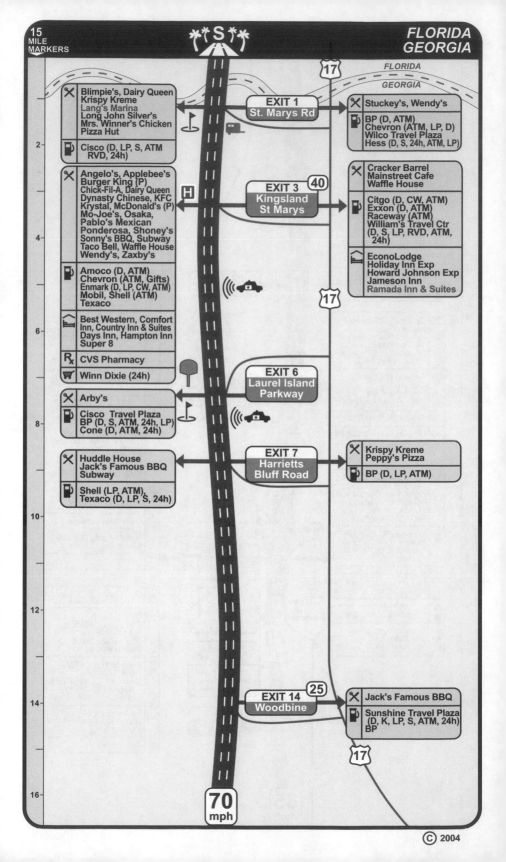

15 MILE MARKERS

FLORIDA GEORGIA

FLORIDA
GEORGIA

EXIT 1
St. Marys Rd

✕ Blimpie's, Dairy Queen
Krispy Kreme
Lang's Marina
Long John Silver's
Mrs. Winner's Chicken
Pizza Hut

⛽ Cisco (D, LP, S, ATM)
RVD, 24h)

✕ Stuckey's, Wendy's

⛽ BP (D, ATM)
Chevron (ATM, LP, D)
Wilco Travel Plaza
Hess (D, S, 24h, ATM, LP)

EXIT 3
Kingsland
St Marys

✕ Angelo's, Applebee's
Burger King (P)
Chick-Fil-A, Dairy Queen
Dynasty Chinese, KFC
Krystal, McDonald's (P)
Mo-Joe's, Osaka,
Pablo's Mexican
Ponderosa, Shoney's
Sonny's BBQ, Subway
Taco Bell, Waffle House
Wendy's, Zaxby's

⛽ Amoco (D, ATM)
Chevron (ATM, Gifts)
Enmark (D, LP, CW, ATM)
Mobil, Shell (ATM)
Texaco

🛏 Best Western, Comfort
Inn, Country Inn & Suites
Days Inn, Hampton Inn
Super 8

℞ CVS Pharmacy

🛒 Winn Dixie (24h)

✕ Cracker Barrel
Mainstreet Cafe
Waffle House

⛽ Citgo (D, CW, ATM)
Exxon (D, ATM)
Raceway (ATM)
William's Travel Ctr
(D, S, LP, RVD, ATM,
24h)

🛏 EconoLodge
Holiday Inn Exp
Howard Johnson Exp
Jameson Inn
Ramada Inn & Suites

EXIT 6
Laurel Island
Parkway

✕ Arby's

⛽ Cisco Travel Plaza
BP (D, S, ATM, 24h, LP)
Cone (D, ATM, 24h)

EXIT 7
Harrietts
Bluff Road

✕ Huddle House
Jack's Famous BBQ
Subway

⛽ Shell (LP, ATM),
Texaco (D, LP, S, 24h)

✕ Krispy Kreme
Peppy's Pizza

⛽ BP (D, LP, ATM)

EXIT 14
Woodbine

✕ Jack's Famous BBQ

⛽ Sunshine Travel Plaza
(D, K, LP, S, ATM, 24h)
BP

70 mph

© 2004

☆ MASSACHUSETTS ☆

It was President Dwight D. Eisenhower, while leading the Allied forces in Europe, who noticed the German autobahns and how crucial a highway system was for a nation's defense. The reason Interstates go around major cities rather than through them is because it would be harder to destroy them in case of war. In 1956, Eisenhower signed the Federal Aid Highway Act birthing the National System of Interstate and Defense Highways, wherein the federal government would pay 90% of the costs paving the way for the post war boom of roads for Americans and contributing to their love of automobiles.

Exit 10: Furlong's Cottage Candies – Stop the car!. You are about to pass a 90-year-old homemade chocolate store. They are famous for stemmed cherries dipped into fondant and then milk or dark chocolate. Stan likes the cream centers - they offer 18 different ones (pineapple, ice cream drop, pistachio, marshmallow, coconut), but for Sandra it's the chocolate covered nuts or apricots (there's also orange peel, brazil nuts, ginger, prunes). People who love hard and chewy candy will enjoy molasses sponge, peanut butter bolsters and caramash. Sugar free treats are here, and most everything can be shipped home. ☞ Head west up Coney St. to US 1 and turn right to 1355 Providence Highway (US 1). ☎ 781-762-4124.

Exit 9: FunWay – We're not sure if your kids will do any eating if you stop at this cafe, but they sure will enjoy the break. There's mini golf, bumper boats, a go-kart track, batting cages and a game room. You can play a round of pool if you're not elbowing your place in line with the kids to join their fun. And oh yes - you can eat salads, chicken, ribs, steak, sea scallops casino, linguine with clam sauce, sandwiches (bbq chicken wrap, chicken parmesan) and pizza. Summer weekends feature dance parties. ☞ From I-95 exit 9, head south on US 1 (Washington St) for about 2 1/4 miles to 2 Washington Street on you left. www.funwaycafe.com ☎ 508-668-2000.

Exit 8: Ward's Berry Farm – If you want to pick up fresh food for the car, you can't get much fresher than a farm stand store. In season there's strawberries, blueberries, raspberries, tomatoes, cucumbers, peas, peaches, honey, squash, Asian eggplants etc. They make freshly squeezed juices and smoothies from the fresh fruits, and pies and preserves: jalapeno tangerine jam, cherry butter, pink grapefruit marmalade and nuts in clover honey. In the fridge there's quick lunch food: grilled chicken and corn chowder, scallion humous, eggplant parmagiana, Mrs. Ward's meatballs in sauce. Fair trade coffee is sold here to have along with the home made bread, muffins, cookies.

Ring... Ring... Ring... It's for you

Exit 12: Alexander Graham Bell invented the telephone here in Boston. He was born in 1847 in Edinburgh, Scotland, moved to Ontario, Canada and then settled in Boston. Throughout his life, Bell had been interested in the education of deaf people. This interest led him to invent the microphone, and in 1876 his "electrical speech machine," which we now call a telephone. If you think about it, this paved the way for the Information Superhighway we rely on today.

In season, you can pick berries or pumpkins or take hayrides. There's even an indoor petting zoo cared for by the local 4H club and an outdoor playground, including toy tractors.

Jim and Bob Ward's dad purchased land in 1981 for his "retirement"; he bought 7,000 blueberry bushes to start a farm. Neither Jim nor Bob had any farming experience, but when their father died they decided to run the 150-acre farm. Their mother is the backbone of the farm. Starting in February, she transplants every seedling in the greenhouse, and in May she herself starts doing all the baking for the farm stand. All crops are hand harvested, and there are many other steps done by hand. Everything they produce is sold in this farm stand store or to specialty restaurants, groceries, and a cooperative, Coastal Growers. ☎ 781-784-3600.

Mile 9 Northbound: Massachusetts Info Centre – Here's a place to stop and ask questions about things to do in the area or to use the direct dial phones to 9 motels. Pick up flyers and FREE coupon motel booklets and take advantage of bathrooms. There's vending machines and a picnic area here. ◑ Sept-Mar Daily 8-6, Mar-Aug 8-8.

Exit 3: Capron Park Zoo – If the kids need a bit of an airing, why not let them run about in this intimate zoo with a rainforest display, a nocturnal building and more. The park around it is a nice place for a picnic lunch. Go

> **Exit 8:** On Thanksgiving in 1903, at his grandparents' homestead in Fairhaven, Franklin Delano Roosevelt made quite a "startling announcement" to his mother Sara that he had become engaged to (Anna) Eleanor Roosevelt.

see Edgar Allen Crow and Kazoo, a prairie dog, that are an inseparable pair who "talk" to each other. They have an adopt-an-animal program (you can choose perhaps a diadem snake, flying fox or snow leopard) which could add to road trip fun if every time you pass here, you can check up on "your" special friend. ◑ Daily 10-4 ☞ From I-95 exit 3 head east along South Avenue (Rte 123) to County St. Turn left and follow the signs to the zoo at 201 County St. www.capronparkzoo.com ☎ 508-222-6202.

☆ RHODE ISLAND ☆

Exit 29S or 28N: Blackstone Valley Visitor Center – Well, here not only do you get a clean bathroom, friendly advice and brochures, but a gift shop with original items by Rhode Island artists: hats, soaps, glass wine stoppers, jewelry, herbal teas, wooden walking sticks, beaded lamp finials and oh yes, Starbucks coffee. There is a changing art gallery exhibit and a film about the rise and fall of the American Industrial Revolution. ◑ Daily 9-5. ☞ See directions to the Slater Mill museum below. The visitor center is around the corner at 175 Main St. www.tourblackstone.com ☎ 800-454-2882 or 401-724-2200.

Exit 29: Samuel Slater Canal Boat – What a way to break up a long drive. Get lulled to sleep overnight in a floating B & B - a 40-ft British canal boat which has berths for four, a head with shower, galley/dining area and unfortunately a TV, VCR, radio, phone and microwave.

As a millennium project, the Blackstone Valley Tourism Council commissioned the boat and named it in honor of the father of the American Industrial Revolution. It's a reminder of the 20 years (1828-1848) when canal boats were a common sight on the river and the Blackstone Canal. The canal linked Worcester, MA and Providence, RI and was used to transport goods and passengers during the early stages of the region's manufacturing growth until 1848, when railroads replaced the canal. If you stay overnight, you can book the boat for a clambake or a cruise, and you may get to see swans, great blue herons and turtles. www.tourblackstone.com ☎ 800-454-BVTC or 401-724-2200.

Exit 28N or 27S: Slater Mill Living History Museum – In 1789, 21-year-old Samuel Slater left England with some knowledge of textile machinery, having been a manager in the Arkwright Mills in Derbyshire. With financial support from Moses Brown, he built this water-powered mill, and within the year was able to produce cotton yarn.

One of these machines could supply a weaver with the same amount of yarn as 10 hand weavers. This was the first factory in America, and it helped transform the area so much that by 1820 processing cotton became the backbone of Rhode Island's economy. Besides the mill, the museum displays the history of US textile manufacturing.

On site is the Wilkinson Mill, built of rubble stone in 1810 by Oziel Wilkinson's son David, and used as a machine shop and textile mill. Here you can view a replica of a mid-breast waterwheel using river power to move wood-working and metal-working machinery. Moved to the site is the Sylvanus Brown House (1758), which is now used for spinning and weaving demonstrations and which sports a textile and dye garden. ◗ May 1st -Sept 30, Tues-Sun 10-5. ☞ From I-95 Southbound: Take exit 29 (Downtown Pawtucket), Turn right at the second stop sign onto Broadway. Make a right turn at the traffic light onto Exchange Street, then turn left

at the next traffic light onto Roosevelt Avenue. Slater Mill is on the left after City Hall. Northbound: Take exit 28 (School Street), turn left at the bottom of the ramp and go through the light, down the hill, bear right across the river and turn right onto Roosevelt Avenue. Slater Mill is on the right at 67 Roosevelt Ave. www.slatermill.org ☎ 401-725-8638.

Exit 27: Modern Diner – Diners started out in Providence to serve night workers when restaurants were closed, and were a precursor to today's fast food. One of the first of these restaurateurs in R.I. was Walter Scott, who galloped around in 1872 in his horse-drawn canteen serving light food, pies and coffee.

This "Modern Diner", opened in 1941, is a Sterling Streamliner that was factory-built and customized. What's neat about the menu here is that it is schizophrenic - the oldsters can still have their classic menu, featuring their famous "Jimmie Gimmie" (2 poached eggs on an English muffin with sliced tomatoes, topped with melted cheese and bacon), while the youngsters trek in for the modern twist on it: "Eggs St. Nick" (2 poached eggs with fried onions and leeks set in a potato skin).

Daily lunch specials (meatloaf, liver & onions, Del Monico steak, corned beef and cabbage) remain the same, but brunch on the weekends will bring butterscotch almond coconut pan-

Exit 22: Edgar Allan Poe took a special liking to the Athenaeum library. In 1753 he spent many days and nights here courting Sarah Whitman by reading poetry to her. 251 Benefit St. ☎ 401-421-6970.

cakes, custard French toast with Kentucky bourbon sauce or lobster Benedict. ◐ Mon-Sat 6-3, Sun 7-2. ☞ From I-95 exit 27 take George St. (Rte 1) South, angling to the left at the fork, and you will see ther diner ahead of you at 364 East Ave. ☎ 401-726-8390.

Baubles, Bangles and Beads

Exit 22: Women of the world should be thankful that in 1794 Nehemiah Dodge, a Providence gold-smith, developed the process for plating base metal with gold. Most of the sparkly gold costume jewelry that adorns us today can be traced back to his invention.

Exit 22: Haven Bros. – It doesn't get more quirky than this. Haven Bros. Diner, which stands night duty on the Fulton St. corner of City Hall, began in 1888 as a wooden lunch wagon with oak interior and rustic scenery painted on the sides. Anna Coffey Haven passed it on to her sons, Tom and Henry, who are the Bros. in its name. In 1949, Catherine Haven Gannon replaced the wagon with the steel trailer that remains today.

In 1986, city planners were trying to attract new business downtown and tried to give the diner the boot because of its "unattractive" quality, so by a Mayor's order it was moved 3 blocks away to W. Exchange Street.

The people of Providence started an overwhelming protest to the Journal, and the Mayor's office was flooded with requests by mail and phone pleading for the diner to stay at City Hall. "I never realized that so many people would care so much about a truck that sells hot dogs", exclaimed Mayor Paolino. The 18-wheeler was allowed back to its privileged spot (with its free electricity hook-up to a lamp-post!), and the mayor helped celebrate its 100th anniversary in 1988 with a hot dog and champagne party.

Between 5 pm and 3 am Sun-Thu and 5 pm-4 am Fri & Sat, you can join senators, cops, truck drivers, bar hoppers, hospital shift workers and motorcycle gangs for the burgers, (veggie ones too), fried eggs, grilled cheese, chili dogs, beans and even the New England regular - a lobster roll. Corner of Dorrence and Fulton. ☎ 401-861-7777.

Exit 22: "Kee–mo–sabie" – Roger Williams, with his tolerence for all beliefs, befriended the Wampanoag and Narragansett tribes. They later deeded him land in 1636 and, as payment Canonicus, one of the chiefs, was allowed to take what he wanted from Williams' trading post. In 1643 Williams published "A Key into the Language of America", which covered both translations of Narragansett words and observations of their culture. He spent his life forging closer ties to the Native Americans, defending their rights and acting as a mediator for the Massachusetts colony, even though he had been thrown out of it. Willams had had the audacity to question English charters which just took land from Native Americans. His deep respect for tribal rights was extraordinary for those times.

The Exterminator

Mile 35.5, between exits 18 and 19 on the West side: Get the kids ready to catch a glimpse of the 9 foot high, 58 ft long purple termite named "Nibbles Woodaway" which sits quite close to and overlooking the highway. This hurricane-proof 2 ton bug, 928 times the size of the household variety, must be hard to get rid of - it's been sitting on top of the New England Pest Control Building for 24 years. The steel wire-mesh-fiberglas creature is not only a landmark on the road, but also a movie star, having appeared in *Dumb and Dumber* and on the *Oprah Winfrey Show*. The company dresses the bug for holidays: Uncle Sam hat for July 4, witch's hat and broom for Halloween and a red blinking nose and antlers for Christmas.

Exit 21: Regal Reptiles – This is a low-key, kid-friendly center that breeds and sells reptiles and has set up exhibits of 500 snakes, lizards, frogs, geckos, turtles and baby alligators. You can take a photo with an alligator, giant tortoise or huge snake. There's a gift shop with slimy (but fake) reptiles to buy, books, alligator skulls, tortoise shells, wooden puzzles, tons of T-shirts and even a frog lamp. If you're lucky you'll get to see staff feeding the gang - we caught frogs being fed crickets. ◐ Daily 11-7. ☞ I-95 Exit 21. Northbound, turn left onto Broadway, then next left onto Service Rd 7 (Southbound, keep straight on Service Rd past Broadway). Second street after Broadway is Washington St. - turn right for 2 blocks to 425 Washington St. on the right. www.regalreptiles.com ☎ 401-277-9000.

Exit 18N or 19S: Russian Sub Museum – It is a totally weird feeling to be walking through an "enemy" cruise missile submarine. It is also a great idea to contrast this one with the USS Nautilus in Groton, down the road a piece. If you can fit through the round portal at the entrance, you will be allowed to slink through this deceivingly crudely finished but highly electronically sophisticated (Kasatka satellite downlink - way back then!) 1965-built ship.

How did we wind up with this Cold War souvenir? After the fall of the Iron Curtain, an enterprising Russian sold her to a Finn who tried to turn it into a restaurant (We are still trying to figure out where they cooked or sat). It failed, and was brought to St. Petersburg, FL as a tourist site. That didn't work either, so it was purchased by Paramount and used in the movie "K-19:The Widowmaker", and was eventually put up on eBay and brought here. Now in an ironic twist, it sits here to raise money for the restoration of the USS Saratoga, an aircraft carrier that this sub had stalked in its it heyday.

Project 651 (NATO named: Juliette 484) subs were developed by the USSR in the 1950's to provide nuclear strike capabilities against mainland US cities like New York and Washington, and wore a second skin of rubber sound-absorbing tiles, which with their low magnetic signature, very cleverly made them difficult to track.

It is hoped that this sub will re-unite in Quonset Point with her former adversary for peaceful and educational purposes. ◗ Sat-Sun 10-6, but during school vacations and holidays, 11-5 weekdays. ☞ From I-95 Exit 18, keep right off the ramp if you're heading North (left if South) towards Allens Ave. Turn left for about 0.8 mi. to Collier Point Park on the right hand side and turn up the access lane. www.russiansubmuseum.org ☎ 401-521-3600.

Exit 15: Bugaboo Creek – In this Canadian themed (talking fir trees and mooseheads) restaurant, you'll find the warmth of a rustic mountain lodge at the end of an adventurous mountain climb. In 1910, Conrad Kain and his team were some of the first to climb to the summit of a rugged range in the Canadian Rockies. In one climb, a mate exclaimed, "This is a veritable bugaboo," borrowing a mining term used by prospectors to describe a dead-end lead. Kain took his scoff as a challenge and vowed to reach the top of the spectacular range and name it the Bugaboo Mountains (officially Bugaboo Glacier Provincial Park).

Adjectives to describe the food are borrowed from Canadiana: Moosebreath burger, Dog Team sandwich, Snowbird, Cariboo, Mountie. For all you hungry climbers, expect to find Prime Rib and hearty steaks, baked onion and ale (Canadian beer, eh!) soup and Canadian salmon, but also chicken, salad and sandwiches for the others. ◗ Mon-Th 11:30-10, Fri & Sat 11:30-10:30, Sun 12-9. 30 Jefferson Blvd., just on the hill

to the east from I-95. Other location on I-95: Exit 4 in Delaware. ☎ 302-283-0615 www.bugaboocreeksteakhouse.com ☎ 401-781-1400.

Drinking a Cabinet

In RI, if you ask for a milk shake, they will give you milk and syrup, but if you want what most Americans call a milk shake, with ice cream mixed in, you must order a cabinet. The term's origins are unknown, but the most commonly accepted thought is that milk shake blenders used to be shipped in heavy wooden cabinets.

There are also über-cabinets with 3 or 4 scoops of ice cream, which have been made famous by a 70-year-old regional chain called Newport Creamery, and are called Awful Awful®, short for awful big, awful good. They are nearly impossible to finish; the chain has a standing offer to "Drink 3, get one free!".

The homegrown flavor choice is coffee, due to Rhode Islanders' love of coffee milk. Nowadays, you can get reduced fat cabinets, or at Newport Creamery, outrageous flavors: Oreo®, Strawberry Banana Chip, Cappuccino Crunch & Choc O' Nutter. If you must try one on this trip, there's a location in the Warwick Mall at Exit 12.

Exit 12: Warwick Mall – Kids will love the Carousel food court, and you'll all enjoy Rhode Island's famous Newport Creamery for "cabinets" (shakes). Macy's, Filene's and JC Penney are the anchors, and there's Lane Bryant, Old Navy, Abercrombie & Fitch for the clothes, Aldo for shoes, Firestone if

you're having tire trouble and even a RI Costume store. ◑ Mon-Sat 10-10, Sun 12-6 ☞ Take exit 12B off I-95 Southbound or exit 11 Northbound, onto I-295 north, and exit immediately at exit 2, right into the mall. (Note that the Rhode Island Mall is just on the other side of 295) www.warwickmall.com ☎ 401-739-7500.

WARWICK'S "BAD BOY"

Exit 10: Warwick was founded by Samuel Gorton, who was a bit of a renegade. He was thrown out of Plymouth Colony, Portsmouth and even from the tolerant Roger Williams' Providence, and had disagreements with Aquidneck and Pawtuxet. To avoid persecution, he and a band of followers bought land from the Narragansett Indians, called the Shawomet Purchase. Somehow, this caused trouble again, this time with the Massachusetts Bay Colony, and he and his cult followers were sent to prison for blasphemy.

After serving his sentence, he sailed back to England and was promised protection by the Earl of Warwick, an important member of Parliament at the time. He returned to the New World and renamed Shawomet to Warwick, after his protector, the Earl.

Exit 3: Boucher's Wood River Inn Restaurant – Here's a family owned resto for your basic food: a soup of the day, fish & chips, meatballs and spaghetti, baby back ribs, shrimp scampi and burgers (made from fresh meat) with a fireplace to warm your toesies. There are daily specials: meatloaf and mashies on Wednesday, shepherd's pie on Monday and an extensive breakfast menu including omelets, Mickey Mouse pancakes and eggs benedict or florentine. 1139 Main St. ☎ 401-539-9800.

Exit 3: The Stagecoach House Inn – Imagine what stagecoach drivers and travelers in 1796 (when this was built) would have thought of the Jacuzzi tubs in their rooms. Have a soak, romance by the fireplace and enjoy your breakfast on the deck overlooking Wood River listening to the waterfall. There are shops on the lower level for books, gifts or The Village Baker & Cafe for sandwiches to go (spinach/cheese or chicken calzones) and divine desserts: Oreo bomb, peanut butter delights, cinnamon twists, fig squares and the ones we took home - brownie on a stick. 1136 Main St. www.stagecoachhouse.com ☎ 888-814-9600 or 401-539-9600.

Exit 3: Golf Central – Kids getting crabby in the back seat or do you need to get out and stretch those tight shoulder muscles? Right here you have an option of driving some golf balls, hitting in the batting cages or playing 18 holes of miniature golf. ◑ Summer, Mon-Thurs 7-10, Sat & Sun 7-11, rest of year til dusk. Route 138. ☎ 401-539-2383.

Mile 9 Northbound: Rhode Island Welcome Center – You are always welcome to pick up any flyers on the State. Ask for travel info, use the clean rest rooms, try the vending machines or enjoy the picnic area. ◑ Daily 8:30-6. ☎ 401-539-3031.

Exit 2: Enchanted Forest – Low key fun for toddlers and younger children, with nursery rhyme attractions like the brick cottage from "The Three Little Pigs" or the shoe from the "The Old Woman who Lived in a Shoe" from Mother Goose and other storybook favorites coming to life. Older kids will enjoy the bumper cars, tilt-a-whirl, ferris wheel, roller coaster, batting cages or miniature golf. ☀ May-Labor Day, 10-5; Sept, weekends only 10-5. ☞ From I-95 Exit 2 head North toward Hopkinton on Woodville Alton Rd for a short bit until it comes to an end. Turn right along Main St until you see the attraction on your right. www.enchant edforest-ri.com ☎ 401-539-7711.

☆ CONNECTICUT ☆

Exit 92: Raspberry Junction – Though about 3 miles off the exit, those of you who love to buy handmade items will go nuts over the 300 artisans represented here selling: weathered wood, hand knits, doll clothing, placemats, music boxes, bibs, stitched sayings on pillows, pins, candle holders, tapestry purses, wooden hair clips, wreaths and more. Besides all that in this 10,000 sq ft. post and beam barn, there's a coffee shop. ☀ Mon-Thurs 9-5, Fri 9-7, Sat 9-6, Sun 12-6. ☞ From I-95 Exit 92, Follow Rte. 2 West for 3 miles. 417 Route 2. www.raspberryjunction.com ☎ 860-535-8410.

Mile 108 Southbound: Connecticut Welcome Center – It always pays to stop at Welcome Centers for their clean rest rooms, coupon booklets and friendly advice. This one has a canine rest area, trailer parking and picnic tables. ☀ Summer Daily 8-6, Sept Daily 8-4, Oct-May Thurs-Sun 9-4.

A UNIQUE ORDINARY

Exit 92: Randall's Ordinary Inn and Restaurant offers a unique opportunity to experience life in the 1600's sleeping in the farm house, log cabin or silo suite (all now very upscale with colonial style canopy beds, rockers, handwoven blankets). Dinner can be authen-

tic colonial cuisine prepared in an open-hearth fireplace or traditional favorites such as Nantucket scallops, roasted duck and roast turkey, all served by a wait staff garbed in period clothing while a harpist spins colonial melodies.

John Randall originally purchased this property in 1680, his son John Randall II built the existing dwelling and then for more than 200 years this farm was occupied by 10 generations of Randalls, and John's ghost seems to still be in residence.

The family became ardent abolitionists before and during the Civil War and were one of the first to free their slaves. This home was a stop on the Underground Railroad. Ask to see the trap door (in The Keep/Hearth Room) that leads to the basement root cellar where slaves were hidden. ☞ From I-95 Exit 92, turn North on Rte 2, and the Inn is located 1/2 mi. on your left. www.randallsordinary.com ☎ 877-599-4540.

Between Exit 89-90, Mile 100 Northbound only: Hoxie Scenic Overlook – You might want to take a stretch here and look out over the pretty Mystic Seaport. The seaport in its heyday was busy with fishing, sealing and whaling, and at one time had more than a dozen shipyards building sloops, schooners, brigs, ships and steamers. It was the 2nd busiest (after Boston), launching ships during the Civil War. The bluff on the right was the scene of a Pequot Indian War. Looking East, you can see in the distance, at Mystic Seaport (originally George Greenman & Bros Shipyard), the masts of the 1841 Charles W. Morgan, a whaling ship, the square-rigged 1882 Joseph Conrad, the sailing schooner L.A. Dunton and many more.

Exit 90: Mystic & Shoreline Visitors' Information Center – Friendly Theresa, Marterese and crew will help you find a hotel or something fun to do in Mystic, if you'd only stop in and ask. The motel discount coupon booklets are here, and even if the center is closed, you can use the FREE hotel reservation night phones located outside, and pick up the popular tourist site flyers there too. ◗ Sept-June Mon-Sat 9:30-5, Sun 10-5; June-Aug Mon-Sat 9-6, Sun 10-5. www.mysticinfo.com ☎ 860-536-1641.

Exit 90: Mystic Aquarium & Institute for Exploration – The sea lion (Coco, Surfer and Tabor) show is bound to please the whole family, since they have been trained as "deep-sea divers" to retrieve sunken objects and carry cameras to record underwater action. Don't miss the Immersion Institute, with robots and the deep-sea camera's live video feed of California coastal waters.

Besides the 30,000 gallon coral reef display and 500 exotic fish, famous underwater explorer Dr. Robert Ballard and his team's findings are on view: see John F. Kennedy's PT 109. Check out the frogs, the weird, slimy shapes, colors and sizes and the new Sting Ray Touch Pool. You can sign up for contact programs with beluga whales and African penguins. ◗ June-Labor Day Daily 9-6; Rest of year 9-5. www.mysticaquarium.org ☎ 860-572-5955.

Exit 88: Mystic Marriott and (Elizabeth Arden) Red Door Spa – We have found very few 5-star properties directly on the I-95 exits, so this one is an oasis in more ways than one. Yes, there is the known luxury of a Marriott hotel, and this one not only has an upscale dining room

(Octagon) and a Starbucks in the lobby, but a luxury Red Door Spa attached to it.

What better way to make your drive more relaxing than to come in and get all those kinks smoothed out of your body with a shea butter massage (even toes and ear lobes) on an ergonomic heated table, cozy warm cocoon towel wraps and eye pillows to soothe. Spa ◗ Mon-Fri 8-9, Sat 8-8, Sun 8-7. 625 North Rd. www.reddoorsalons.com ☎ (hotel) 860-536-5150; ☎ (spa) 860-446-2500.

Exit 86: USS Nautilus and U.S. Navy Submarine Force Museum – The story of the US Navy's "Silent Service" and "sharks of steel" is depicted here, starting the from Bushnell's Turtle, which served in the American Revolution. David Bushnell, who lived here in Connecticut, developed a hand powered submarine, called the Turtle, which tried to attach a 150-lb explosive charge to the British HMS Eagle hull in the NY harbor. The attempt failed due to the Eagle's copper-sheathed bottom.

Learn about the modern Seawolf, Los Angeles and Ohio class submarines and get hands on in a control room (from the USS Bill Fish) or try one of the 3 periscopes. There is no doubt that the highlight of the experience is going aboard the Nautilus, the

U.S.'s first nuclear powered submersible and the first ship to make it to the geographic North Pole. You must go to see how the men slept, figure out where they kept their clothes and gear and imagine 120 of them cooped up here. ◐ May-Oct, Wed-Mon 9-5, Tues 1-5, Nov-May, Wed-Mon 9-4. ☞ I-95 Exit 86, and follow Rte 12 North about 1.7 mi. to the sub base. Turn left on Crystal Lake Rd. and follow the USS Nautilus signs to the museum. 1 Crystal Lake Rd. FREE www.submarine museum.com and www.ussnautilus.org ☎ 800-343-0079 or 860-694-3174.

Exit 85: America's most famous traitor, Benedict Arnold, arrived on Sept 6,1781 with 1,700 British soldiers and attacked Fort Griswold. The 140 American soldiers were able to withstand 2 battles, but succombed to the 3rd. Lt. Col. William Ledyard surrendered by offering his sword to a British officer, who accepted it and then drove it right through him. A massacre followed this act, with 80 Americans killed after this offer to surrender. Dear Benedict, a native of Connecticut, kept busy by setting fire to New London, burning down 150 buildings, supposedly with pleasure. This was one of Britain's last actions in the North.

Exit 84: Note that the front doors of the 1833 Robert Mills U.S. Custom House & Museum of Maritime History are planks from "Old Ironsides". This is where the ship Amistad was docked for more than a year when it was brought to shore in 1839. It is the oldest operating customs house in the nation. 150 Bank St. ☎ 860-447-2501.

Exit 84: Nathan Hale Schoolhouse – Revolutionary War notable Nathan Hale was a school teacher in East Haddam and New London. "He was a happy and faithful teacher, everybody loved him. He was sprightly, kind, intelligent and ever so handsome." Hale was very athletic, and his broad jumping, high jumping and football kicking made him famous at Yale.

In July, 1775 he closed the schoolhouse doors and joined the patriots. In the summer of 1776, George Washington was desperate for information on the strength and intentions of the British, so he asked for a volunteer to spy on them. Nathan Hale exchanged his uniform for a plain brown suit and broad-brimmed hat and grabbing his Yale diploma, pretended to be a schoolmaster. He crossed the L.I. sound and headed for Manhattan, where he was captured on September 21, 1776.

The intelligence reports found on his person caused British General William Howe to order him hanged the next morn without trial. His dying words have turned him into one of the most famous patriots, "I only regret that I have but one life to lose for my country." You can still go visit both the schoolhouses he taught in, at 28 State St. in New London or on Main St., East Haddam (if you want to take a 10-mile detour). ◐ Both are open June-Sept 1, Sat & Sun 12-4 and by appt. ctssar.org/sites/e_hale_ schoolhouse.htm ☎ 860-873-3399 FREE.

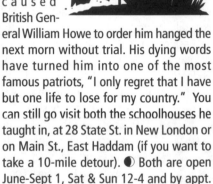

Exit 82: Crystal Mall – If you are in some sort of need of a mall, this one, with its signature Waterford Crystal chandelier, has 130 options on 2 floors. Jazz up your vacation with Frederick's of Hollywood, find Euro fashions at H&M (for kids too!), find car ideas at Game Stop, and for cranky travelers, perhaps "Crab World". If you need one, there's 10 wireless communication stores and complimentary wheel chairs. ◐ Mon-Sat 9:30-9:30, Sun 11-6. ☞ Head

Exit 67: James Gallery & Soda Fountain – Anna Louise James was the first African American woman and one of the first women, period, to become a pharmacist in the state in 1911. She was one of the first women to register to vote when the women's suffrage was passed in 1920. You can visit her pharmacy at 2 Pennywise Lane. ☎ 860-395-1229.

North on Hartford Turnpike (Rte 85), left for Northbound travellers, for about 1/4 mi. www.shopsimon.com ☎ 860-442-8500.

Exit 67: Mill Rock Mini Golf – Give the kids (and you) a bit of a break on this mini golf course sitting on an exit. The holes have a bridge, a waterfall, cave, a shallow pond, a water fountain and if you are really lucky and are there at the right time, one hole is close enough to watch real trains passing on the tracks. ◑ May-Sept 11-11. ☎ 860-395-1882.

Mile 65 Northbound: Connecticut Welcome Center – It always pays to stop at Welcome Centers for their clean rest rooms, FREE coupon booklets and friendly advice. This one has a canine rest area. ◑ Daily 8-6 Memorial Day to Columbus Day, Sept: Daily 8-4, Oct-May: Thurs-Sun 9-4.

Exit 65: Tanger Outlets – For those who love to shop, here's 65 stores with a variety for all: J.Crew, Old Navy, Pfaltzgraff, Cool Brands 4 Kids, Fuller Brush and more. It has a homey village architecture reminiscent of a New England train station, and for fun you can check out both a restored 1902 cruising yawl and the last working steam engine in the state. ◑ Jan-Mar: Sun-Thu 10-6, Fri & Sat 10-9, Apr-Dec: Mon-Sat 10-9, Sun 10-6. www.tangeroutlet.com ☎ 866-665-8685 or 860-399-8656.

Exit 63: Clinton Crossing Premium Outlets – Names, names names, they're all here: Barneys, BCBG Max Azria, GF Ferre, Versace, Donna Karan, Calvin Klein, Waterford Wedgwood, Dooney & Bourke, Coach and about 65 more. Wheelchair and stroller rental available. ◑ Jul-Sept: Mon-Sat 10-9, Sun 10-8; Oct-Dec and Apr-June: Mon-Sat 10-9, Sun 10-6; Jan-Mar Sun-Wed 10-6, Th-Sat 10-9. www.premiumoutlets.com ☎ 860-664-0700.

ROUND AND ROUND

There are now less than 200 antique wooden carousels left in the U.S., and Connecticut is lucky to have 12 locations with carousels, 5 of which are the antique wooden ones. Along I-95 you can have fun hopping on and off 6 of  them: Exit 28: Beardsley Zoo Carousel, 1875 Noble Ave, Bridgeport ☎ 203-394-6565; Exit 50: Lighthouse Point Park, 2 Lighthouse Rd, New Haven ☎ 203-946-8327; Exit 62: Lenny and Joe's Fish Tale Restaurant, 1301 Boston Post Rd, Madison ☎ 203-245-7289; Exit 71: Carousel at Old Lyme, 75 Hartford Ave. Sound View Beach ☎ 860-434-3908; Exit 83: Ocean Beach Park, 1225 Ocean Ave., New London ☎ 860-447-3031; Exit 90: Mystic Carousel & Fun Center, 193 Germanville Ave.

Exit 62: Lenny & Joe's Fish Tale Restaurant – In 1979, Lenny and Joe opened up a roadside clam stand with 4 picnic tables, and offered overly generous portions with friendly service. Now, over 25 years later, they have grown to 2 restaurants with many of the same friendly staff offering only the freshest fish and seafood in a casual atmosphere. The portions are definitely shareable, and you won't have to negotiate what to eat if you just order the seafood platter, which has clam strips, scallops, shrimp and scrod. Whole clams with "firm, flavorful bellies" are a specialty.

In the summer there's a lobster shack offering fresh lobster or chunky buttery lobster rolls, and the ice cream stand opens. This location has outdoor seating and a beautiful carousel for the kids. ☞ From I-95, head South toward the Hammonasset State Park and turn left at Boston Post Road (Rte 1). The restaurant is 300 yards on your left at 1301 Boston Post Rd. www.ljfishtale.com ☎ 203-245-7289. Other location at Exit 64: Westbrook, 86 Boston Post Rd. ☎ 860-669-0767.

Exit 59: Shoreline Diner & Vegetarian Enclave – It was rare, driving the length of this highway, to find a vegetarian restaurant. This diner has 2 locations with not only creative veggies (grilled tempeh with wild rice cake, sauerkraut, & maple mustard on rye, grilled polenta with portobello mushroom sauce with cucumber salsa, vegetable strudel, veggie medley caesar salad), but with a full diner menu as well.

Yes, it goes from pancakes to club sandwiches, burgers and steak, to fresh seafood and Italian pasta, but expect some interesting twists on the regular: a tuna sandwich with wasabe mayonnaise, salmon and asparagus fettuccini, poached eggs with spinach and feta, 14 yummy desserts and a favorite for a New Yorker: egg creams. ◖ 7 am to midnight. 345 Boston Post Rd. ☎ 203-458-7380. Other location at Exit 24: Fairfield Diner, 90 King's Highway cutoff ☎ 203-335-4090.

Exit 56: Hilltop Orchards Country Store & Bakery – The main reason for stopping here is the famous homemade pies. The story begins in 1867, when Samuel Cooke returned from the Civil War and bought this land and, like his family who had been here since 1640, planted an apple orchard. Two of his sons opened the first roadside stand, and it was Florence Cooke, the wife of Samuel's grandson Nelson, who accidentally started the pie story.

After baking pies with her mother-in-law Edith Cooke, she brought one to the dairy bar in the roadside stand to slice up for customers. Customers clamored for whole pies, so Nelson, Florence, Edith, and Phyllis Ceccolini (Florence's Mom) started their famous pie business, which has been acclaimed on national television and made it to the front lines of the Vietnam war.

Yes, there's the apple flavor, but try one of the 15 others, like: Coconut Custard, Key Lime, Chocolate/Lemon, Peach Melba or Pineapple.

The other big deal here is the Yankee Candles in 60 scents, from Banana Nut Bread, Aloe Vera and Wild Pansies to Clean Cotton, Coconut Bay or Cucumber and Cantaloupe. There are Ty™ plush toys, maple products from Vermont

and 30 flavors of Jelly Bellies™ too. In the summer, there's a rack of tourist brochures. ◑ Daily 9:30-5:30 ☞ Head North from 95 up Leetes Island Rd to its end at Main St. Turn right up Main St. to 616 E. Main St. ☎ 203-488-0779.

Exit 54: Lenny's Indian Head Inn – This wooden structure, set on the marshes with its well worn varnished wooden booths, is your Kodak shot of a New England seafood shack. The food is worth the detour off I-95 just to taste Grandma Georgianna Moon's tangy clam soup recipe and their magical way of deep frying fish without you being able to discern that oil was involved. The platter with clams, shrimps, scallops and scrod was not only huge but delicious. The dippable zuppa d'clams is a popular starter.

This is a second generation family business, with sister Kim Conlin up front, and such attention to freshness that some days the boys of the family, Tom and Chris, are out fishing for your dinner. Carnivores please note that their burgers have been voted the best in at least one contest, and there's also hot dogs, steaks and an outdoor deck in warm weather. Cash only, but there's an ATM in front. ☞ From I-95 Exit 54 take Cedar St. South toward the water until it ends in 1/2 mi. at Main St. Turn left and take the right fork as it turns into S Main St., which ends in 3 blocks at Montowese St. (Rte 146). Turn right and continue for 1.4 mi. to 205 S Montowese St. on your right. www.LennysNow.com ☎ 203-488-1500.

Exit 47: Historic Mansion Inn – This inn, built in 1812 for a sea captain, was then bought in 1862 by Mr. Parmalee, co-founder of the Baldwin Piano company and (due to a fire in his piano factory) inventor of the fire sprinkler system. He installed "The Fireman That Never Sleeps" here in his own home, so this inn was the first residential building in the world to have its own fire sprinkler system. Some of the orig-

inal pipes and valves are still working! Doll lovers will enjoy the collection of handmade dolls designed and crafted by Mrs. Mastrobuono, one of the current owners. www.thehistoricmansioninn.com ☎ 888-512-6278 or 203-865-8324.

Take a Bite of Hamburger History

Exit 47: Louis' Lunch (The birthplace of the hamburger) – In 1900, a customer asked Louis Lassen for a meal on the run. He broiled some chopped beef on a vertical cast iron grill and used the same grill to toast some bread to put it on. Today you can take a bite of history cooked on that very grill (they sure knew how to build them in those days), but remember - only onions, cheese or tomato are acceptable garnishes (no mustard or ketchup here).

This century-old family business holds such a special place in the hearts and stomachs of the locals that when it was threatened with demolition, many helped preserve it in a fun way. After managing to find a place for it to be relocated (well, 3 of its walls, anyway), supporters sent thousands of bricks from every corner of the globe for the 4th wall.

Third generation Ken Lassen, Louis' grandson, will give you a "tour of the walls", if you'd only ask. To this day customers are still on the run, and seats are so few that voices yelling "to go" are still the order of the day. ◑ Tues & Wed 11-4,

Th-Sat 12-2. ☞ From I-95 Exit 47 (Rte 34, a left exit if you're Northbound) head toward Downtown New Haven. Keep right immediately and take Exit 1. Continue on the service road to Church St and turn right for 2 blocks and make a left onto Crown St. The restaurant is on your right on the 4th block. 261-263 Crown St. www.louis lunch.com ☎ 203-562-5507.

Exit 47: Peabody Museum of Natural History – There is no question that the star of this small museum is the 67-foot brontosaurus skeleton. He's there along with Triceratops, Stegosaurus and others in the Great Hall of Dinosaurs under Rudolph F. Zallinger's famous mural "The Age of Reptiles".

The museum's collections began in the 1870's when Othniel Charles Marsh (George Peabody's nephew) led four Yale expeditions to the American West searching for fossils. The amazing dioramas of animals (timber wolf, bighorn sheep, polar bear) in their habitats were painted by J. Perry Wilson and Francis Lee Jacques assisted by Ralph C. Morrill, who created the lifelike foregrounds. See if you can join the visitors' game of trying to figure out where foreground ends and background begins. At the bison diorama we learned that the U.S. Government encouraged the elimination of the herds of buffalo to control the Plains Indians whose culture and economy depended on them.

The rest of the museum is filled with the birds and minerals of Connecticut, evolutionary human origins, Connecticut Indians and the spooky hall of ancient Egyptian with real "live" dead mummies. This year there's a special exhibit til June, 2005 on "Dinosaur Eggs, Nests and Young". ◑ Mon-Sat 10-5, Sun 12-5 ☞ Take Exit 47 to the left off I-95 and get off immediately at exit 1. Continue down the service road to the second street, Church St., and turn right. Follow Church St for 7 blocks, where it turns into Whitney Ave. The museum is 4 blocks ahead on your left side. You'll find a large parking lot just past the museum. 170 Whitney Ave. www.peabody.yale.edu ☎ 203-432-5050.

Exit 47: Yale University – You can say you "went to Yale" after taking the FREE campus walking tour. The student-led 75 minute tour covers the history, architecture and traditions (you visit the statue of Theodore Dwight Woolsey and get to rub his foot for good luck) as you walk on the same ground as many U.S. Presidents through Old Campus, College courtyards, Sterling Memorial Library and get a glimpse of a Gutenberg bible in the Beinecke Rare Book & Manuscript Library. You can also pick up a self-guided walking tour map called the Yale Blue Trail for $1, which explains info about each site. ◑ Walks are Mon-Fri at 10:30 & 2, Sat & Sun 1:30. ☞ Go to the Yale Visitor Center at 149 Elm St. www.yale.edu/visitor ☎ 203-432-2300.

Exit 47: If you hang out in the sculpture garden of the Yale Gallery, you may someday marry a President of the U.S. Firstly, that's where Hillary and Bill supposedly had their first date and secondly, the last 4 Presidents were Yalies.

Best Pizza in the Whole U.S.?

Exit 46: Amistad – In 1839, Africans illegally captured and held by Spanish slave-traders aboard the schooner Amistad revolted and took over their ship. Led by Sengbe Pieh, the 53 Mende (now Sierra Leone) Africans were arrested for mutiny and murder in Connecticut waters. Former President John Quincy Adams represented them when the case went to the Supreme Court, which led to their release in 1841, and they came back to live in Farmington.

James Pennington of the Colored Congregational Church in Hartford, himself an escaped slave, formed the Union Missionary Society to raise funds to send them back to their homeland, and created a mission there. Some slaves returned to their homes, yet others stayed to work at the Mission.

Sarah Magru (one of the children on the ship), after returning home, came back to the US to study at Oberlin College, then took her skills to Africa to teach at the Mende mission. Many of the future leaders of Sierra Leone were educated at schools established by the Mende mission.

This "Baltimore" style schooner has been recreated and has a home port in New Haven from May thru August, but makes its way to national and international ports to serve as a monument to the millions of souls that were broken or lost as a result of the transatlantic slave trade. To find the schedule: www.amistadamerica.org. ☎ 203-498-9000 or 866-AMISTAD.

Exit 47: It is definitely worth a detour into New Haven for a bite to eat on Wooster Street, acknowledged by foodies as offering the best pizza in the US. There is a continuing rivalry between the lovers of Pepe's (Frank Pepe Pizzeria Napoletana #157) version or Sally's (#237), but you should note that pizza sauce is in their blood, since they're actually third cousins. The one-way street will also take you past two locations of Tony & Lucille's Little Italy, Consiglio's, The Spot (a Pepe's annex), Abate and Tre Scalini. For dessert it is tradition that you stop at Libby's Italian Pastry Shop.

Frank Pepe, the most famous name on the strip, started out as a baker, eventually spreading sauce on top of his bread. His signature pizza is one with white clam sauce on it, but there's also sausage, spinach, bacon, mushroom, onion, pepper and pepperoni to choose from. He opened his first shop in 1925 and moved to this one about 1936.

Flora Consiglio, widow of Salvatore Consiglio (Frank Pepe's nephew) who opened Sally's in 1938, offers her famous delectable oblong pizza with its thin crispy crust in a decor that hasn't changed in decades. If either restaurant offers seasonal specialties like broccoli di rape, zucchini or yellow squash, do try them. They use over a ton of coal a week in original coal-fired ovens, which adds to the unique taste of both pizza parlors.

Consiglio's, established in 1938, is one of the street's more complete dining establishments, serving veal, pasta, beef and chicken or even pepper-encrusted tuna with tomato. You can try Tre Scalini, a relative newcomer, which offers white-tablecloth dining with dishes ranging from rigatoni in vodka sauce to filet mignon with prosciutto, goat cheese and pecans in port wine sauce. Tony & Lucille's I (#127) opened in 1953 and was so popular for calzones, etc. that it outgrew

CT 47 – CT 46

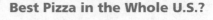

its 40-seat trattoria and opened #II across the street in 1977 with seating for 100.

Tradition dictates that after you've eaten, you waddle down the street to Libby's (#139) for dessert. This ice cream parlor hasn't changed its look much in 82 years, but sure has kept up with its offerings. It is the Ben & Jerry's of canoli, with about 16 flavors: pistachio, heath bar, double chip, raspberry, cookies and cheese, cappuccino and canoli pignole (pine nuts). The 4th generation is now making the Italian ices in 20 flavors, and sure, there's all your favorite traditional Italian desserts too.

You can't help noticing the new arch installed over the midpoint of Wooster Street (because you will be waiting outside in lines for tables) welcoming visitors to New Haven's Little Italy and acknowledging the relatives who dared to come over to the New World and start a way of life that continues into 3rd and 4th generations today.

> ### Heads in the Clouds?
>
> Legend has it that Yale students invented the game of Frisbee using empty pie plates from Mrs. Frisbie's pies and flung them across the New Haven Green.

ster in puff pastry covered with lobster bisque sauce. Their clam chowder was chunky and deliciously spicey and so were the mussels, and even their simple broiled fish platter was yummy. Carnivores will be happy to know that their roast beef has won awards.

They menu will have anything you want and each of the portions is big enough for a family of 4 (there is a charge for sharing). Note that Mon-Fri there's an Early Bird Special for $9.99 on selected menu items (call for exact times). ☞ I-95 Exit 44, left onto Kimberley Ave. for 0.35 mi, then left at the second traffic light (First Ave., then turns into Beach St.) and follow to the water for 1.2 mi. 19 Beach St., West Haven. www.resourcelinks.net/cgalley2.htm ☎ 203-932-1811.

Exit 44: Nick's Luncheonette – Some towns are lucky enough to have a friendly hangout where all the locals go to chow down. Nick's is that kind of place, with a buzzing, hopping, crowded, elbow to elbow party going on. Your basic breakfast and lunch menu is there, but they do get creative too, and offer Reese's pieces™ or banana pancakes, Greek omelette and kielbasa or grilled pastrami and eggs. Do not miss their home fried potatoes; take some to go if you have no time to stop and eat. ◐ Mon-Fri 5 am-3 pm, Sat 5 am-2:30pm, Sun 5 am-1:30 pm. ☞ I-95 Exit 44, left onto Kimberley Ave. for 0.35 mi, then left at the second traffic light (First Ave.) Nick's is on the left at 423 First Ave. ☎ 203-937-9036.

Exit 44: Captain's Galley – Some of our new-found favorite seafood dishes we discovered in this family restaurant. Firstly, seafood a la vodka, which doesn't taste like vodka but is light cheesy, tomatoey, creamy and is full of shrimp, lobster and scallops served on pasta, and secondly, lobster pie, which is chunks of lob-

Exit 43 Northbound: Baby Club of America Warehouse Outlet – This is a catalog or online shopping com-

pany, but since the depot is right here, you can shop and save on name brand and hard to find baby products. The big deal here is all the clearance items scattered about. Members get an extra 10% off. ◑ Mon-Fri 10-6, Sat 10-4. ☞ Northbound: Take I-95 Exit 43 and turn right onto Campbell Ave. for 1/4 mi. Southbound: Exit 43 and turn left onto First Avenue to the first street, Richards St., and turn right for 3 blocks until it ends at Campbell Ave. Make a left onto Campbell. You'll see the store on your left in about two blocks. 721 Campbell Ave. www.babycatalog.com ☎ 800-Playpen or 203-931-7760.

Exit 43: In 1895, when she was voted into West Haven's Engine Co. # 1, Carrie Rockefeller is believed to be the first female to become a firefighter in the US. She was cited "for her valuable services in helping to pull the apparatus".

General George Washington rode up it from Philadelphia to British-held Boston trying to figure out how he would combine the ragged units of volunteers into a coordinated fighting army. When the British left Boston, Washington raced with his men on horseback down the road to try to save New York City, but failed. The road was then filled in droves with military men deserting the army. But in 1789 Washington, now as President, rode the road in triumph with cheering crowds greeting him in every town along the way.

Exit 39: Boston Post Rd. – This old road runs parallel to I-95, especially around this area and from New Haven to NY, and still bears the same name as it did 300 years ago. It was just a wilderness trail when on January 22, 1673 the first mail on the continent was sent from New York to Boston, taking the rider "only" two weeks! America's earliest highway became part of the King's Highway, which traveled very much the same route as I-95 from Maine to Florida. By 1730 it "only" took 4 weeks to post a letter from Boston to Williamsburg.

Many of the revolutionary heros used this road to achieve the goals of Independence. Paul Revere rode to New York on it to report how he and 49 other men "painted as Indians" boarded 3 English ships and dumped 342 chests of tea into the Boston Harbor. Samuel Adams and his cousin John Adams (later President) traversed this road back and forth to Philadelphia and the First Continental Congress.

Exit 39: HoJo Mini Golf – In a truly retro course that was designed in 1978, you can putt through the lion, zebra, rocket or hippo holes, and if you hit the clown's nose on the last hole, you win a FREE game. ◑ Summer 10-11, Rest of year, Sat & Sun 10 5. Located on the side of the Howard Johnson Motel. ☎ 203-878-4611.

Exit 39: The Lily Pad – If you can't find a lily pad floating in the Wepawaug River behind this 1820 home, perhaps you can be satisfied with the waterfalls. Located on a quiet street within short walking distance to the downtown green, you are made to feel at home by Charles and

CT 44 – CT 39

Lily Flannigan. He's the owl, up at night if you come in late, and Lily is the early bird who has home baked goods and freshly cut fruit waiting for you in the morning. One guest room is kept scent-free for guests with allergies. www.bedandbreakfast.com ☎ 203-876-9996.

Exit 32: Hudson Paper Company – Craft lovers: stop right here. This is a real wholesale outlet which is open to the public for all things paper. The business opened in 1908 and is still run by the same family and is still making some boxes on a circa-1880 machine. Looking for hat boxes, gift boxes, rolls of craft paper, rolls of wrapping paper, ribbon, clear bags, department store bags, paper lunch bags - they have them all. There's one room for party needs, paper placemats, plastic serving stuff, themes, colors, metallic twist ties - you just never know what you might score here. ◐ Mon-Wed & Sat 9-5, Thurs & Fri 9-7, Sun 10-3. ☞ From I-95 EXit 32, head West on W. Broad St. passing under a Railroad bridge. Then make your first left into the parking lot behind the building. The retail store entrance is on the right side. 1341 W. Broad St. ☎ 203-378-8759.

Exit 31: Stratford Antique Center – Just what every antique fan needs for a pit stop on your drive - a 16,500 sq. ft. blue building right off an exit and full of 200 dealers. Opened in 1992, the booths are neatly organized and full of furniture, glassware, artwork, brass and copper and collectibles. ◐ Daily 10-5. 400 Honeyspot Rd. www.stratfordantique.com ☎ 203-378-7754.

Exit 27: The Barnum Museum – Here's your chance to run away from your car trip and join the circus for a moment. Kids and kids-at-heart will be fascinated by the life and legacies of P.T. Barnum - entrepreneur, politician, journalist and showman. Learn the story of Tom Thumb (and Mrs Tom - Lavinia Warren) and see their carriages, furniture and clothing. Discover Jenny Lind, "the Swedish Nightingale", William Brinley's miniature hand-carved 5-ring circus, Jumbo the elephant, and check out Barnum's biggest hoax.

You can see the splendor of a room in his home and wallow in the eccentricities of his multi-faceted life. ◐ Tues-Sat 10-4:30, Sun 12-4:30. Northound: Take Exit 27 (Lafayette Blvd) and continue to the 5th traffic light to Main St. Turn left on Main. Museum is on the right. Southbound: Take Exit 27 (Lafayette Boulevard), stay in right lane, continue to State St. Turn right on State, continue to 2nd light and turn right onto Main. Museum is one block down on the left. 820 Main St. www.barnum-museum.org ☎ 203-331-1104.

Exit 27A: Beardsley Zoo – Just the right size for a zoo break, this 1922 Olmstead-designed park has 120 species of animals to enjoy. Mr. Bald Eagle is the first to greet you, and then you can go on to the Tropics Rainforest with a free flight aviary, a New England farmyard with goats to feed, bunnies to pet and a dairy, the Alligator Alley and a walkthrough prairie dog exhibit.  North and South American animals include a maned wolf, toucan, otters, ocelots, the smallest primate: a pygmy marmoset and the largest rodent: a capybara. Don't forget a ride on the Carousel and notice the beautiful New England foliage. ◗ Daily 9-4. ☞ I-95 Exit 27A to Rte 8 & 25 for 2 1/2 mi. and get off at Exit 5 (Boston Ave). At the light at the end of the ramp, turn left to the 4th traffic light. Then turn left onto Noble Ave. to 1875 and the Beardsley Park on the left. www.beardsleyzoo.org ☎ 203-394-6565.

Exit 24: Super Duper Weenie – When Gourmet magazine rates a place "one of America's ten best hot dog joints", we have to investigate. The split and grilled dogs will tickle your taste buds no matter where you are from, because they salute all the regions.

The New Yorker has sauerkraut, onion sauce (just like the "dirty water" hot dogs on the streets), mustard and hot relish, while the Chicagoan has the required lettuce, tomato, mustard, celery salt, hot relish and pickle, and if you're from Dixie, you can eat the one with meat chili and cole slaw. If you must, there is also grilled chicken, veggie burgers, sausages, tuna salad, burgers, grilled cheese and nuggets. All of their condiments are home-made (they even grow some of the veggies!). Their crispy salt and pepper fries are great with everything, and they even have freshly brewed tea and exciting homemade soups in season (go early - they sell out fast). ◗ Mon-Wed 11-4, Thurs-Sat 11-8, Sun 11-6. From I-95 Exit 24, go around the roundabout to the South side of I-95, heading down Black Rock Turnpike. You'll find weenies on your left just as you leave the roundabout. 306 Black Rock Turnpike www.superduperweenie.com ☎ 203-334-DOGS.

Exit 21: Rawley's Drive–In – Who would ever think that to do some celebrity watching (David Letterman, Meg Ryan, Martha Stewart, Dennis Quaid, Mike Wallace, Paul Newman have all imbibed), you should hang out at a hot dog joint? Well, not just any joint. This over-50-year-old busy, tiny (4 booths, 6 stools) place is always packed with regulars who pine for the deep fried dogs which are rolled on a griddle with a spatula and plunked into a toasted, buttered French bakery roll and topped with the "works": relish, sauerkraut, mustard, raw onions and - if that wasn't enough fat for you - real bacon bits.

You can wash it down with a chocolate milk shake, and for the rest of you there's burgers, grilled cheese and tuna. To keep yourself busy while you wait (this is not fast food) you can read the names and initials carved into the walls and tables. ◗ Mon-Sat 11-6:45 ☞ From I-95 EXit 21 turn South down Mill Plain Rd under the train tracks to Post Rd (US 1). Turn tight, and Rawley's is on the next block on your right at 1886 Post Rd. ☎ 203-259-9023.

Exit 21: The Chocolate Shoppe – We are suckers for a place to buy chocolates, so this one with its handmade truffles (perhaps some Jack Daniels?), chocolate dipped Oreos, cherry cordials and Ashers, Godiva, Lindt, Perugina or Ghirardelli lines fits the bill. Even sugar-free needs are covered quite well, with a choice of chocolate covered cherries, pretzels and peanut butter cups. Popular candy like the 21 colors of M & M's, 21 flavors of Jelly Bellies, caramel corn, fruit slices and maple candy round out the offerings. 1614 Post Rd. ☎ 877-234-9210.

Exits 16-14: During the French and Indian War, 1754-1763, Colonel Thomas Fitch led the troops from Norwalk. His sister Elizabeth arrived to see him off, and was dismayed by their dishevelled uniforms. To spiff them up, she ran to the chicken pen, took some feathers and placed one in each man's cap.

They rode to Fort Crailo near Albany, New York, where British Army Surgeon Richard Shuckburgh, amused by their garb, exclaimed "Now stab my vitals, they're macaronis!" (This was a slang term for dandies who affected foreign mannerisms and fashions). He proceeded to write a derogatory verse dedicated to them called a "New England Noodle". Everyone sing along now...

"Yankee Doodle went to town
A-ridin' on a pony
He stuck a feather in his cap
And called it macaroni. "

A doodle was a put-down to mean simpleton or a do-little. The tune used was popular in Britain with many different verses, but one sheet music version that has survived goes:

"Brother Ephraim sold his Cow
And bought him a Commission;
And then he went to Canada

To fight for the Nation;
But when Ephraim he came home
He proved an arrant Coward,

He wouldn't fight the Frenchman there
For fear of being devour'd. "

The Americans wound up liking the tune and turned the derision around, making it popular. It became the principal American battle theme of the Revolution, and eventually a greater symbol of humiliation to the British than it had been to the Americans. It was actually played victoriously in 1781 as the beaten British forces filed out of Yorktown to end the Revolutionary War.

Exit 15: Silvermine Tavern – Whatever you are in the mood for - wild times on Jazz evenings (Thurs thru Sat) or quiet dining overlooking the tranquil mill pond with swans and ducks - this 200-year old country inn offers both plus creaky wooden floors and character.

The St. John family who arrived from England in 1757 were the first to lay claim to a 200-acre homestead here. It was later owned by Faith Baldwin, the writer, and the coach house was said to be used as a "still" during Prohibition. In 1846 it was owned by Henry Guthrie, who ran a shipyard and water-powered mills along local rivers. The post and beam construction and the rippled window glass date from that time.

In 1908, Ike and Anna Helfant raised six children and ran a cozy country store here, where Johnny Gruelle, creator of Raggedy Ann and Andy was known to visit. The current owners, the Whitmans, bought in 1955 and carry on the tavern tradition with a gourmet restaurant, popular Sunday champagne brunches and famous honey buns (even your B&B breakfast includes them along with Hawaiian Kona coffee). Don't forget to walk around to the waterfall. ☞ Exit 15 (Rte. 7 north) and take Rte. 7 to Exit 2. Turn right at the end of the ramp. At the second stop light (by Wendy's) turn right; at next stop light, by a Shell gas station, turn right onto Silvermine Ave. and follow it for about 3/4 mi. At the 2nd stop sign bear right and continue on for 1 1/4 miles to the Tavern. 194 Perry Ave. www.silverminetavern.com ☎ 203-847-4558.

Exit 14N or 15S: Coastal Fairfield Visitor Center – Located in the Gate Lodge at Mathews Park, this little tourist pit stop has info about the region and the State, and they book hotel rooms in their area. Yes, the FREE coupon books are there and restrooms are located outside the office. ◗ Mon-Fri 8:30-5:30. 297

West Ave. www.coastalCT.com ☎ 800-866-7925 or 203-853-777.

Exit 14N or 15S: Stepping Stones

For children ages 1-10 or children at heart (couldn't get Stan out of here), enjoy this interactive learning environment for entertainment, expression and imagination. You can explore in water play: where it comes from or goes and what it does, through pools, cascades, a streambed, a vortex and a fog machine. Practice conservation in the new Rainforest Adventure using 40 multi-sensory games and problem solving activites.

Learn to express yourself using secret messages, instruments from around the world, sound effects and video images. Role play in a train, a helicopter, submerged in a research submarine or figure out the principles of motion, gravity and velocity with race cars, light and machines. ◐ Tues-Sat 10-5, Sun 12-5, (summer Mon 10-5 too). ☞ Northbound: From I-95 Exit 14, go through two stop signs to a stop light. Turn left onto West Ave and proceed under two overpasses. The museum is on the right, in Mathews Park. Entrance is between two stone pillars at stop light. Southbound: From I-95 Exit 15, bear right down the hill. Turn right onto West Ave. The museum is directly on the right, in Mathews Park. Entrance is between two stone pillars at stop light. Mathews Park, 303 West Ave. www.steppingstonesmuseum.org ☎ 203-899-0606.

Mile 12.5 Northbound: Con-

necticut Welcome Center – It always pays to stop at these centers to find out about things to do in the area, pick up FREE motel coupon books and use the clean rest rooms. This one has one of the busiest McDonald's in the US, since it is the first service area on I-95 since upper NJ. ◐ Summer Daily 8-6, Sept-June Daily 8-5. ☎ 203-655-8289.

Exit 8: Antique Alley – Anyone who loves antiques is going to have to stop the car right now and plan to spend the night. This old industrial neighborhood is slowly evolving into Antique Alley. The dozens of businesses are far from being considered "stores".

Fancy retail antique shops usually have chock-a-bloc warehouses where they store everything that doesn't fit into their main place of business. Here they have opened those vast spaces and let you see it all. You have to drive around from building to building to view the treats. Some options: Debbie's Stamford Antiques Center, 735 Canal ☎ 888-329-3546; Braswell Galleries, 733 Canal ☎ 203-899-7420 ; Stamford Auction Gallery, 737 Canal ☎ 203-357-0753; Hidden Galleries, 481 Canal ☎ 203-323-9090; Harbor View Center, 101 Jefferson St. ☎ 203-325-8070; Antique and Artisan Center, 69 Jefferson St. ☎ 203-327-6022.

One of the enterprises has over 100 dealers in one spot. A very convenient "U-Haul" depot is located in their midst, so if you wind up with an impulse purchase, you can drag it home. ◐ Mon-Sat: 10:30-5:30, Sun 12-5.

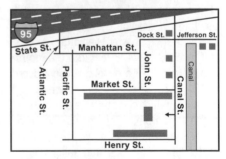

Exit 3: Bruce Museum of Arts and Science – This gem of a museum has little hors d'oeuvres which are sure to please the palate of many in your car. It mixes up 19th and 20th century American paintings, minerals of the world (some in drawers with fun names like "It's a bad hair day"), the mammals and birds of New England, decorative arts and Native American cultures.

CT 14 – CT 3

Children and adults alike love the cave-like mineral gallery, with its fluorescent niche, the wigwam (listen to native story-telling), live-animal marine touch tank and the 1,200-lb touchable meteorite. The specialty shows are of high quality and eclectic; coming up this year: Great Women, Great Science, Rubens Oil Sketches, China Trade and New England. Call for others and for dates. ◗ Tues-Sat 10-5, Sun 1-5. ☞ Turn right at bottom of exit ramp (left if you're coming from the North). Follow Arch Street as it curves past Steamboat Rd. Go straight across to Museum Drive. 1 Museum Dr. www.brucemuseum.org ☎ 203-869-0376.

☆ NEW YORK ☆

Exit 19: Playland Amusement Park – Built in 1928 with Art Deco structures, this is America's first totally planned amusement park, sporting 50 rides for children and adults, a beach, boardwalk, swimming pool, lake boating, picnic area, FREE entertainment, mini golf, indoor ice-skating and FREE admission. What a concept - you only pay for the rides you want to go on!

The Dragon Coaster, even after 70 years, still plunges you 128 feet into the mouth of a dragon. The Carousel was constructed in 1915 with its 66 elaborate horses and 3 chariots, which circle the rare Gavioli band organ with monkey ornaments. The Derby Racer is one of only 2 known original rides of this type in the U.S., and gallops along at 25 mph, imitating the motion of real steeplechase steeds. Besides the fun rides, there's fun foods like funnel cakes, Dippin Dots ice cream, Nathan's hot dogs or Carvel soft custard. ◗ Closed Mon. Varies daily between 12-11, May-September. www.ryeplayland.org ☎ 914-813-7000.

Exit 17 Northbound: Walter's Hot Dog Stand – is just that, a stand, with no inside seating. You cannot miss this copper roofed Chinese pagoda made in the attention grabbing style of its day, but quite incongruous with this tree-lined street in a NYC  suburb. Opened in 1919, the stand moved here in 1928, and the hanging lanterns and bamboo-style letters are still the calling card of Walter Warrington's trademark protected hot dog recipe.

The dogs have been specially blended so they don't shrink, curl or burn as they sizzle split on a grill which has been coated with a secret sauce. They are dropped into a toasted bun with home-made mustard that is dotted with little bits of pickle in it. You can buy jars to take home.

While you wait, read the postcard collection from around the world attesting to Walter's as the best hot dogs. The most treasured one dates to 1929 and was sent from Antarctica by Willard Van Der Veer of the Admiral Byrd expedition. ☞ From I-95 exit 17, continue to Chatsworth Ave and turn right over the highway for 4 blocks to Palmer. Make a left on Palmer and proceed for almost a mile to 937 Palmer Ave. on your left. www.waltershotdogs.com

Exit 16: MacMenamin's Grill and Chef Works – This is situated in what was a munitions factory, but is now very New York loft-like, warmed by cherry and oak woods, a brick fireplace and an open kitchen. You can enjoy upscale dining: gorgonzola salad, stir-fried soba noodles, lamb osso buco with polenta, crispy roast duck, stone oven pizzas, steaks and a raw bar. If you live nearby, there's a professional or recreational cooking school, and what fun - cooking parties! 115 Cedar St. right beside I-95. www.macmenaminsgrill.com ☎ 914-632-4900.

Exit 13: Wonder Hostess Bakery Thrift Shop – If someone in the car has the munchies, you might as well stop at a factory outlet store like this one and get a snacks as low as 7/$2.99. You can pick from fudge brownies, Twinkies, Hohos, Funnybones, Coffee Cakes, Yodels, Donettes, Hostess cupcakes, Honey Buns, fruit pies, Fruit and Grain cereal bars and Sandra's favorite Ring Dings.

You can buy bread and jam to make sandwiches, Utz chips (honey BBQ, cheddar, sour cream), instant soups and there's even sugar free snacks: chocolate sandwich cream cookies and wafers. ◐ Mon-Sat 8:30-6, Sun 9-5. ☞ From I-95 Exit 13 turn left on Tillotson Ave and left again onto Conner St. (Southbound, just turn right on Conners at the gas station). Just as you pass Hollers Ave., you'll see the plant on you left, and the store is just behind it.

Exit 3 Southbound: Mario's – An anchor in Belmont, Bronx's "Little Italy", 5 generations of the Migliucci family have been turning out fresh, robust Neapolitan food since 1919. The family left Naples in the early 1900's and opened the first Italian restaurant in Egypt. It was a success, but they decided to come to America and open Mario's on the site where it stands today. It is said that they were the first to sell pizza by the slice, originating one of America's first street foods.

In 2000, they earned a James Beard Award, chosen by a 17-member committee of leading food editors and restaurant critics, which recognized Mario's as a "restaurant with timeless appeal, beloved in its region for quality food that reflects the history and character of its community". ☞ From I-95 Exit 3 turn North up 3rd Ave for 3/4 mi. and turn right on 184th St. for 2 blocks to Arthur Ave. Turn left up to 2342 Arthur Ave. on your right side. ☎ 718-584-1100.

Exit 2B Northbound: White Castle – We were terribly excited when we found a White Castle hamburger joint on I-95, because Sandra has been addicted to their signature Slyder since she was a child, and has been the "pusher" to get everyone else addicted too. These are teeny 3 bite (2.5" square) 100% beef burgers cooked by placing the baked buns on the top of the burgers and a bed of fried onions, which helps absorb the delicious steam grilled flavor.

In 1949, after an employee suggestion, 5 evenly spaced holes were added (or subtracted?), which allow the steam to completely pervade the burger, enhancing the flavor and allowing the patty to cook faster, eliminating the need to turn the burgers over and increasing productivity and quality.

Started in 1921 in Wichita, Kansas, White Castle's medieval motif was inspired by Chicago's famous Water Tower, and some of the first establishments sported rooftop battlements and a turret. Way back in 1931, they began to use frozen beef patties to assure quality, and developed the crush-resistant cardboard carton that is specially lined to keep the perfect square burgers steaming and also promote the carry-out idea by ensuring that each sandwich reaches its destination looking and tasting as fresh as when it came off the grill.

By 1961 White Castle had served 1 billion hamburgers, more than any other hamburger chain in the U.S. Sandra was saved in 1987 when the hamburgers and cheeseburgers became available frozen in grocery stores throughout the U.S. Wash the burgers down with a chocolate thick shake, which is so thick you need a spoon to eat it. Sometimes she will weaken and have a side of the fried clam strips or chick-

> The construction of the Empire State Building was begun in October 1929, the month the stock market crashed. During the Depression it was referred to as the "Empty State Building".

NY 19 – NY 3

en rings. The burgers started out at 5¢, and even after all these years with inflation have only made it to 48¢. They got the nickname of Slyder because they are soft and seem to melt in your mouth and just slide down so easily. Yum! The joint we found is just north on Webster Ave from I-95, on the left side. www.whitecastle.com

The Sale of the Millennium

Exit 1: The sale of the millennium was the $24 price tag on Manhattan Island. On August 10,1626 the legend goes that the West India Company paid that much in trinkets to Native Americans living there at the time. But there is really no proof that they ever paid in beads.

William Verhulst, who was to become the 2nd governor of New Netherlands and Peter Minuit, who would be the 3rd, left Amsterdam in January 1625 on the ship Orange Tree. The West India Company, which was financing the colony gave Verhulst these instructions:

"In case any Indian should be living on the aforesaid land or make any claim upon it or any other places that are of use to us, they must not be driven away by force or threat, but by good words be persuaded to leave, or be given something therefor to their satisfaction, or else be allowed to live among us, a contract being made thereof and signed by them in their manner, since such contracts upon other occasions may be very useful to the Company." [A.J.F. van Laer, trans. 1924 Documents Relating to New Netherlands 1624-1626 in the Huntington Hartford Library, San Marino CA, pp. 51-2.]

When Minuit became governor, he wrote a letter dated 11 May 1626 to one of the other colonists instructing him to buy Manhattan Island, which incidentally had not been the colony's first choice. Further proof of the sale appears in another letter to the board of the West

Indies Company: "They report that our people are in good heart and live in peace there; the women have also borne some children there. They have purchased the Island Manhattes from the Indians for the value of 60 guilders; 'tis 11,000 morgens (about 22,000 acres) in size." [E.B. O'Callaghan, ed. 1856 Documents Relative to the Colonial History of the State of New York. Albany. Vol. 1, [p. 37.]] That is the only information relating to the sale, as the deed has been lost. The fable was probably started by Martha J. Lamb in "History of the City of New York" [1877: New York, Vol. I, p. 104], who first wrote: "He [Minuit] then called together some of the principal Indian chiefs and offered beads, buttons and other trinkets in exchange for their real estate. They accepted the terms with unfeigned delight, and the bargain was closed at once."

Then to make matters worse, in 1892 J.G. Wilson, in "Memorial History of the City of New-York", quoted and repeated Lamb's insinuations as fact. His 4 volume set was considered the basic work for a long time, and this influenced historians for years to come.

Anyway, Minuit and others built Fort Amsterdam at the very bottom of the island, which eventually became the village of New Amsterdam. In 1664 the British, annoyed at the competition for world trade, seized it and renamed it New York after James, the Duke of York, who became King James II.

☆ NEW JERSEY ☆

THE MISSING LINK

The New Jersey Turnpike is not really a part of I-95, though logically people use it as such, so we have drawn it that way (I-95 really goes through Pennsylvania but the signage is so poor that we feel motorists will get lost). It has been discussed for many many years to include the NJ Turnpike as part of I-95 but the southern 51 miles are still not even part of the Interstate system and remain solely a state road. The Federal Highway Administration objects to placing I-95 markers on this section, and the State of New Jersey has so far found that it is not worth upgrading the standards nor making an application for its designation.

Between Exit 18 & 17 Northbound and Southbound, Mile 116: Vince Lombardi Service Area

- Don't forget to come and pick up your FREE motel discount coupon booklets which offer great deals along the way. New Jersey service centers are open 24 hours and have excellent lit up hotel/motel boards with phones to call for reservations. This state has the best service area bathrooms on I-95. Take advantage of them. Vince Lombardi's most famous quote is "Winning isn't everything; it's the only thing.", and that motto drove him as a coach from the New York Giants to the

Green Bay Packers (5 NFL titles and the first 2 Super Bowls). His lifetime coaching record was an outstanding 94-34-6.

Exit 16W Southbound or 17 Northbound: Meadowlands Sports Complex

– Jock Alert!! You are now passing Giants Stadium, the home of the New York Giants and the New York Jets. Across the road is the Continental Airlines Arena, home ice of the New Jersey Devils hockey team since 1981. The arena is also the home to the New Jersey Nets, the Seton Hall basketball teams and various other sporting events and concerts. Meadowlands Racetrack offers horse racing.

Exit 16W Southbound or 17 Northbound: Secaucus Outlet Stores

– It's a bit complicated to absorb this original factory town, so we'll start by telling you to follow Meadowlands Parkway off Route 3 between the 2 branches of the Turnpike here, until you come to a street called American Way (can't forget that). You'll soon pass Gucci and London Fog, and turn left on Enterprise Ave just between Calvin Klein and Mikasa. On the way, you'll have passed the parking lot of the Harmon Cove Outlet Cen-

---

Turning Lemons into Lemonade

Exit 69: Hackensack was once covered with so many cedar trees that it enticed lumbermen to move here. They cut trees, and without today's lumber management eventually decimated the area, leaving clay-bottomed swamps. But this was not so bad. The clay made good bricks. A brickmaking industry thrived from 1870 to the 1950's, providing bricks for Newark, Paterson, New York City and as far away as Providence RI.

---

ter on your right (the closest thing here to an outlet mall that you might know). The first thing you need to do is to pick up one of the various FREE guides (Secaucus Outlet Centre, Secaucus Guide Book, Secaucus Shopping Directory), which all include maps to many of the buildings that house shops; the rest you will find while poking around.

New Jersey does not charge sales tax on clothing or shoes. Smart shoppers know they should try to buy in one of the 30 Urban Enterprise Zones where, retailers charge only 3% tax - half the normal rate. To find them: www.state.nj.us/commerce/UEZ locations.shtml

The original name for an "outlet" meant the factory store. It was a small area behind a plant where companies could get rid of surplus, unsold, out-of-season goods at bargain prices to their employees, the locals or other bargain-hungry adventurers. In the 1970's, when the concept caught on in a big way because owners saw this as a source of ready cash, and other clever businessmen realized there was surplus in all industries, they banded together and formed the newer "outlet mall".

The Secaucus area is a real functioning one, as it encompasses the receiving and distribution centers for Metropolitan NYC area firms. The warehouses are where the unsold goods are stored and where the department stores return items because of warranty damages or errors.

You need a car to traverse the far flung industrial park, some buildings having a show window on the ground floor (a throwback to the "factory store"), interspersed with groups of newer outlet buildings.

Outlets sell the current season's merchandise (at 40-60% off), whereas the retail stores could already be selling next season's fashions. So if you visit Secaucus in the summer you will find summer clothes, whereas regular malls are already focusing on back-to-school and fall merchan-

dise. You will discover brands like: Gucci, Jil Sanders, Chaus, Tahari, Liz Claiborne, Mikasa, Kenneth Cole, DKNY Jeans, Lenox, Tommy Hilfiger, YSL, Aeropostale, Bally, Natori, London Fog, Reebok and Levi's. Since so many of these goods are manufactured in places like Singapore, South Korea, Hong Kong and China, Secaucus is about the closest you are going to get to the factory without flying to the Far East. ◑ Mon-Wed 10-6, Thurs 10-8, Fri & Sat 10-7, Sun 11-6 ☎ 877-688-5382 or 201-348-4780.

Exit 13A: Jersey Gardens – This is New Jersey's largest outlet mall, with 200 indoor stores. Female alert - Sandra's favorite DSW Shoe Warehouse is in here, for teens Hot Topic for music or how about a Good Fortune Bonsai shop? Clothing stores abound: BCBG Max Azria, Daffy's, Off 5th-Saks Fifth Avenue, Aeropostale, Quiksilver and Kid's Outlet. They offer a Kids Club. ◑ Mon-Sat 10-9, Sun 11-7. www.jersey gardens.com ☎ 908-354-5900.

Exit 13: Giovanni da Verrazzano, an Italian explorer, navigated this part of the New World for France before toddling on up as far as Newfoundland, noticing Manhattan Island along the way. The Verrazano Narrows there were named after him (slightly different spelling, tho) and later the bridge from Brooklyn to Staten Island. His explorations established King Francis I's claim to the New World, so he sent Verrazzano back for two more voyages. Unfortunately on his final trip he stopped off at an island, probably Guadeloupe (little bit of a vacation?) in the West Indies and was gobbled up by cannibals.

Between Exit 12 & 11 South-bound, Mile 92.9: Thomas Edison Service Area – Don't forget to come and pick up your FREE motel discount coupon booklets, which offer great deals along the way. New Jersey service areas are open 24 hours and have excellent lit up hotel/motel boards with phones to call for reservations. This state has the best service area bathrooms on I-95. Take advantage of them. ☎ 732-636-0580

Thomas Alva Edison did all of his inventing very close to here in Menlo Park and West Orange. Known as the inventor of the incandescent electric lamp (electric light bulb), he also patented 1,368 other inventions in diverse fields including: the phonograph, motion picture machine, universal stock ticker, paraffin paper (first used for wrapping candies), carbon telephone transmitter "button", which led to the microphone and much later on to the solid state "diode" or transistor used in today's electronic devices, fluoroscope (for X-rays), pre-cast cement, iron ore rolling machine, dictating machine (which enabled the user to hear repetitions and even make corrections), telescribe (recorded both sides of a telephone conversation) and thousands more.

Between Exit 11 and 12 North-bound, Mile 92.9: Grover Cleveland Service Area – Don't forget to come and pick up your FREE motel discount coupon booklets which offer great deals along the way. New Jersey service areas are open 24 hours and have excellent lit up hotel/motel boards with phones to call for reservations. This State has the best service area bathrooms on the route. Take advantage of them.

Grover Cleveland was President of the U.S. twice - the only one to ever do that!

He first won in 1884 by fewer than 25,000 votes, then lost the re-election to Benjamin Harrison (although he actually won a larger popular majority, he received fewer electoral votes), then regained the Presidency in 1892.

He started out as a lawyer in Buffalo N.Y., became Mayor of Buffalo in 1881, and later Governor of N.Y. Cleveland was not comfortable with the amenities of the White House, writing "I must go to dinner, but I wish it was to eat a pickled herring, a Swiss cheese and a chop at Louis' instead of the French stuff I shall find.". He was the only President married in the White House, marrying 21-year-old Frances Folsom in June 1886 (he was 49).

He is thought of as an honest politician in a time when graft, bribery and corruption ran rampant. (What, you thought things were different back then?) After leaving the White House, Cleveland lived in retirement in Princeton, N.J. til his death on June 24, 1908.

Exit 8: Battle of Monmouth – On June 27, 1778, the main British army under Sir Henry Clinton abandoned Philadelphia and were headed to New York with a baggage caravan that was 12 miles long. Washington saw this as an opportunity to attack an exposed, strung out enemy by surprise just around this area.

General Charles Lee was leading the attack, scattering his 5,000 men. When advised that the advantage would be lost if he didn't apply more force to the enemy, he replied "Sir, you do not know the British soldiers. We cannot stand against them". His lines soon fell apart.

George Washington, who was coming in from Valley Forge with the main army of 8,500, met Lee's men in retreat. For once, the ordinarily restrained commander-in-chief let himself go and "swore 'til the leaves shook on the trees". Soldiers stopped in their tracks and stared at the stately man on the large white horse who began darting up and down the line, personally turning back the retreat.

A young Marquis de Lafayette remembered the moment the rest of his life. Washington rode "all along the lines amid the shouts of the soldiers, cheering them by his voice and example and restoring to our standard the fortunes of the fight. I thought then, as now, that never had I beheld so superb a man". Washington relieved Lee of his command. By the time he had the army turned around, his great white horse had died from exhaustion.

The battle was a political triumph for the Continental Army, for they had met the British in an open field and forced them to retreat. Monmouth was the last major battle in the North. It left enough of an impression on London that they recognized a stalemate and shifted their attention to the South. Washington took satisfaction in knowing that his men would turn and follow when he called.

Courtesy: Elk Forge B&B

Between Exit 8A and 9 Northbound, Mile 78.7: Joyce Kilmer Service Area — Don't forget to come and pick up your FREE motel discount coupon booklets which offer great deals along the way. New Jersey service areas are open 24 hours and have excellent lit up hotel/motel boards with phones to call for reservations. This State has the best service area bathrooms on the route. Take advantage of them. ☎ 732-257-6103.

Joyce Kilmer was an editor, critic, lecturer, soldier and was best known as a poet, especially for his poem called "Trees". He enlisted in the Army during World War I, but while scouting for a machine gun nest in France, he was shot in the head and died at 31 on July 30, 1918.

"Trees" was written at Kilmer's home in Mahwah, New Jersey on February 2, 1913; it was written in a little notebook in the afternoon, in an upstairs room which offered a window overlooking a wooded hill. On one page, the first two lines of "Trees" were written, with the date, February 2, 1913, and on another page, farther on in the little book, was the whole poem. It was dedicated to Kilmer's mother-in-law (Wow!), who was well-loved by all her family.

> **High Flyers**
>
> Both Charles Lindburgh, first to fly from New York to Paris, and Edwin E. (Buzz) Aldrin, second to walk on the moon, are New Jersey boys.

Trees (For Mrs. Henry Mills Alden)

I think that I shall never see
A poem lovely as a tree.
A tree whose hungry mouth is prest

Against the earth's sweet flowing
breast;
A tree that looks at God all day,
And lifts her leafy arms to pray;
A tree that may in Summer wear
A nest of robins in her hair;
Upon whose bosom snow has lain;
Who intimately lives with rain.
Poems are made by fools like me,
But only God can make a tree.

$$$ BOOKS ON AUDIO

We are audio book junkies. Once you get hooked, long road trips go by so fast, and you actually don't mind traffic jams. Here's 2 suggestions of how to get them reasonably. Cracker Barrel Old Country Stores help us get our fix by offering 200 titles to choose from, including best sellers, with a money saving deal. You buy one at prices from $12.99 to $48, and when you finish the book, you return it at the next Cracker Barrel on the road and they give you back your money minus $3.50 for each week you've had it. You can mail them back if you've forgotten to return one. www.crackerbarrel.com

Secondly, Audible, Inc. is an online company that offers you 18,000 titles that you can download for $14.95 for 1 book/magazine/newspaper per month or $19.95 for 2 titles. (You could finally make your way through the Sunday NY Times this way.) If you take a year's subscription, they will give you their Audible MP3 player for FREE or you can play them on a Pocket PC, Palm Handheld, Apple Ipod or a variety of other devices. There's a 50% off first month trial offer. We use Audible books with a tape adapter in the car on our trips. www.audible.com

Between Exit 8A & 8 South-bound, Mile 71.7: Molly Pitcher Service Area – Don't forget to come and and pick up your FREE motel discount coupon booklets which offer great deals along the way. New Jersey service areas which are open 24 hours have excellent lit up hotel/motel boards with phones to call for reservations. This State has the best service area bathrooms on the route. ☎ 609-655-1610.

The Battle of Monmouth (see Exit 8) produced a heroine. Mary Ludwig followed her husband John Hays to war. In the 100 degree temperature, the soldiers were dropping from thirst, so Molly used an artillery bucket filled with spring water to offer drinks to the troops. Soldiers seeing her moving across the terrain called "Here comes Molly with her pitcher!". She also nursed the wounded that day.

When her husband fell beside a cannon he was manning, she took the rammer staff and worked the rest of the day swabbing and loading the gun under heavy fire. Folklore has it that General Washington himself thanked the barefooted, powder-stained "Molly Pitcher" and issued her a warrant as a non-commissioned officer. You can see the paintings of this story in the entrance to the service area. ☎ 609-655-1610.

When is a gas station more than a gas station?

Well, gas stations sure have come a long way since they diversified beyond selling fan belts and spare tires. Now it is unusual to see one without at least a mini-mart attached to it. However, if you really look around, you'll be surprised at the things you might find.

Along I-95 we have found: fireworks, country hams, live bait, live crabs and fishing gear, a peanut outlet, key making, fresh jumbo eggs, dry cleaning, muscadine cider, trees, books on tape, guns, shrimp meal, clay, car detailing, bird houses, bows & arrows and very interesting take-out food: hot boiled peanuts, Claxton fruit cakes, or fried gizzards and livers. One even had a mart with a drive through window, so you don't

NJ 8-8A

even have to get out of your SUV to pick up your milk, cigarettes, etc. The strangest one had a sign that said "Armed guard after hours". We're suggesting you skip that one.

Between Exit 7A & 7 Southbound, Mile 58.7:

Richard Stockton Service Area – Don't forget to come and pick up your FREE motel discount coupon booklets which offer great deals along the way. New Jersey service areas are open 24 hours and have excellent lit up hotel/motel boards with phones to call for reservations. This State has the best service area bathrooms on the route. Take advantage of them.

Richard Stockton, not a well known name, was an American hero who was born in Princeton on October 1, 1730. He was the first signer of the Declaration of Independence from New Jersey (one of 5). Stockton was a well respected lawyer, came from a wealthy and distinguished family and had been presented to the Court in England when he traveled there.

In the autumn of 1776, as a member of the Continental Congress, he was sent to Saratoga, New York to give a report on the state of the army. He wrote that the New Jersey soldiers were "marching with cheerfulness, but (a) great part of the men (are) barefooted and barelegged... There is not a single shoe or stocking to be had in this part of the world, or I would ride a hundred miles through the woods and purchase them with my own money".

For his efforts upon his return, he was captured by the British and put in prison. Though he had escaped death twice before in his life (once by a thug in Edinburgh and again when he missed a ship that later sunk), his confinement was so severe that his constitution never recovered. As if this wasn't enough, his lands and animals were destroyed, his papers and library burnt and his fortune greatly reduced. He died an invalid in Princeton on February 28, 1781.

Exit 7A: Six Flags – If you need to bribe the kids to be quiet in the back seat, this 140-acre park has 13 roller coasters and a new SpongeBob SquarePants™ 3-D simulator, a fast-paced, underwater escapade. There's the Superman-Ultimate Flight coaster, where you tilt face-first into flying position suspended from the track above.

If you want to visit the park efficiently, you can sign up for Fast Lane, the virtual queue system, by making reservations on the most popular rides; for a fee, you get other discounts and paging. You can also buy guided and self-guided V.I.P. Tours. Bounce Back allows you return visits at greatly reduced prices.

On hot days there's Hurricane Harbor, with 20 water slides, a million gallon wave pool, and for the folks - the longest lazy river. Or try the 350-acre, 4.5 mile world's largest drive-thru safari, with 1,200 animals from six continents - it's FREE with the theme park ticket purchase. A V.I.P program here offers a Behind-the-Scenes tour. ☞ From Exit 7A take I-195 East about 10 miles to Exit 16A (Rte 537 West) and follow it 1/2 mile to the entrance. www.sixflags.com ☎ 732-928-1821.

Courtesy: Six Flags

Why Did Washington Cross the Delaware?

Answer: To Get to the Other Side.

Exit 7: You've probably seen the famous painting of George Washington crossing the Delaware. If not, you have at least heard that expression. Well, what does it mean? On Christmas night 1776, Washington had to take a gamble in what was the bleakest time of the war. He wrote, "I think the game is pretty near up". As his troops shivered with hunger and disease, the British and Hessian soldiers were snug in their winter quarters on the NJ side of the Delaware River. On this holiday eve, the enemy feasted on goose and tankards of rum, and the sentry guards were less alert, since they knew the poor condition of the Revolutionary troops, and besides, the river was full of ice.

Washington's many shoeless ("Some of them have tied old rags around their feet") troops crossed the icy waters in the dead of night in a snowstorm, and left bloody footprints in the snow. Even their musket powder became soaked, and they were told to use their bayonets.

Two thousand four hundred men (including 2 future Presidents - James Madison and James Monroe - as well as future Supreme Court Justice John Marshall and famous rivals Aaron Burr and Alexander Hamilton) made it across.

They caught the Brits and Hessians in a drunken slumber; the Hessians standing guard in the storm thought the first Continentals were their relief party. The Revolutionaries managed to get them to surrender in 40 minutes. No Americans were killed, though a couple had frozen to death. They captured over 900 prisoners, 1,000 muskets and 40 horses.

The incredible victory flashed through all of the colonies, changing the minds of many battle weary soldiers, and turned the tide of the war. The army that had been on the brink of falling apart now felt that all was not hopeless and planned for the campaigns ahead.

Between Exit 7 & 7A Northbound, Mile 58.7: Woodrow Wilson Service Area – Don't forget to come and pick up your FREE motel discount coupon booklets which offer great deals along the way. New Jersey service areas are open 24 hours and have excellent lit up hotel/motel boards with phones to call for reservations. This State has the best service area bathrooms on the route. Take advantage of them.

Woodrow Wilson, the 28th President of the U.S. from 1913-1921 (during WWI), went to Princeton University in 1875 (it was called College of New Jersey back then). He returned as a professor in 1890, later becoming the University's president in 1902. From there he went on to become New Jersey's governor in 1910 and then President. Wilson manoeuvred some major legislation through Congress. The first was one we still suffer over: a graduated Federal income tax, but he also passed the Federal Trade Commission to prohibit unfair business practices, a law prohibiting child labor and

From the 1870's until the recent off shore move, New Jersey was the number one producer of embroidery and lace in the world. Even today more than 10,000 people in over 500 companies are sewing away on fast "Schifflis" machines creating bedspreads, curtains, men's and women's clothing and emblems for the military.

another limiting railroad workers to an 8-hour day.

He is well remembered for planting the seeds of the United Nations. He went before Congress in January 1918 with his Fourteen Points. The last one established "A general association of nations... affording mutual guarantees of political independence and territorial integrity to great and small states alike". After the Germans signed the Armistice in November 1918, Wilson went to Paris and came back to the Senate with the Versailles Treaty containing the Covenant of the League of Nations, which was the forerunner of the United Nations.

An Early Reservation

Exit 5: The Lenni-Lenapes were the first settlers of this area. In October, 1677 the ship *Kent* deposited some Englishmen and founded the town of Burlington; they were a fair enough lot and actually bought their land. The Native Americans sold more and more to the new settlers until 1801, when there was only 100 of the tribe left. The land that they lived on was the first Indian reservation in the US.

Between Exit 4 & 5 Northbound, Mile 39.4: James Fenimore Cooper Service Area – Don't forget to come

and pick up your FREE motel discount coupon booklets which offer great deals along the way. New Jersey service areas are open 24 hours and have excellent lit up hotel/motel boards with phones to call for reservations. This State has the best service area bathrooms on the route. Take advantage of them.

James Fenimore Cooper was the first famous American-born novelist, having made his name by the stories he wrote about the American frontier in his *Leatherstocking Tales*. He created a typical 18th-century frontiersman named Natty Bumpo, who lived close to nature. The settlers who moved in around him brought civilized ways that changed his wilderness. Cooper wrote over 30 novels, the most famous probably being "Last of the Mohicans" in 1826.

He was born in Burlington County on September 15, 1789. His father was a Judge, a representative of the 4th and 6th Congress, and made his money as a land developer. The family moved to Cooperstown, New York, which was named after the family, and James roamed the forest and developed a love of nature which was later relayed into his books.

Cooper was thrown out of Yale because of his capers, one of which included

---

FREE motels breakfasts have become cookie cutter copies of each other. We have stayed in almost every brand of motel on the I-95 exits, and the FREE breakfasts seem to come out of the same commissary: plain or blueberry bagels, cream cheese, jams, perhaps peanut butter, sliced bread, 3 kinds of cold cereal, apples (always the Delicious kind), bananas, 3 kinds of tiny danish, orange juice, coffee and cold French toast to be microwaved. Occasionally there will be a burst of excitement when we see hard boiled eggs, biscuits and gravy, or a waffle-maker. We shouldn't complain, because after all this is all FREE, and it certainly is enough to get you started in the morning, but it is kind of boring to see no individuality amongst the chains. It is interesting to note, though, that when you stay in the higher priced hotels, you never get a FREE breakfast!

training a donkey to sit in a professor's chair. He joined the Navy, and the sea experiences later inspired his sea stories.

He mostly lived his life as a gentleman farmer, and only started writing in 1820 on a dare from his wife. From 1826 to 1833 they lived in Europe while he served as the US consul at Lyons, and they travelled a great deal. He became friends with Sir Walter Scott and Marquis de Lafayette, but eventually returned to New York.

Mind Bog-gling

Elizabeth Lee, a cranberry grower in South Jersey, decided, instead of tossing them out, to boil some wrecked berries with sugar and spices, She liked the tasty jelly so much she started a company called "Bog Sweet Cranberry Sauce", which eventually became part of the Ocean Spray cranberry cooperative company.

TRUCK STOPS

It really is a myth that if you see trucks parked at a restaurant, you know the food is good. What you know is that there is room to park trucks there and you will find basic cooking, not exotic fare. However, you should stop at one of the many humongous truck plazas along the way, just for the fun of it. First of all, the gas prices are usually excellent. If you need to take a shower, wire money, buy long distance phone cards, play video games, use the internet, amble through an interesting store with travel/auto products you will not come across in

the ordinary gas mini marts, or perhaps just chat with truckers, these places are fascinating.

Between Exit 4 & 3 Southbound, Mile 30.2: Walt Whitman Service Area – Don't forget to come and pick up your FREE motel discount coupon booklets which offer great deals along the way. New Jersey service areas are open 24 hours and have excellent lit up hotel/motel boards with phones to call for reservations. This State has the best service area bathrooms on the route. Take advantage of them.

Walt Whitman, born on May 31, 1819, spent the last years of his life in Camden after living in Brooklyn, Long Island, New Orleans, and Washington D.C. He is best known for his definitive poetry book "Leaves of Grass" (1855), which is an American classic. Though known as the father of free verse, he was a printer, teacher, journalist, editor, Civil War hospital worker and finally a civil servant in Washington. He wound up in NJ when he had come to visit his dying mother at his brother's house. A stroke in 1873 led to life in the NJ countryside, where he lived until his death in 1892.

Between Exit 2 & 1 Southbound, Mile 5.4: Clara Barton Service Area – Don't forget to come and pick up your FREE motel discount coupon booklets which offer great deals along the way. New Jersey service areas are open 24 hours and have excellent lit up hotel/motel boards with phones to call for reservations. This State has the best service area bathrooms on the route. Take advantage of them.

Clara Barton, born on Christmas Day 1821, began her work as a teacher in Bordentown, New Jersey in 1851. When she was only 11, she nursed her brother David who was badly injured in an accident, for

NJ 5 – NJ 2

2 years, and the lessons learned were of much use to her later on.

As a teacher, she was so upset by the number of poor children who could not afford to go to school that she offered to teach for free for 3 months if the town would make the school free for all. The concept was so successful that a larger school had to be built, but she quit when they wanted her to be overseen by a male principal.

In 1862, during the Civil War, she got government permission to accompany the sick and wounded as they were being moved. She heard about terrible shortages of field supplies, so she set about supplying their needs, tearing up old sheets for towels and handkerchiefs and cooking for the troops. Then, with her characteristic independence, she advertised for provisions in a newspaper, and when the public sent enormous donations, she set up a distributing agency.

For 4 years after the war, Clara supervised a Federal search for missing soldiers. By 1869 she was traveling in Europe and offered her services to help tend to civilian victims of the Franco-Prussian War. While In Geneva she learned of the International Red Cross, and brought the concept back to America.

She took on the formation of this agency practically single-handedly, educating the public through brochures and speeches and paying calls to cabinet heads and Congressmen. Her efforts were successful, and it was founded in the US in 1881. She served as its first president, and for the next 23 years directed its relief activities, retiring at the age of 82 and living to the ripe old age of 91. She certainly lived up to her nickname, "Angel of the Battlefield".

Play Ball!

Exit 1: New Jersey Mud – If you are a baseball nut, look down at the Delaware River as you cross over it here, because this is where the famous Lena Blackburne's Baseball Rubbing Mud comes from.

In 1938 when an umpire complained to Blackburne, a 3rd base coach for the old Philadelphia Athletics, about the condition of the balls which were rubbed with mud made of water and dirt from whatever field they were playing on, he went looking in the Delaware River until he found some muck (the whereabouts of the mud hole is still a dark secret) with a perfect texture - a cross between chocolate pudding and whipped cold cream.

Nowadays, every major and most minor leagues in the US use this mud to mask the ball's shine and improve the pitcher's grip. The mud's source  was willed to a close friend, John Haas, who had worked with Blackburne on his mud-finding exploits. Haas eventually turned over the enterprise to his son-in-law, Burns Bintliff. Burns in turn passed it on to son Jim and his family. Other kinds of mud and even mechanical methods have been tried to de-slick baseballs, but they couldn't make the grade - only good ole New Jersey mud will do.

Between Exit 1 & 2 Northbound, Mile 5.4: John Fenwick Service area – Don't forget to come and pick up your FREE motel discount coupon booklets which offer great deals along the way. New Jersey service areas are open 24 hours and have excellent lit up hotel/motel boards with phones to call for reservations. This State has the best service area bathrooms on the route. Take advantage of them. ☎ 856-299-8246.

John Fenwick, a Quaker, landed in these parts in 1675 to start a settlement without fear of persecution. He named it Salem from the Hebrew word for peace, and the county is still called that. He was probably a better leader than businessman, because financial troubles led him to turn the holdings over to William Penn, who had started another Quaker colony called Pennsylvania on the other side of the Delaware River. He died only a few years later in 1683.

☆ DELAWARE ☆

Exit 14: Bowlerama – Open for over 40 years, this fun spot has 74 lanes for your bowling pleasure. During the week take advantage of the kids' 2 hour special ($6) which runs from 9-4 and includes bowling, hot dog, french fries, soda, balls and shoes. On the weekend there's a family fun pak (Rent-A-Lane)  between noon and 3. For $30 per lane you get 2 hours of bowling, shoe rentals and $1.50 off a large french fry & pitcher of soda.

For a cosmic adventure try Xtreme™ bowling with black lights, glow-in-the-dark bowling balls and fluorescent pins. If you want to grab some fast food, the Fast Lane grill offers up jalapeno dogs, grilled cheese, kielbasa, cheese twigs, breaded mushrooms, chicken Caesar, BLT, pizza and breakfast, or just stop in for a peach tea. ◗ Mon-Thurs 9-11, Fri 9-12 am, Sat 10-11, Sun 9-11 (more hours in winter). ☞ Take the I-95 New Castle / Wilmington Exit and head North on Rte 9 through first traffic signal. You will see McDonalds on the right and Bowlerama will be on your left at 3031 New Castle Ave. www.bowlerama.us ☎ 302-654-0704 or 302-654-0263.

Exit 14: Mike's Famous Harley-Davidson – If you've ever pined to drive a Harley-Davidson, you could own the road for a moment with a rental if you are licensed for a bike (includes helmet, rainsuit, emergency assistance). Kids young and old will enjoy browsing through the showroom imagining themselves aboard a Harley.

If you can't own a Harley, you can still buy a piece of the action with Genuine Harley-Davidson MotorClothes™ and merchandise like helmets, jeans, jackets, pins, patches, wallets, jewelry and other souvenir items.

Next door, visit the Museum of the American Road, which is not quite opened but offering a free exhibit about the feats of Dave Barr, double amputee rider and Guinness Book of World Records holder, and you can see the only Harley-Davidson® motorcycle to be ridden around the world. And if you're already a biker, there's a service department here. ◗ Mon & Tues 9-6, Wed-Fri 9-8, Sat 8-8, Sun 10-6. 2160 New Castle Ave. www.mikesfamous.com ☎ 800-FAMOUS-HD or 302-658-8800.

Exit 13: Entenmann's Bakery Outlet – Head right here If you want to load up on inexpensive sweet snacks for the car or to buy discount bread (Arnold or Freihofer, Thomas' muffins) to make lunches.

Markdowns and overstocked Items (with a red line) are fresh and are only there because of their appearance or incorrect weight. Market returns (black lines on box at 50% off) are unsold from regular stores. Daily Specials did not sell out and are further reduced to sell quickly.

The Freezer Plan is a deal which gives you an extra 10% off if you spend $20 or more, and you could spend that easily by scooping up the super cinabons, crumb cakes, raspberry danish, chocolate variety pack of donuts, lemon crunch cake, marble light loaf, pecan danish ring or the healthier Rold Gold cheddar honey mustard or onion pretzels. Seniors get 10% off every day, and everyone gets a "How are you?" from the friendly staff. ◗ Mon-Sat 9-5, Sun 9-4. ☞ I-95 Exit 13 (New Castle Dover exit) and keep left off the exit if you're Southbound, right if you're heading North, to 1505 North Dupont Pkwy. ☎ 302-328-2510.

Mile 13: I-95 crosses the Christina River here. Swedes arrived in 1638 on *The Key of Kalmar* and the *Griffin*. They named the river you are now crossing after their 12-year-old Queen, Christina, and then they bought the land from the Native Americans and built a small fort. Since they were accustomed to long cold winters they thrived here, building the first log cabins in America, and soon numbering at least 1,000 living between here and Philidelphia. In 1655, the Dutch arrived in an armada of 7 ships with 600 men, so the Swedes, with very little ammunition, surrendered. Only 9 years later, the English came along and took over. Though the Swedes didn't last they left their mark, as their log cabins became a permanent feature of the American frontier.

Between Mile 2 & 3: Legend has it that the Stars and Stripes were unfurled for the first time in the only Delaware Revolutionary battle fought on or about September 3, 1777, called "the Battle of Cooch's Bridge", which occurred about a mile to the east of here.

Mile 5 Northbound and Southbound: Delaware House Service Area and Visitor Center – The name says it all. Stop in for your flyers, FREE motel brochures, clean restrooms and friendly traveling advice.

Exit 1: Mason-Dixon Line – The royal charters that established Maryland and Pennsylvania and granted them to the Calvert and Penn families did not coincide, and there was a great deal of confusion as to where the boundary lay. They brought the matter to the British court, and England's chief justice declared a border. A whole decade later, the two families agreed on the compromise and decided to get the new boundary surveyed.

Surveyors available in the colonies were no match for the difficult job, so two experts from England had to be brought over. Charles Mason and Jeremiah Dixon, an astronomer and a surveyor, spent from 1763-1767 surveying the north-south line now separating Delaware and Maryland, and then went west to survey the east-west line dividing Maryland and Pennsylvania. Before leaving the New World, they were both admitted as members of the American Society in Philadelphia for "Promoting Useful Knowledge". Fifty years later, in the Missouri Compromise of 1819-1820, which covered the slavery issue in new territories admitted to the Union, an imaginary line along the Maryland-Pennsylvania border and beyond separated the free States from the slave States. It was called the Mason-Dixon line, because its first east-west segment coincided with theirs. Eventually it came to be known as the boundary between the North and South.

☆ MARYLAND ☆

Exit 109: Elk Forge B & B – Only about 2 1/2 miles off I-95, you could sleep nestled in 5 acres of woods and gardens in a colonial manor house which has been newly updated into an inn and retreat. The 12 freshly renovated rooms (Internet, hot tubs, fireplaces, VCR's) are each beautifully themed to a nearby area (Pennsylvania Dutch, Philadelphia). If your bones are weary from your car journey, try the small spa on the premises for a massage, body wrap or facial to soothe it all away. Eating breakfast or afternoon tea et with silver and china in the cheerful solarium overlooking the lawns and woods will make you feel like the lord or lady of the manor. www.elkforge.com ☎ 877-ELK-FORGE or 410-392-9007.

> Crabs are monogamous, mating only once in their lifetime.

Exit 100: North East – For the charm of small town life, take a quick pit stop along South Main St. There is no overwhelming history to bore you with (okay George Washington's brother and father held an interest in the Principio Company, an iron works nearby) so you can just enjoy the handful of friendly gift shops and restaurants.

Animal lovers can head to The Bay Dog (#6) for all things dog (sox, picture frames, figurines, T-shirts), while Quackers (#7) is obviously about ducks and for outdoorsy folks (loved the "Endangered Feces" shirt) and Wild Birds Unlimited (#6) can help you with backyard bird feeding, plush birds, or fountains. Beans, Leaves, Etc. (#2) is for specialty coffees, teas and gourmet goodies. Our personal favorite, Herb's Tackle Shop (#4), is for those bloodsucker worms you've been hankering for, and if Herb's not around you can just throw some coins in the vending

machine out front and out pops... worms! Antique shops dot the street and the biggest is in an old 5 & 10, called the 5 & 10 Antique Market (#3), with 2 floors holding about

60 invisible dealers who are not there, so you simply choose from the display cases and pay at the front.

If you only have time for one pit stop, make it to the Shoppes of Londonshire (#7), and especially to Victoria's Touch/Where Butterflies Bloom, where Ron, Jenene or Rondi will help you select painted buoys, walking sticks, cloisonne enameling, plush hand puppets, Tula rush hats, reproduction home accent pieces, 65 varieties of vegetable glycerine soaps and candles, and there's Cafe-Chez Cameron & Bakery for eats in the mall too. To rest up after all this walking, have a cuppa at The Victorian Tea Cup (#5), where they serve a proper English tea all day long, with homemade Devonshire cream, homemade scones and tea sandwiches. ☎ 410-287-9500 for tea.

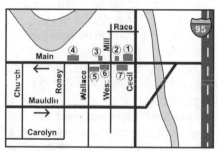

Exit 100: Steak & Main – Stop here for an upscale lunch or dinner. Starters might be tuna or beef carpaccio with capers, relish, asiago cheese on mixed greens, oysters Rockefeller or a salad of Boston bib and radiccio with pan seared rare ahi tuna or chicken in a mango vinaigrette. Yes, there's perfectly turned out steaks (you could have one with rock shrimp and boursin cheese on top) or sauteed veal with crab and asparagus in a chardonnay reduction or grilled honey chipolte Chilean sea bass.

Do not miss the house specialty - fried cheesecake (do you hear your arteries slamming shut?), which is a donut flavored crunchy crepe with melted sweet cream cheese inside - a heavenly ending, or go light with one of 6 sorbets or 3 gelatos. Here's a way to have fun, reserve Tony's table - a glass table perched on a handmade ship's wheel so it can turn in both directions - and then you can taste your neighbor's food. 107 S. Main St. (#3 on map) ☎ 410-287-3512.

Exit 100: Tailwinds Farm – Wow, a bed and breakfast where you can get up in the morning and go horseback riding! This farm family takes in travellers, be they the human kind or the animal kind (horses, dogs, etc). Ask about riding lessons, horse-drawn carriages, hay rides and pony rides.

JoAnn Dawson, the "farmers' wife", was written up in the NY Times, Baltimore Sun and was on Good Morning America for her role as a wrangler and appearance in Oprah Winfrey's "Beloved" film (and after that, The Sixth Sense, Hack, Jersey Girl). You could be riding one of those quiet dependable horses used in a film.

Enjoy a walk in the fields and woods, visit with Jeepers the goat, gather your own eggs for breakfast in the hen house or just watch the horses graze from your window. Same day reservations possible. www.fairwindsstables.com ☎ 410-658-8187.

Exit 100: Woody's Crab House – If you must have your fill of Maryland's famous crabs, you can head over to this wood-slatted fancy crab "shack" for a crab cake dinner, crab imperial, crab au gratin or jumbo lump crab salad which are made fresh every day. Hardshell bluefin crabs were voted best by Chesapeake Bay magazine - they serve them here seasoned and steamed. Healthy homemade vegetables, homemade crab bisque or Maryland crab soup round out the meal.

You could go farther asea for gulf shrimp, little neck clams, Alaskan king crab legs, a catch of the day (broiled, blackened or stuffed), their famous Carolina shrimp burger or have a landlubbers' chicken or ribs. Vegetarians are not forgotten, and are offered a sack of veggies. Big and small kids will enjoy munching on the free peanuts while you wait. ◗ Sun-Thurs 11:30-9, Fri & Sat 11:30-10 (closes one hour earlier in Fall and Winter). ☞ From I-95 Exit 100, take North East Rd. (route 272) south for 2.3 miles until it turns into Main Street. Woody's will be one block down on your right, 29 S. Main St. www.woodyscrab house.com ☎ 410 287-3541.

Mile 98 Northbound and Southbound: Chesapeake House – These are busy full service centers with the usual friendly tourist advice, flyers, FREE motel coupons and clean restrooms. However, this State info center also offers fax machines, ATM, mail and hotel reservations and a picnic area. ☎ 410-287-2313.

Exit 93: Prime Outlets at Perryville – You can't see this from the exit, but trust us - it is hiding down in a valley. First, a store with hard-to-find items: D & R Square Dance & Western Wear, and then there's an L.L. Bean Factory Store, Mikasa Factory Store, totes/Isotoner/Sunglass World and Peruvian Connection. ◗ Mon - Sat 10-9, Sun 11-6. ☞ I-95 Exit 93 and turn left on Perrylawn Dr. (Rte 275 South) to Heather Lane (you'll see a Pilot Truck Stop). Turn right and continue down the hill to 68 Heather Lane. www.outletsonline.com/nepomd.htm ☎ 410-378-9399.

Exit 89: The Underground Railroad was neither underground nor a railroad, but the name given the concept of a secret network of roads, waterways, trails and hiding places called "stations" (barns, churches, basements and woodsheds) which, with help from anti-slavery activists (who were breaking the law by assisting), led enslaved people from bondage to freedom.

In 1793 the US passed a Fugitive Slave Act, which allowed for the capture and return of any runaway living in a "free" state. Harford County's location near the Mason-Dixon Line and on the Chesapeake Bay made it a strategic point along the Underground Railroad, since slaves and indentured servants hid in the many coves. Rock Run Mill in the Susquehanna State Park was nicknamed "The Promised Land", since it would provide both refuge and a place to pick up provisions for the ferry journey across the river leading farther north.

In Connecticut, you can visit the Joshua Hempstead House and sleep or eat in Randall's Ordinary, other stops on this route, while Farmington was considered "Grand Central Station". The route ran through the New England states and ended in Ontario, Canada. If the slaves were lucky enough to make it that far, the British authorities declined to honor the US demands to return them.

Mile 82 Northbound and Southbound: Maryland House – These are busy full service centers with the usual

friendly tourism advice, flyers, FREE motel coupons, clean restrooms and a picnic area. This State info center also offers fax machines, an ATM, mail box, postage stamps and can make hotel reservations. ◗ Daily Winter 9-5, Summer 8:30-6. ☎ 410-272-0176.

Mile 56: The Star Spangled Banner – When driving through the Fort McHenry Tunnel, you are now driving under the very water that Francis Scott Key was stuck in on September 13 and 14, 1814 during the War of 1812. Key, a lawyer, had boarded the British flagship to secure the release of a friend.

Mary Young Pickersgill and her daughter Caroline had sewn a gigantic flag with 15 white stars and 15 red and white stripes which fluttered defiantly on the ramparts of Fort McHenry. It was so large that it could not be stitched in their home, so they had completed it in a Baltimore brewery.

As Key waited out the 24 hours in "shock and awe", the British fired off 200-lb. bombs which were supposed to explode on impact, but instead often blew up prematurely in mid-air. At night they sent up signal rockets which burned in flaming arcs across the sky. Through all of that, at dawn Key was amazed to see Mary's flag sill waving and the fort intact.

Overcome with emotion, he wrote some phrases on the back of a letter. It was his brother-in-law who suggested singing the poem to the meter of a British drinking song, "To Anacreon in Heaven" (must have been real catchy with those words). The song was an instant hit, but it took Congress until 1931 to designate it the US

> **Traffic Jam**
>
> **Exit 59:** If you're caught in traffic around Baltimore or Washington D.C. and think you're going really slowly, think about the patriots who rode horseback on this road. Thomas Jefferson complained that he could do at most 3 mph.

MD 100 – MD 56

national anthem. If you want to see the flag, it is still a moving site; it is hanging in the Smithsonian Institute, which is down I-95 a bit.

Why not sing along through the tunnel in Francis' honor?:

Oh, say can you see, by the dawn's early light,
What so proudly we hailed at the twilight's last gleaming?
Whose broad stripes and bright stars, through the perilous fight, O'er the ramparts we watched, were so gallantly streaming?
And the rockets' red glare, the bombs bursting in air,
Gave proof through the night that our flag was still there.
O say, does that star-spangled banner yet wave
O'er the land of the free and the home of the brave?

On the shore, dimly seen through the mists of the deep,
Where the foe's haughty host in dread silence reposes,
What is that which the breeze, o'er the towering steep,
As it fitfully blows, half conceals, half discloses?
Now it catches the gleam of the morning's first beam,
In full glory reflected now shines on the stream:
'Tis the star-spangled banner! O long may it wave
O'er the land of the free and the home of the brave.

And where is that band who so vauntingly swore
That the havoc of war and the battle's confusion
A home and a country should leave us no more?

Their blood has wiped out their foul footstep's pollution. No refuge could save the hireling and slave
From the terror of flight, or the gloom of the grave:
And the star-spangled banner in triumph doth wave
O'er the land of the free and the home of the brave.

Oh! thus be it ever, when freemen shall stand
Between their loved homes and the war's desolation!
Blest with victory and peace, may the heaven-rescued land
Praise the Power that hath made and preserved us a nation. Then conquer we must, when our cause it is just,
And this be our motto: "In God is our trust."
And the star-spangled banner in triumph shall wave
O'er the land of the free and the home of the brave!

Exit 53: Oriole Park at Camden Yards – This baseball field is located in what was a railroad center, and is only 2 blocks from the birthplace of baseball's most legendary hero, George Herman "Babe" Ruth. His father operated Ruth's Cafe on the ground floor of the family residence located at Conway Street and Little Paca, which amazingly is now center field at Oriole Park! Tours of the park lasting 1 1/4 hours are given all year round, rain or shine. www.TheOrioles.com ☎ 410-547-6234.

Mile 48: The World's First Telegram – This was dispatched on the B&O railroad's right of way between Washington and Baltimore which passes beneath the highway here and runs parallel to I-95. One telegraph unit was set up in the Supreme Court chamber and the other in the B&O's Pratt St. Station in Baltimore. On May 24, 1844 Samuel Morse's dots and dashes were received in the first telegram which read "What hath God wrought?".

Morse trained as a painter and studied at Yale, but it was a chance meeting on a ship with Dr. Charles Thomas Jackson that set him on the path toward telecommunications. Since he had sketched for so many years, he could visualize and draw the ideas in his head. He also realized that he would need a code for each letter to communicate. He took time to study the English language to determine the most popular letters and numbers, and it was his brilliant idea to assign the simplest patterns to the most common letters, which led to his greatest contribution: the Morse Code. His inventions began one of the most important revolutions in American history: the communication revolution.

Mile 37 Northbound and Southbound: Maryland Welcome Center – These are busy full service centers with the usual friendly tourism advice, flyers, FREE motel coupons, clean restrooms and a picnic area. This State info center can also make hotel reservations. ◐ Daily Summer 8:30-6; Winter 9-5. ☎ 301-490-1333.

Exit 23: College Park Aviation Museum – How appropriate to house an aviation museum at the oldest continuously operated airport in the world. The first person to greet you is Wilbur Wright - who else? This animatronic life-like man tells you how he came to this airfield in 1909 to teach military officers how to fly. The gallery contains historic and reproduction aircraft associated with the history of the airfield, as well as hands-on activities for children of all ages. Look for exhibits on the first US Postal Air flight in 1918 and the first controlled helicopter flight by H. Berliner.

The airport runway is just outside the rear glass windows of the museum, so you can watch take-offs or landings as today's pilots take to the sky. ◐ Daily 10-5. ☞ From I-95 Exit 23, go south on Kenilworth Ave (route 201) until the light at Paint Branch Pkwy. Turn right until Corporal Frank Scott Dr., make another right and follow signs to the museum. www.college parkaviationmuseum.com ☎ 301-864-6029.

Exit 15: Everlasting Life is a way of life. This group of African Hebrew Israelites of Jerusalem have set up a community-owned cooperative which encompasses a communal center with a health food supermarket, restaurant, bakery, take-out counter and juice bar (Source of Life).

Vegetarian food is hard to come by on I-95, so it was a real find to discover a soul vegetarian gourmet one. From the hot spinach dip to the barbeque twists, Jamaican curried tofu, smothered cabbage and onions and "grab cakes" to the munchie baskets of cauliflower southern fried in a wheat/cornmeal batter, this complex is sure to please the healthier side of you. The informal juice bar has lighter fare of shakes, smoothies, about a dozen salads and hot plates. 9185 Central Ave. www.everlastinglife.net ☎ 301-324-6900.

Exit 7: John Wilkes Booth fled through these parts after assassinating President Abraham Lincoln in Ford's Theatre in Washington, DC on April 14, 1865. With David Herold, a fellow conspirator, he stopped at

MD 53 – MD 15

the house of Dr. Samuel Mudd to get treatment for a broken leg which happened in his leap to the stage. He arrived at Dr. Mudd's around 4 a.m. on April 15, 1865. Dr. Mudd set, splinted, and bandaged the broken leg, and they stayed

---

Oops, Important Errors

Did you know that Timothy Matlack, the calligrapher who personally wrote the Declaration of Independence, made 3 errors in the writing of it? Two of them have been corrected by the addition of a ^ with the corrections inserted above the word: the word "representative" was spelled "represtative" and the word "only" was omitted. The third error could not be changed, since an extra letter was written in the line "Nor have we been wanting in attentions to our Brittish brethren".

---

steak and of course, fried chicken, all cooked to order by this second generation of Henry's. Fresh cornbread is made daily and it is used for the turkey and chicken stuffing, or you can have your BBQ sandwiches made on it. And don't forget that sweet

until the next afternoon. Mudd's handyman, John Best, made a pair of rough crutches for Booth. Mudd was paid $25 for his services.

Within days Dr. Mudd was under arrest by the US Government and was charged with conspiracy and with harboring

Booth and Herold during their escape. He was sentenced to life in prison and missed the death penalty by one vote. However, because of outstanding efforts as a physician during a yellow fever epidemic at the prison, he was granted parole after only 4 years by President Andrew Johnson.

Exit 3B: Henry's Soul Cafe – With its slogan "Home of the Sweet Potato Pie", you can expect that there will be collard greens, okra, chitterlings and pigs feet on the menu as well. For the rest of the less daring, head for the meatloaf, freshly fried fish (trout or whiting), country style

potato pie for dessert. ◑ Sun 12-8, Mon 11:30-7, Thurs-Sat 11:30-9. ☞ I-95 Exit 3B (Forest Heights) onto Indian Head Highway. Restaurant is on the left at 5431 Indian Head Highway. www.henryssoulcafe.net ☎ 301-749-6856.

Exit 3A: Oxon Cove Park/Oxon Hill Farm – If you need a breath of fresh air or if the kids need to blow off some steam, or if you are looking for a place to picnic, get off and enjoy this FREE National Park Service site. The park varies from low flat river shoreline to high river terraces offering open grassland, deciduous forest, marsh and swamp ecosystems. On a clear day , the 2-mile easy loop walk even offers a glimpse of the Washington Monument.

The little farm has horses, cows, sheep, goats, pigs, rabbits, a chicken coop, deer, a duck pond and herb garden. If you stop at the right time of day, there are daily programs for cow milking, a chicken program, wagon rides or ranger talks about the history of the farm.

The property goes back to Dr. Samuel and Mary DeButts who bought it in 1811. In 1814 they watched in horror with divided loyalties as the War of 1812 was fought on their doorstep. The fires from the burning of the Presidential White House and other buildings glowed on the walls of their own white house. Across the Potomac, in the Alexandria Harbor, sat the British warships, and the city surrendered to them. No wonder the DeButts went off to visit their daughter in Virginia.

In 1891 (and until the 1950's), the U.S. Government bought it and established a farm for St. Elizabeth's Hospital, allowing patients to work the farm for therapy and to grow their own food. Hours: Daily 8-4:30. ☞ I-95 Exit 3A and bear right on the exit ramp onto Oxon Hill Road. Follow signs to the farm (a quick right turn). 6411 Oxon Hill Rd. www.nps.gov /nace/oxhi ☎ 301-839-1176.

☆ VIRGINIA ☆

Exit 177: Alexandria Visitor's Center – When you go up the staircase in the charming historic Ramsay House don't be surprised if the ghost of Mr. Ramsay passes you. He and other spectres are encountered in the nightly ghost walks, or you can join spook-free walking tours or just ask for friendly advice. Pick up the scrap-book-able *Proclamation of The Mayor of the City of Alexandria*, proclaiming you an "Honorary Citizen for the Day", which includes 24 hours of FREE parking at the meters in town. On the weekends there's a FREE Dash About shuttle,

and on Saturdays there's still a Farmer's Market in Market Square. There are combination passes called Patriot, Liberty or Key, which can save you money on sites. ◑ Daily 9-5 ☞ From I-95 Exit 177B, head North up S. Patrick St. (US 1) for 3/4 mile to King St. Turn right to 221 King St. on your left. www.funside.com ☎ 800-388-9119 or 703-838-4200.

Exit 177: Carlyle House – In 1741 John Carlyle, 2nd son of a wealthy Scottish family, emigrated to Virginia to work as a representative for William Hicks, an English merchant. He first achieved enormous financial, then romantic, success by marrying Sarah Fairfax, daughter of one of Virginia's most influential families. This Georgian Palladian manor house was built on 2 of the most expensive lots in the city with Potomac River views and access to Market Square.

Carlyle became one of Northern Virginia's most influential men, and it was in this house that the legendary conference of 5 colonial governors and General Edward Braddock, Commander in Chief of His Majesty's Forces in North America, decided on a tax on "all his Majesty's dominions in America" (to fund the French and Indian War), the first colonial tax. A succession of taxes followed, which eventually led to resentment against England and cries of "taxation without representation", and the American Revolution. ◑ Tues-Sat 10-4:30, Sun 12-4:30. 121 N. Fairfax St. just N of King St. ☎ 703-549-2997.

Exit 177C: The Carriage House B & B – For those of you who enjoy being surrounded by nature or who like privacy or want the feel of home, this B & B offers you, down your own driveway, a French Country decorated apartment that sleeps 5. You'll be sitting on your deck above the carriage house for the same price as others are paying for a high end plastic motel room. If you are staying a few days in the

MD 3 – VA 177

area, this is but a 5 minute drive from old town, so you can use it as a jumping off point for Alexandria, Washington DC (take the metro in town), Mount Vernon and more. www.aabbn.com ☎ 888-549-3415 or 703-660-9420.

Exit 177: Christ Church – This church building was begun in 1767, and its fame rests on the fact that both George Washington and Robert E. Lee worshipped here. As you enter, on your far left towards the front you can notice Washington's pew (#60) - it is the only one remaining in its original double configuration. Robert E. Lee (# 46 on the right), the Confederate General, was actually married to Washington's step-great grand-daughter, Mary Custis. He was confirmed here, together with two of his daughters. A silver

plaque on the chancel rail marks the spot. Regular congregants refer to the chapel's geography as the Lee side or the Washington side. Notice an original boot scraper outside building. Perhaps one of these gentlemen used it.

During the Civil War, Col. Orlando Willcox of the Union Army wrote of Washington's connection to the church, "There I could almost feel his imposing presence...". It is a tradition for the President of the United States to visit here at some point during his administration, usually on a Sunday near Washington's birthday.

Presidential visits have also happened in conjunction with other important events. A notable one was the January 1, 1942 visit by President Franklin Roosevelt and British Prime Minister Winston Churchill for the World Day of Prayer for Peace during World War II. ☞ From I-95 Exit 177B, head North up S. Patrick St. (US 1) for 3/4 mile to Duke St. Turn right for 4 blocks to Washington St., then make a left for 3 blocks to 118 N. Washington St. www.historicchristchurch.org

Exit 177C: Collingwood Library and Museum on Americanism – This property was originally part of George Washington's River Farm. It is part research library of Americanism including, amazingly, George Washington's diaries, Paul Revere's lantern from Boston's Old North Church (see story), 6,000 books on patriotic subjects and 600 volumes of geneaology from the Mayflower Society of Washington D.C. The other part is a wee bit of a museum which is easily traversed in under an hour.

Kids would enjoy the Sioux chief headress with 87 eagle feathers, Uncle Sam's outfit, flags of all the States and Medal of Honor winners. There are replicas of The Declaration of Independence and the Magna Carter.

Facing the front door there is a huge old holly tree where you can hide inside and have a secret picnic on a bench. (Glad George didn't cut that one down!). Entrance is FREE or you may just want to stretch your legs walking around the grounds and go down for the water views. ◑ Mon, Wed-Sat 10-4, Sun 1-4. ☞ From I-95 Exit 177C, take S Washington St. (which turns into the George Washington Memorial Pkwy) heading South (right turn) for 4 1/2 mi. and turn left at Collingwood Rd., then right on East Boulevard Drive to the parking area. 8301 E. Blvd Dr. www.collingwood library.com/collingwood.html ☎ 703-765-1652.

The Official Paul Revere Old North Church Lantern

ONE IF BY LAND OR TWO IF BY SEA?

Exit 177: In the Collingwood Library and Museum on Americanism hangs the lantern from the belfry of Boston's Old North Church that was used to signal to Paul Revere that the British were coming. Do you know which it was - one if by land or two if by sea? Here's the verse in the Longfellow poem that addresses it:

"Meanwhile, impatient to mount and ride,
Booted and spurred, with a heavy stride
On the opposite shore walked Paul Revere.
Now he patted his horse's side,
Now he gazed at the landscape far
and near,
Then, impetuous, stamped the earth,
And turned and tightened his saddle girth;
But mostly he watched with eager search
The belfry tower of the Old North Church,
As it rose above the graves on the hill,
Lonely and spectral and sombre and still.
And lo! as he looks, on the belfry's height
A glimmer, and then a gleam of light!
He springs to the saddle, the bridle
he turns,
But lingers and gazes, till full on his sight
A second lamp in the belfry burns."

from "Paul Revere's Ride"
by Henry Wadsworth Longfellow.

Exit 177: Dr. James Craik was surgeon-general, so it was his duty to accompany George Washington during every battle he fought in the Revolutionary War. Unfortunately, without modern antibiotics, he was unable to save the Father of our Country from a simple throat infection that led to his death in 1799. The home of Dr. James Craik is still there at 209 Prince St.

Exit 177: Hard Times Cafe – Chili in all its firy glory is served up in 4 styles - Texas (just the beef Ma'am), Cincinnati (a bit sweeter), Terlingua Red (with tomato sauce) or Vegetarian (veggies and heat).

In 1980, Fred and Jim Parker mortgaged their homes and opened this cafe to salute the Southwestern Depression era chili parlors and to recall the Hard Times that people like their Dad lived through. Circa 1930 photographs of western life and back-lit silhouettes of western scenes fill the walls; those and other architectural details are in the style of Thomas Molesworth, a designer of dude ranches in the 1930's and 40's. This location also displays flags given to them by various Congressional delegations from nearby DC.

To choose your flavor of chili, you are offered a tasting plate in the beginning so you can figure out which suits you. After that you decide how you want the chili served: with beans, on spaghetti, on a healthy salad, in a soft tortilla, on a burger or a hot dog or in a 1940's Frito chip pie. You can also order chicken, burgers, salads and there's a kids' menu. Speaking of kids, they love to choose songs on the real juke box. Finish off your meal with a root beer float. ◑ Sun-Thurs 11 am to midnight, Fri-Sat 11-1. 1404 King St. Other locations on I-95: Exits 130, 156 and 169. www.hardtimes.com ☎ 703-837-0050.

Exit 177: Civil War Prisons – The U.S. government operated 5 prisons in Alexandria during the Civil War, including the Slave Pen on Duke St. and Prince St. Prison, which is still here as a large brick building on the southeast corner of Fairfax and Prince St. (It's a private residence - yoiks!).

For the most part, most offenders kept here were for desertion, and were eventually just returned to their regiment without pay. In July 1864, Capt. Rufus Pettit, an especially cruel officer, was appointed to oversee the prisons. He often tortured suspected deserters until they confessed, whether they were guilty or innocent. Thankfully, he was eventually court-martialled and removed from the U.S. Military.

Exit 177: Stabler–Leadbeater Apothecary Museum – Founded in 1792 by Quaker pharmacist Edward Stabler, this business remained in the same family for 141 years until 1933, when the Depression forced them close. They chose to simply lock the door, and inadvertently preserved history. Fortunately over 8,000 items, including the old account books, prescriptions, early medical wares, apothecary containers, documents and journals all remained in their original drawers, providing a living history of the city. Everything you see now is just about the same as George Washington, James Monroe and Robert E Lee saw them. Look for the note Martha wrote to them for George's ailments. ◗ Mon-Sat 10-4, Sun 1-5. 105 S. Fairfax St. ☎ 703-836-3713.

- - - - - - - - -
Whose Side are you on Anyway?

Confederate General Robert E. Lee married Mary Anna Randolph Curtis. Her father was George Washington Parke Curtis, who was Martha Washington's grandson. Who do you think Mary Anna was rooting for in the Civil War?
- - - - - - - - -

Exit 177: Torpedo Factory Art Center – From 1918 thru WW II this building produced torpedo shell casings and other weapons. The 9920 MK-14 green torpedo you now see in the main hall salutes that era. Now what we have is a great concept of about 165 artists renting reasonably priced work space in this steel and glass airy building, which offers water views and has light coming in from every angle.

We, the public, are allowed to wander through and watch them work on painting, jewelry, sculpture, ceramics, wearables, printmaking, glass, photography or fiber art and are able to buy their work on the spot without the cost of the middle man.

Some of the spaces are co-ops for groups of artists. On the third floor is the Alexandria Archeology Museum, which traces the history of the city going back 9,000 years. In a small corner you can discover diagrams of 23 miles of trails in the city to be covered by foot, bike or car. ◗ Daily 10-5. 105 N. Union St. at the corner of King St. right down by the river. www.torpedofactory.org ☎ 703-838-4565 X3.

Exit 176A: Pearl's Discount Arts and Crafts – Are the kids getting antsy in the car? Stop here and get them some arts and crafts supplies to keep them busy for a few hours or days: color or paint by numbers sets, bead or stringing kits, fimo and clay, a greeting card kit, and more paper, pencils and Crayola crayons than you could ever imagine.

For activities for when you arrive at your vacation destination, there's painting kits, travel easels, needlework supplies, radio kits, toe painting sets or why not paint on an apron, a scarf or our personal favorite - an umbrella. Pearl started in 1933 in NYC as a paint store. Since the 1960's the flagship store has been on Canal St, near Soho, so you are shopping in the same company as the NYC art community. ◐ Mon-Sat 10-8, Sun 11 to 6. 5695 Telegraph Rd. www.pearl paint.com ☎ 703-960-3900.

WASH YOUR WINDSHIELD WITH HOLY WATER?

Exit 170: Arlington Temple United Methodist Church in Rosslyn has a gas station underneath it. William P. Ames, Jr. was a very far thinking son. He donated the piece of land where the church stands in honor of his father. Churches, as we

now know, tend to have dwindling congregations and wind up having to close up shop. Mr Ames solved the problem by having a tenant (the gas station) pay rent, and also built Ames Office Building on the rest of the land. Though locals used to call it "Our Lady of Exxon" after the first tenant, it is now a Chevron station.

Exit 169B: Talbots Outlet Store– In the Springfield Tower Center, look for clothing deals for women who wear sizes petite right up to 24W. There's a bit of things for kids and men. Expect discounts of 25% to 70% from the past season's merchandise and from their catalogs. If your'e lucky, you'll catch them at a 50% off sale moment. It's hard to find an outlet store for Talbots, so we're lucky here. ◐ Mon-Fri 10-9, Sat 10-

Sunday in the Park with War

In July of 1861, Washingtonians traveled in their "Sunday best" to Judith Henry's farm in Manassas Junction. They brought their picnic lunches, blankets and fans to loll away the afternoon watching, through binoculars, a battle between North and South. Expecting a swift painless demise to the South, they were horrified to experience a bloodbath killing 900 men. This battle jolted the North and Washington leaders into realizing that a Civil War had really begun. A year later, in one of the US's bloodiest days, 24,000 men died in yet another Confederate victory here.

6, Sun 12-5. ☞ Take I-95 Exit 169B and follow Franconia Rd. (Rte 644) to the first right turn (Backlick Rd.). Turn right for 1 block to Talbots at the corner - 6825 Bland St. www.talbots.com ☎ 703-644-5115.

Exit 163: Fairfax County Visitor Center is located in the Comfort Inn at this exit. Helpful advice from Nancy, Jean or Linda, informative flyers, coupon books and clean bathrooms in the motel await you. ◐ Daily 9-5. www.visitfairfax.org ☎ 800-732-4732 or 703-550-2450.

Exit 160: Prince William County Visitor Information Center – For information on the area, come into this cute town and check it out and what you can do around the area. ◐ Daily 9-5. See the main Occoquan story and the map below for directions. 200 Mill St. www.Occoquan.org ☎ 800-388-9119 or 703-491-4045.

Exit 160B: Occoquan – If you want to stretch your legs in a little old town on a river just 5 minutes off the exit, head for this artsy craftsy place. Occoquan is a Dogue Native American word for "at the end of the water". Captain John Smith of Jamestown fame made it all the way here on one of his forays, and

VA 177–VA 160

reported that "Dogues", surly hostile Indians, lived nearby.

The river setting made it a natural choice for early tobacco farming, forges, grist mills, saw mills, cotton mills and store-houses, with cargo leaving for Europe and the West Indies - until the river silted up. The first commercial ice storage house in the area was here, and Merchant's Mill, the first automated grist mill in the nation, lasted here for 175 years before being damaged by fire.

The Occoquan Post Office was the main delivery point for mail between North and South, so this was quite a bustling city up to the early 20th century when, in 1916, a fire devastated much of the town and then, in 1972, Hurricane Agnes hit hard again, destroying the Pratt iron-truss bridge.

The merchants' association dates from around that time. It encouraged reju-venation to a new citizenry of artsy types who have opened over 50 charming bou-tiques in all the ups and downs and alley-ways of the old town's buildings. Look for everything from Irish and Celtic art to cook-ware, loose teas for tea parties (even tea hats), quilting supplies, folk art, a woman's book store, weather vanes, doll houses, Americana, whimsical wear-ables, soft dolls, garden accessories, unique jewelry, Victorian lace and the best home-made pies on I-95.

Please note that the town is haunted by ghosts (pick up the guide in the vis-itor's center to find them) who rearrange things in stores, tread footsteps, leave behind flowers, flicker can-dles or show up as a Con-federate soldier. ☞ From I-95 Exit 160B, take Gordon Blvd (Rte 123) 3 traffic lights north for about 3/4 mile to

the Historic Occoquan sign. Turn left and then make the 1st right onto Washington St. down to Mill St. at the bottom. You can turn left or right here - the town of Occo-quan is at your feet. www.occoquan.org

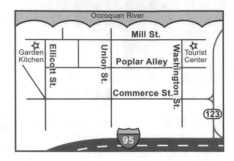

The Pie Lady

Exit 160: The Garden Kitchen – This is the home of Marie-Claire's pies. Yes, it's a café too, but this is the kind of cafe where you must start with dessert. A landmark for 30 years in the cute town of Occoquan, located in a 150 year-old house, its narrow stone and brick stairway surprises you when it opens to a lovely quiet garden away from the bustling street.

Inside the colonial dining rooms or on the terrace and patios, you must dig in to the Key Lime Cheesecake, Sinful Chocolate Cake or 14 daily Cream Pies (Coconut, Butter-scotch, Peanut Butter) and Fruit Pies (Cherry, Blue-berry, Sweet Pota-to) or brownies, cookies, cinnamon rolls and some sugar-free choices. Oh yes, there's quiches, sand-wiches (grilled Dijon chicken sal-

> ### Shh! Don't Tell Anyone
>
> **Exit 150:** During the Second World War, the Army used the thick forest and vast 17,000 acres in Prince William Forest Park to train spies. The Office of Strategic Services (OSS), which became the CIA, operat-ed training schools. Area A agents learned to gather infor-mation and they practiced their skills in nearby communities, and Area C agents were taught to train radio engineers to relay secret messages from agents who were behind enemy lines.

Courtesy: Garden Kitchen

ad) and soups too. Marie-Claire says, "Happiness is still homemade", so please treat yourself to a pie for the road - they're worth every calorie. ◑ Mon-Fri 9-4:30, Sat & Sun 9-5:30. ☞ See the main Occoquan story and map for directions. 404 Mill St. www.GardenKitchen.com ☎ 703-494-2848.

Exit 156: Potomac Mills – This enclosed, one-mile long outlet mall has over 220 stores and even Mills TV, an in-mall television station broadcasting store specials. Grab a bite in one of the 25 in-mall eateries or attached restaurants. Some popular outlets for you to find bargains in are: L.L. Bean, Royal Doulton, Etienne Aigner, Lego, Stride Rite/Keds/Sperry, Urban Planet, Daffy's, Bible Factory Outlet and an unusually large number of diamond and jewelry shops. Here's a new one for us: Armed Forces Recruiting Station, perhaps the "deal" is free travel! ◑ Mon-Sat 10-9:30, Sun 11-7. www.potomacmills.com ☎ 800-VIR-MILLS or 703-643-1855.

Exit 152: Weems–Botts Museum – Parson Mason Locke Weems, a bookseller from Dumfries, wrote the biography "Life of Washington", in which he recounts a story about Washington as a young lad "barking" a cherry tree and then confessing to his father, "I cannot tell a lie". This story took on a life of its own, and helped to make George Washington a national hero for all time. It was the 2nd best selling book in America (after the Holy Bible) for years, and was in continuous publication from 1800 to 1927.

His original book shop is now this museum. Reportedly, he played the devil's instrument, the fiddle, outside his shop to attract customers from the major east-west high-

way. Guess he was one of America's first marketing geniuses.

The name Botts refers to Benjamin Botts, who purchased the building from Weems in 1802 and who was on the team defending Aaron Burr in his treason trial. They were successful, and Burr was not convicted. Botts and his wife Jane were killed, along with the Governor of Virginia and other prominent state leaders, in a theater fire in Richmond, Virginia in 1811.

You can picnic here, but I don't think there's a cherry tree to sit under. ◑ Tues-Sat 10-4. ☞ From I-95 Exit 152 take Rte 234 East towards Dumfries and turn right at US 1. Continue for just under a mile, keeping right where the road splits, and make a right onto Duke St. at the museum sign. The Museum is 2 blocks up the hill on the left. Please do not park in the apartment building's lot. 3914 Cameron St. www.geocities.com /hdvinc ☎ 703-221-3346 or 703-221-2218.

Exit 150: Globe and Laurel – Major Rick Spooner and his wife Gloria are the hosts at this pub, which is located only a rifle shot from the entrance to the Quantico base. If you are fascinated by military people and paraphernalia (some date back before the Civil War), don't miss this spot, frequented by the who's who of the Marine Corps (notice the personalized pewter mugs hanging from the bar). There is a display which traces the evolution of the U.S. Marine emblem, insignia of Marines of the world on the walls, and the ceiling is plastered with civil police shoulder patches, which is probably one of the largest collections in the world.

The pub was intriguing enough for Patricia Cornwell to use it as a location in two of her mystery novels. Food is reasonably

VA 160 – VA 150

priced, with the popular Maryland crab cakes, roast prime rib of beef, Norwegian salmon with a garlic, ginger and white wine marinade or duck a l'orange. A cute Marine salute: desserts are called Ruffles & Flourishes, and there is no charge for "young recruits" under 5. ◐ Mon-Fri 11:30-1:30 and then Mon-Sat 5-9:30 ☞ From I-95 Exit 150A head East on Route 619 for one block and turn left on Jefferson Davis Highway (US 1) to number 18418 on your left. www.heritagestudio.com/spooner.htm ☎ 703-221-5763.

Mile 137 at the Potomac Creek: Pocahontas Kidnapping –

Look east downstream where the Native American village Patawomeck stood. When Capt. John Smith was captured by Pocahontas' people and was about to have his head smashed, she threw herself in the way and beseeched her father, Chief Powhatan, to spare him, saving his life. Five years later, when the English were upset with the Chief for taking some rifles, they kidnapped her. While in Jamestown, she fell in love with John Rolfe and their marriage brought peace for 10 years to the area. In 1616 she even traveled to England with Rolfe and had an audience with the King and Queen, but fell ill and was buried there.

Exit 150: Quantico – This is the only town in the US that is completely surrounded by a military base. In order to get to your home, you must pass through the gates of the base.

Exit 133: Best Inn – This chain of inns, suites and motels offers "evergreen rooms" which filter both air and water to provide an odor-free, allergen free, clean water guest room. The air filter incorporates a pre-filter, a HEPA-type particle filter and an odor module. The drinking water filtration is cer-

tified to National Standard Foundation Standard #42. If that wasn't enough, the shower filter offers a chlorine free soft water massage.

Mile 132 Southbound: Virginia Welcome Center – It always pays to stop off at these centers for clean bathrooms and the FREE motel discount coupon booklets and all the flyers from places to visit all around the State. Don't forget to chat with the friendly and helpful staff who can answer many questions. ◐ Daily 8:30-5, Summer Daily 8:30-6.

Exit 130: Central Park Mall – This is one of the new type of separate-store malls. If you have the patience to keep driving around, you might find: Eddie Bauer, Tweeter for high end audio, Zany Brainy for games to keep the kids busy, Funland for a break or Maggie Moo's for mix-in ice creams and fruit smoothies. The Look of Europe is a mix and match shop with many fabric, color and pattern choices allowing a woman to create a unique look, and they even make alterations to the clothing's size or style for free. www.centralparktoday.com/STORES /index.htm ☎ 540-786-1405.

Exit 130: Fun-land – If your seatmates are driving you crazy in the car, help is at hand for kids from 3 to 93. This indoor/outdoor amusement area, located in the Central Park Mall, offers the slow fun of the carousel right up to the challenge of a rock climbing wall. There's a roller coaster, a flight simulator, laser ball batting cages, laser tag and 140 arcade games (not for those sensitive to noise) where you can win

coupons and redeem them for prizes.

Outside in decent weather there's go karts, bumper boats and cars, miniature golf and batting cages. Parents can retire to the cafe and Subway shop for the simple adrenaline buzz of coffee. Look for daily specials: on Mondays you get 60 tokens for $10. Okay, we'll admit that we had fun here and spent far too long choosing our silly prizes (candy, slinky, rings, hair clips, pencils all the way up to stuffed animals and Harley racers) with coupons that we won. ◑ Sun-Thurs 10-9, Fri & Sat 10-12 am; Summer 10-12 am daily. 1351 Central Park Blvd. www.cpfunland.com ☎ 540-785-6700.

> **Exit 75:** What color was George Washington's hair and eyes?
>
> Answer:
> Reddish brown hair and blue eye

Exit 130: Carl's – This 2nd generation family-owned walk up frozen custard stand is a ritual stop for native Fredericksburgers (don't ya just love that name!). It was designed (building and signage) and opened by Carl and Margaret Sponseller in 1953 in a former gas station, and is now honored to be on the Virginia Landmarks Register. The choice of St. Anne St (#2200) was deliberate, for not only was that one of the main downtown arteries, but it was along US 1, at the time the busiest North/South highway in the US.

Frozen custard takes soft ice cream, mixes it with eggs, and then the mixture is cooked before it is frozen. The 3 flavors, Vanilla, Chocolate and Strawberry are still the same recipes and have been churning out of the same machine since the 1940's.

We had a serious standoff choosing our favorites among the flavors. If the pale chocolate has a really familiar taste to you, that's because they use Hershey syrup in the mix.

Though we are admitted chocoholics, Sandra actually favored the strawberry, because it tasted like you were biting into a real strawberry - because it really is made with fresh fruit. ◑ Sun-Thurs 11-11, Fri & Sat 11-11:30 (from the Fri before President's Day to the Sun of Thanksgiving). ☞ From I-95 Exit 130A head east on Plank Rd (Rte 3) for 1 1/4 miles, passing (US 1), and turn left on William St. (Business Rte 3) for 1 1/4 miles to Caroline St. Make a left and proceed 7 blocks to Herndon St., where you will turn left for 1 block and right again onto Princess Anne. Proceed to Carl's at 2200 Princess Anne St.

Exit 130: Fredericksburg – Walk in the footsteps of George Washington and James Monroe here, just a cannon shot from I-95. In the 40 square block "Old Town" you'll discover bookstores, art galleries, pubs and more than 350 18th and 19th century houses built on the hallowed ground of the Civil War, with cannonballs still embedded in the sides of buildings. Check out the Hugh Mercer Apothecary shop, an 18th century doctor's office where blood draining and amputating limbs was a common occurrence, or the Rising Sun Tavern, where you will learn about Colonial twice-a-year bathing habits (see story below).

Until the last decade of his life, George Washington spent alot of time here. From the ages of 6 to 16, he lived across the river at Ferry Farm (burned down in 1740, but you can visit the land) and attended school for a term or two. His many relatives and acquaintances lived here, so he

VA 137 – VA 130

would break up his long journey to Williamsburg with a stop at his brother Charles, his mother, his sister Betty's beautiful Kenmore Plantation, attend church services and BBQ's, or hoist a few with friends at Weedon's Tavern.

Ask at the Visitor Center about the Pass to Historic Fredericksburg (40% off 9 historic sites, museums and battlefields) and a FREE Parking permit for metered zones and municipal lots. ◑ Daily 9-5 (summer: 9-7). ☞ From I-95 Exit 130A head east on Plank Rd (Rte 3) for 1 1/4 miles, passing (US 1), and turn left on William St. (Business Rte 3) for 1 1/4 miles to Princess Anne St. Make a right and proceed 3 blocks to Charlotte St., where you will turn left and see the Center on your left at the corner of Caroline St. 706 Caroline St. www.fredericksburgvirginia.net ☎ 800-678-4748 or 540-373-1776.

Exit 130: In Fredericksburg, the Mary Washington (George's Mom) Monument, a 40-ft. version of the Washington monument, marks the burial spot of Mary Washington. The idea was started in 1833 by a wealthy New York merchant named Silas Burrows, but financial problems caused a setback. The project lan-

guished until 1889, the centennial of Mary Washington's death, when a group was chartered with the goal of completing a monument for Mary. It was completed and dedicated five years later, on Mother's Day, May 10, 1894. It is said to be the first monument dedicated to a woman by women. To pay for it, over 100 years ago, a national Mary Washington Memorial Association appealed to women throughout the country, especially those named Mary (talk about clever marketing!), for donations. 1500 Washington Avenue, right in town.

Exit 130: Rising Sun Tavern – Washington's brother Charles had this place built around 1760 as his home, so George was a frequent guest here. Later on it was a tavern and a stagecoach stop. Enjoy the delightfully funny costumed wenches who give living history tours in which you will learn how these sayings got started:

"Not playing with a full deck" — The King put a tax on the ace of spades, so if you played without that card, you avoided the tax

"Fish out of water" or "Drink like a fish" — A fish was embossed on bottom of mugs so if you got to the bottom and saw the fish, he was out of water and you were out of beer

"Caught with fingers in the till" — You sometimes paid for your drinks by yourself using a box which had a locked money drawer. Unsavory characters would try to pry it open, so the owners put a bell in there to catch them with their fingers in the till. The bell ringing in a cash register came from this idea

> ### Stand By Your Man
>
> In the Fredericksburg Confederate Cemetery rest the remains of 3,553 Confederate men and one woman. Lucy Ann Cox hailed from Fredericksburg, and decided to accompany her husband into the field through four years of war with the 30th Virginia Infantry. Hey, how many of you gals would do that?

"Bite off more than you can chew" — A ring of chewing tobacco was passed around the table and you bit off a piece to chew. If you took too much, you'd spit it out on the floor

1304 Caroline St. www.apva.org/apva/rising_sun_tavern.php ☎ 800-678-4748 or 540-373-1776.

Exit 130: Wawa is a chain of mini-mart/gas bars offering freshly brewed coffee (over 125 million cups sold each year), built-to-order hoagies, the Sizzli (TM) hot breakfast sandwich, quality dairy products, Wawa brand juices and teas, ready-to-go salads, fresh fruits and produce.

Over 100 years ago, George Wood's original dairy business was built in a section of Pennsylvania called Wawa, which was named from a Lenni Lenape Native American word in honor of their favored game bird - the Canada Goose. The Wawa Dairy enjoyed a reputation for quality, superior fresh products ("doctor certified" milk) and customer service. Gra-hame Wood, his grandson, founded Wawa Food Markets

on April 16, 1964 in Folsom, Pennsylvania.

Wawa customers are initially attracted to the prices and value of their coffee and gas bars. Coffee is brewed fresh every 20 minutes using their own blend of coffee beans and filtered water and comes in original, dark roast, decaffeinated, flavors (Irish Cream, Hazelnut, Chocolate Macadamia, Vanilla Cream, Caramel) and cappuccino, and you can buy the beans to go. If you bring your own mug in, they will refill it for the low price of $.59 for a 10 oz. size to $.89 for 20 oz up to $1.09 for 32 oz. (now that'll keep you awake on the road for

awhile!) ◑ Daily 24 hours. www.wawa.com

Exit 126: Civil War Life Museum – Terry Thomann is a Civil War buff whose 45 years of collecting artifacts overtook his house.

His hobby became his career 3 years ago when he and his wife, Jane, opened this little museum so he could share his passion with us.

Don't miss the short video of "How to Fire a Cannon"; you wouldn't believe that it takes the coordination of 7 men to do it. Thomann specifically designed rifle viewing cases so that you can see both the front and the back, and had photos of military buttons blown up so you can see all the details. Kids love the soldier dressed in full military gear on a horse. Learn that a "housewife" was the name of a sewing kit.

The gift shop is full of interesting items: civil war soldier chess sets, tiny music boxes, Williamsburg pottery, Confederate money, glass nibbed writing sets, blown glass, carpet bags and some real artifacts, like canteens, buckles, spent bullets, and the forerunner to the electronic organizer: a weekly calendar made on erasable ivory. ◑ Oct-May, Mon-Fri 10-5 , Sun 11-5; June-Sept, Mon-Sun 9-5; closed January (hours may vary, so call first). 4712 South Point Pkwy, just beside the Visitors' Center www.civilwar-life.com ☎ 540-834-1859.

Exit 126B: Spotsylvania County Visitors' Center – Just beside the Massaponax Crossings Mall, here's a center where you can ask your questions about the area or the rest of Virginia, use the clean restrooms, pick up flyers, FREE motel coupon booklets and see a few exhibits from the Civil War Museum located just next door. ◑ Daily 9-5, Summer 9-7. ☞

Fom I-95 Exit 126, take Rte 1 South for 1/2 mi. to SouthPoint Pkwy. Turn left and the office is on your left at 4704 Southpoint Pkwy www.spotsylvania.va.us ☎ 877-515-6197 or 540-891-8687.

Exit 126: Spotsylvania Mall – Anchors here are Sears, JC Penney, Belk, Costco, Hechts and Dick's. There are some un-mall like stores in this one, for instance: Avon or Dippin' Dots ice cream treats, but then you'll find a Disney Store, Michael's Arts & Crafts, Sam Goody for car music, Hat World and Victoria's Secret for fun. ◑ Mon-Sat 10-9:30, Sun 11-6 137 Spotsylvania Mall. www.spotsylvaniamall.com ☎ 540-786-6660.

Mile 108 Southbound: Petersburg Information Center – In the rest area you will find this quick pit stop to pick up information about the area. Don't forget to look for your FREE motel discount booklets. It's a good time to use rest rooms, and there's a picnic area.

Exit 104: Russell Stover Candies Factory Outlet – What heaven: not only an award winning (Best Taste in America by American Tasting Institute) chocolate warehouse at the side of the road, but discount chocolate! Take a FREE taste from the open box as you walk in to whet your appetite.

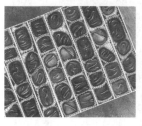

There are first quality boxes (W h i t m a n Samplers, Truffle Assortment, Cherry Cordials), intermediates and the "seconds", which are to the left of the store, mostly in white boxes or bags. These have only slight imperfections or are overstocks - believe us, they taste exactly the same as the firsts.

You can get individual boxes of just your favorite ones (raspberry parfaits, coconut creams, nut delights) without having to rummage though a whole assorted box. Look for sugar free chocolates, holiday special boxes and individual small packs for car snacks. The staff will happily create-a-gift with your personal selections. Room for RV parking. Yum! (Another fancier location - ice cream parlour, candy kitchen and one little corner in the right back for sale boxes- at Exit 98, Santee). ◑ Mon-Sat 9-5, Sun 12-5. ☞ In the Amoco lot on the east side of I-95 Exit 104, you will see a sign that says turn right at the next light. You will find the outlet at the junction of Rte 799 and Enterprise Parkway in the Carmel Church business park at 23361 Business Center Court. www.russellstover.com ☎ 804-448-1169.

Mile 96-95: Revolutionary War Hero – Marie Joseph Paul Yves Roch Gilbert du Motier, Marquis de Lafayette passed the South Anna River here on May 29, 1781 on retreat from British Maj Gen. Cornwallis. Lafayette did not enjoy the French court life, so he bought his own ship and joined the American cause and fought without pay "near the person of George Washington till such time as he may think proper to entrust me with a division of the army".

He suffered the 1778 winter in Valley Forge along with Washington so a strong friendship was forged which lasted their lifetimes. He was eventually entrusted with the defense of Virginia. When Cornwallis showed up with 7,000 men and he was outnumbered, he retreated. Later when he joined up with Washington and the Continental Army at Yorktown, VA they trapped Cornwallis, ending the Revolutionary War.

Exit 92: Ashland/Hanover Visitor Center/Train Station – Built in 1923 by the Richmond Fredericksburg and Potomac Railroad by W. Duncan Lee (who designed some of those beautiful homes along Monument Ave in Richmond), this Visitor Center is worth a mention for its embarrassing historical value. It is still functioning as an Amtrak train depot, but its divided floor plan is a reminder of the segregated South.

There were separate ticket windows, waiting areas, restrooms, and water fountain for whites and African Americans. An original baggage cart sits outside exactly where it has always stood. Two of the original benches are here, and a third is in the Smithsonian. The station has been used as a set for the filming of the movie "Major Payne" and the television series "Legacy". A sign outside explains Ashland's role during the Civil War. ◑ Daily 9-5. ☞ From I-95 Exit 92 head West along England St (Route 54) for 1 1/4 miles until you get to the train tracks and the station. www.town.ashland.va.us ☎ 800-897-1479 or 804-752-6766.

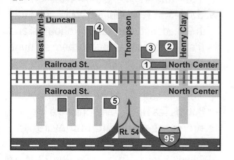

Exit 92: Ashland – Go to the Visitor Center above (#1 on the map) and pick up a Walking Tour map, which hits the highlights of 22 buildings that run on either side of the train tracks. There is no wrong side of the tracks in this town, as both sides make up the town's main street. The exciting part of a stroll here is that the train runs right through the center so if you are here at least an hour, you will get up close and personal with a real live train. Highlights of your walk might include the Ashland Red Caboose (#4) at 105-A Hanover Ave which appropriately sells train memorabilia. And if you yearn for the olden days, Cross Brothers General Store #5 (on the corner of Railroad Ave of Route 54/England St) has been open since 1912 and is still run by someone in the Hawthorne and Willis families. Here everyone knows your name, and if you're sick or infirm, they know that and will deliver your food to your door (or even if you're well!). By now you should be hungry, so head over to Homemade by Suzanne (#3). (see next story).

> **One House to Go, please**
>
> Who would've thought that back in 1908-1940 Sears, Roebuck and Company was selling a mail order catalog of blueprints, instructions and even the building materials for homes called "Book of Modern Homes and Building Plans". At 203 Berkley St. you can see an example of "The Maytown", thought to have been assembled here in 1918. It sports most of its original decorative features, including a corner turret with decorative overhang, full front porch, beveled plate glass in the front door and a bay window with patterned panes. Since the original house did not have running water, the pump still sits in the back yard.

VA 126 – VA 92

Exit 92: Henry Clay Inn – If you ever wanted the feeling of being a Southern manor owner without all the responsibilites, you might want to spend a night at this Georgian Revival (rebuilt in 1992) B & B Inn. Take your mind off the hurried pace of your drive in one of the 14 bedrooms, each one sporting doors leading out to an upper balcony. The rooms are dressed with antiques and have interesting sleigh, pencil post, canopy, acorn post and cannonball beds, and there's a quiet central sitting room with books and games.

Eggs-cellent

In the Virginia Museum of Fine Arts in Richmond you will find the largest public collection of Faberge Easter eggs outside of Russia.

Downstairs you can sit on the rocking chairs and become a trainspotter. The fine dining room is open on the weekends and there's a gift shop with train items and works by local artists.

Henry Clay was an orator and statesman who was born here in Hanover County in 1777. He was known as "the Great Compromiser" and was a candidate for President in 1824,1832, and 1844. ☞ From I-95 Exit 92 (Rte 54) head West for 1 1/4 mi. The inn is on the right, just facing the Vis. Ctr in the train station (#2 on the map). 114 N. Railroad Ave. www.henryclayinn.com ☎ 804-798-3100 or 800-343-4565.

Exit 92: Homemades by Suzanne – Here's a perfect spot to pick up the fixings for a picnic lunch which you could eat inside, or better yet outside, so you can watch the trains go by. Everthing here, even the bread and rolls, is made from scratch. You could stoke up on Brunsick stew or vegetable soup or have one of 15 salads (country ham, black-eyed pea, pearl pasta), quiches, crab cakes and please wash them down with strawberry lemonade. Save room for authentic chess pie in chocolate (brownie lovers will adore this one) or lemon, coconut custard (Sandra's favorite), pecan and a

gorgeous apple pie with cut-out leaves on the crust. Don't worry, you can taste them all because they are also sold by the piece. ◑ Mon-Fri 9-2, Sat 9-3. 102 N. Railroad Ave. (#3 on map). ☎ 804-798-8331.

Exit 83B: Lewis Ginter Botanical Garden – This is an oasis on a driving trip - 82 magnificent acres which started life as Powhatan hunting grounds and was at one time owned by patriot Patrick Henry. In 1884, Lewis Ginter, who was orphaned at 17 and later became a millionarie from tobacco and real estate, developed a Club House here for Richmond bicyclists. It was his niece, Grace Arents, who was inspired to develop the gardens, and her original design is still here; there are more kinds of gardens than we ever knew existed: four season's, healing, sunken, Asian, Rose, wetland, perennial, Victorian, conifer, English cottage, and children's garden (with a botanical maze and an activity center).

For walkers there's a "walk on the wild side" and a woodland walk, a bird trail with 9 feeder stations and birdhouses, and as if all that wasn't enough, there's a huge lush indoor conservatory with exotic and unusual plants from around the world.

You can stop for a bite at the pretty cafe or Robins Tea House overlooking a lake. Do leave some time and money for the extensive gift shop. ◑ Daily 9-5. ☞ From I-95 Exit 83 take E Parham Rd. (Rte 73) West to the first left turn at Brook Rd. Turn down

Brook for 0.88 mi. and then turn right at Lakeside Ave. for 3/4 mi. to the entrance on your right. 1800 Lakeside Ave. www.lewisginter.org ☎ 804-262-9887.

Exit 80: Richmond's populace was ecstatic on April 19, 1861 because Virginia seceded from the Union. They partied while church bells pealed, fireworks lit up the sky, torches burned and the bands played on. Starting on May 29, 1861 and for the next 4 years, President Jefferson Davis led the Confederate States of America from this city.

Soul Searching

Exit 76: Hollywood Cemetery in Richmond has the largest pyramid in the United States. If you visit it, you can also check out the graves of 2 US presidents (James Monroe and John Tyler), Confederate President Jefferson Davis and thousands of Civil War soldiers. This is a garden-style cemetery, so it has paths through hills and valleys and offers a fabulous view of the James River.

Did He Get Liberty or Death?

Exit 75: St. John's Church – We all know the famous words "I know not what course others may take; but as for me, give me liberty or give me death!", which were uttered by Patrick Henry and lit the fires of revolution in 1775. St. John's Church in Richmond was the site of the clandestine Second Virginia Convention where he called his comrades (Benjamin Harrison, Thomas Jefferson, Richard Henry Lee, Edmund Pendelton, Peyton Randolph, George Washington, and George Wythe and others) to arms in a rousing speech. Reenactments of the convention are held on Sundays at 2 p.m. from Memorial Day to Labor Day. Buried in the graveyard are one signer of the Declaration of Independence, George Wythe, and Edgar Allen Poe's mom, Elizabeth Arnold Poe (same initials). So, did Patrick Henry get liberty or death?

Answer: ʎʇɹǝqı˥

Richmond Ambassadors - If you keep seeing people wearing bright yellow shirts and bright smiles, say hello. These are members of the "Clean and Safe" team who are there to escort you or help you (and residents too) find attractions, parking and restaurants or assist in an emergency.

Exit 75: Richmond Visitor's Center – If you decide to drive into Richmond, you can get 2 hours FREE parking in the parking lot (called a deck here) behind the Visitor's Center at the corner of Third and Marshall. Pick up a Richmond Rewards card, which offers you deals (2 for 1, 10% off, free dessert, etc.) in restaurants, museums, sports, specialty boutiques, etc. ◗ Daily 9-5; Summer 9-6. ☞ From I-95 Exit 75 follow 3rd St into town for 2 blocks. 405 North 3rd St. www.visit.richmond.com ☎ 1-888-RICHMOND or 804-783-7450. (Another location: Tredegar Iron Works within the Richmond National Battlefield Park Civil War Visitor Center. 470 Tredegar St. ☎ 804-771-2145)

Exit 74C: Richmond's Capitol – This imposing capitol was built in 1788, and its design in the Classical Revival style had input by Thomas Jefferson, who based it on a Roman temple he saw in Nimes, France when he was Minister there. The statue of George Washington standing under the hidden dome is by Jean-Antoine Houdon, and is the only one he posed for - including having done a life mask in plaster of Paris for it. It is lifesize (all 6'2 1/2", 210 lbs of him) and is made of Italian carrera marble.

If you take the FREE (every 1/2 hour) and interesting tour, you will find out that before the Civil War, Robert E Lee was asked by both the North and the South to lead their forces. He supposedly stood in the

VA 92 – VA 74

rotunda and contemplated his decision in front of this statue and his hero, George Washington, before walking 6 paces into the legislature room and declaring that he could never take a sword against his fellow Virginians. ◐ Mon-Fri 9-5, Sat: 10-4, Sun 1-4. PLEASE NOTE: The building will be closed for restorations from April 2005 through December 2006, except for some weekend tours. ☞ I-95 Exit 74C onto Broad St. Turn right at 9th, and right again onto Marshall St. Turn right onto 10th and cross Broad St into the Bus Loop Parking area. FREE parking on the grounds at the E Grace St. entrance, if there is room. www.legis.state.va.us ☎ 804- 698-1788.

CIVIL WAR FREEBIES

For battle buffs, the civil war can keep you interested for a lifetime. The state of Virginia feeds your need by offering a FREE package all about the different civil war trails throughout the state. These colorful brochures cover the marches chronologically, then go on to write about the battles, the leaders, the technology used, supply and logistics and even acknowledging the black troops and civilians involved. ☎ 888-Civil War.

Exit 69: Candlewood Suites certainly makes you feel at home. This is the first time we have come across a motel with a "Candlewood Cupboard' and its honor system. Since guests are staying here over a longer period of time and are living in their rooms, they offer a very mini mart. Yes, there are packaged foods, freezer meals, toiletries,

cereal and eggs, but there is no salesclerk. You simply take what you want and either drop the money in a slot in the counter or fill out a card with your room number and drop that in the slot and they will add it to your account. How long has it been since they were this honest in your town? wwwcandlewoodsuites.com ☎ 804-271-0016.

Exit 52: The Civilian War – Petersburg suffered the longest siege experienced by any American city, a 10-month battle during the Civil War. The Siege Museum here covers the conflict, and is the only museum in the country which focuses solely on civilian experiences during the war.

Exit 52 Southbound or 50D Northbound: Petersburg Visitors Center, Old Towne – For advice on what to do, where to stay or eat or information for here or site brochures for the rest of Virginia, stop in to the McIlwaine House. Take advantage of clean rest rooms and pick up FREE motel coupons. ◐ Daily 9-5. ☞ Turn West (left if you're heading North, right if South) on Washington St. for 4 blocks to Sycamore St. Turn right for 0.38 mi. into Old Town and turn right on Old St. The Vis. Ctr is straight ahead with a white fence at 425 Cockade Alley. www.petersburg-va.org ☎ 800-368-3595 or 804-733-2400.

> In 1829 a contingent of Petersburg's free blacks sailed to Africa to colonize Liberia. One of them, Joseph Jenkins Roberts, became Liberia's first President in 1848.

Exit 52: The Crater – On June 25, 1864 Union soldiers of the 48th Pennsylvania volunteers, many of whom who were coal miners, began digging a 511 ft. tunnel toward a Confederate fort at Pegram's (or Elliott's)

Salient. The tunnel took a month to dig, and the plan was to explode 4 tons of gunpowder under the area, creating a large gap in their defense line, then pouring troops through the hole. On July 30 at 4:45 a.m. the mine was detonated, and it created a crater about 170 ft. long, 60 ft. wide and 30 ft. deep.

The Union troops rushed forward into the mine, instead of going around it. They got stuck in the tunnel because of the high walls created at the end, and Confederate troops inflicted more than 4,000 Federal casualties. Major Houghton of the 14th New York Heavy Artillery reported that the hole was "filled with dust, great blocks of clay, guns, broken carriages, projecting timbers and men buried in various ways - some up to their necks, others to their waists, and some only with their feet and legs protruding from the earth." and then "blood was streaming down the sides of the crater to the bottom, where it gathered in pools for a long time before being absorbed by the hard red clay." The crater can still be seen at the Petersburg National Battlefield through short trails or a 4-mile drive.

Exit 47: The King's Highway (King's Road, Post Road) – This section of I-95 follows one of the first highways in the US which started in New England and went to Charleston, S.C. and then on through Georgia and Florida. It started out as an Indian trail called the Potomac Trail as it followed the course of the Potomac River. Try to imagine this as a wide dirt road, often muddy, strewn with tree stumps and boulders. Thomas Jefferson wrote that the fastest he could traverse it was at 3 miles per hour.

The Highway was the link between all the colonies which gave them a sense of

> ### Plane geometry or sane geometry?
>
> **Exit 52:** Legend has it that Petersburg's Trapezium House, built in 1817 by an eccentric Irish bachelor, has no right angles. The reason? To prevent habitation by ghosts.

unity. It enabled the movement of mail, newspapers and goods from one end of the New World to the other. It connected with the Boston Post Road in the North - see the story in CT, Exit 39.

Its name was derived from the 18th century order by King George I to build a road "to be used for the subjects of said Lord and the King with their horses and carriages to go and return at their will and pleasure".

Exit 41: Nino's – Right outside a KOA campground and with a captive market, this family-run Northern Italian restaurant tucked in a wooden cabin has been there 20 years, only opening at 5 pm for dinner. All of your favorites, from pizzas to lasagne, eggplant, chicken or veal Parmesan are here as well as 5 sauces to top ziti or spaghetti, but a few like chicken cordon bleu or flounder in lemon butter and shrimp scampi might delight you. Just 1/4 mi. South of I-95 Exit 41 at 2809 Courtland Rd. (Rte 35). ☎ 804-861-3410.

Mile 36 Northbound: Petersburg Information Center – In the rest area you will find this quick pit stop to pick up information about the area and Virginia. Don't forget to pick up your FREE motel discount booklets. It's a good time to use rest rooms and you can picnic here.

Exit 11B: Virginia Products – Those of you who repeat this trip regularly will wind up pining for favorite snacks from Virginia and will make this home-cooked peanut shop a regular stop (the ones sold here earned the Virginia's Finest™ quality distinction from the Virginia Department of Agriculture).

Our family can no longer live without chocolate covered peanut brittle. The large peanut display covers peanut square clus-

VA 69 – VA 11

ters in light syrup, butter toffee coated peanuts and chocolate dipped ones (and double dipped!) sold in season. Pecans are here too - praline covered ones, and then Virginia ham of course, salt-cured and pepper-coated and slab bacon, comb honey, Grave's Mountain jelly and Virginia Brand ones in yummy flavors like blackberry, peach brandy, red pepper jelly, and pecan jam. If you need souvenirs, this mother and daughter team can make up gift baskets to take home, or you can order them online when you get desperate. ◐ Mon-Sat 8-6, Sun 1-6. 1001 West Atlantic St., Emporia, which is just 1/4 mile straight off I-95 to the West. www.vapeanuts.com ☎ 888-790-9096.

Exit 3: Slave Breeding – A slave uprising near here in the summer of 1831 led to even more repressive measures. Virginia's tobacco soil was eroding, so the slave owners began breeding slaves for profit for sale to the more Southern states. The slaves were encouraged to have as many children as possible so they could be auctioned off. In the 1830's Virginia exported more than 10,000 slaves a year, and the total may have reached 300,000, tearing families apart forever. Certainly a very black mark on this country's history.

Mile 1 Northbound: Virginia Welcome Center – It always pays to stop off at these centers for clean bathrooms and the FREE motel discount coupon booklets and all the flyers from places to visit all around the State. Don't forget to chat with the friendly and helpful staff who can answer any questions. ◐ Daily 8:30-5, Summer Daily 8:30-6.

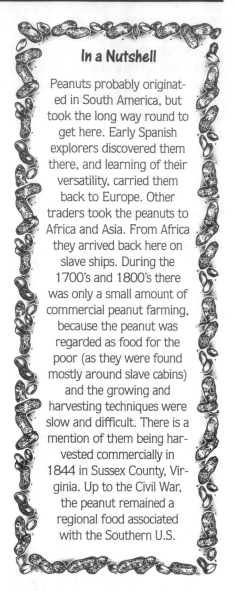

In a Nutshell

Peanuts probably originated in South America, but took the long way round to get here. Early Spanish explorers discovered them there, and learning of their versatility, carried them back to Europe. Other traders took the peanuts to Africa and Asia. From Africa they arrived back here on slave ships. During the 1700's and 1800's there was only a small amount of commercial peanut farming, because the peanut was regarded as food for the poor (as they were found mostly around slave cabins) and the growing and harvesting techniques were slow and difficult. There is a mention of them being harvested commercially in 1844 in Sussex County, Virginia. Up to the Civil War, the peanut remained a regional food associated with the Southern U.S.

motel discount coupon booklets which offer great deals along the way. This is a good moment to take advantage of clean bathrooms. ◐ Daily 8-5. www.commerce.state.nc.us/tourism/welcome ◐ Daily 8-5 ☎ 252 537-3365.

☆ NORTH CAROLINA ☆

Mile 181 Southbound: North Carolina Welcome Center – Don't forget to come and and pick up your FREE

Exit 168: Halifax Resolves – In the Spring of 1776, NC representatives convened near here, far enough away from the British ships gathering on the coast. Cornelius Harnett headed the committee "to take into consideration the usurpations and violences attempted and committed by the King and Parliament of Great Britain against America". The group took 3 days and finally unanimously declared, on April 12, 1776, "that the delegates for this Colony in the Continental Congress be impowered to concur with the delegates of the other Colonies in declaring Independency, and forming foreign alliances...".

These bold colonists in North Carolina were America's first to call for independence, 3 months before the Declaration of Independence. April 12th is celebrated as Halifax Day, with people in period costumes doing Colonial activities, reenactments of encampments, military drills, etc.

Exit 173: New China Restaurant – Located in the Plaza Shopping Center up route 158 on the east side of this exit, this buffet-style mostly Cantonese restaurant is perfect when you want a fast lunch or supper on the road. A real deal is the 6 lunch specials-to-go for as little as $2.99 (11-2:30 p.m.), which include rice and egg roll. The menu lists about 15 spicy dishes for those of you who like that extra bite. Special dishes include ginger prawns, lake tung ting shrimp marinated in a wine sauce, hunan chicken and beef in 2 sauces and more. Vegetarians will be able to order tofu vegetable soup and a choice of six main course dishes. ☀ Lunch buffet 11-4, Dinner Sun-Thurs 4-9:30, Fri & Sat 11-10. ☎ 252-535-2818.

Exit 173: Ralph's Barbecue – We're up to the 3rd generation of Ralph Woodruff's family (granddaughter Kim) running this busy restaurant, which sells 5,000 lbs a week of selected butcher wrapped pork. The lunch and supper buffets are a steal, but you can also order from the menu.

Their North Carolina style barbecue is made daily with no additives or preservatives, and is served dry smoked sliced or chopped (vinegar, crushed red peppers, sugar, salt), along with delicious Brunswick stew, fried chicken, fresh hush puppies, cole slaw, potatoes and collard greens (Sandra can't believe she went back for seconds!). If you don't have time to stop, at least do take-out. ☀ Daily 9-8:30. 1400 Julian Allsbrook Hwy. ☎ 252-536-2102.

Exit 173: Halifax County Visitors' Center – Here's a handy Visitors' Center with a friendly staff to answer all your questions and hand you a free bag of peanuts. This cute little house has clean bathrooms and lots of pamphlets, which are even available when the center is closed (outside on the porch by the front door is a display box). 1640 Julian Allsbrook Highway (Rt 158), 0.4 mile west of I-95. ☀ Mon-Friday 9-5, Sat 10-3 (only June, July & Aug). www.visithalifax.com ☎ 800-522-4282.

> Someone in the North Carolina highway office has a sense of humor. To save lives on the roads, they have come up with these ditties: "Click it or Ticket", "Booze It or Lose It", "Pay Attention or Pay the Price"

Exit 150: Florida Travel Center – All those signs along the highway lead to this business which offers travelers help on all travel needs and information pertaining to Florida. You can buy tickets for Disney World here.

Exit 138: Gardner's Barbecue 'n' Chicken – Okay we'll admit it, we ate fried gizzards and actually liked them, but if you're not game, you can have the fried chicken, fried fish, chicken 'n collards, and of course, the yummy barbecue with

VA 3 – NC 138

some of the 15 sides - collards, yams, butter beans, slaw, squash, etc. Don't miss the little corn sticks or the hush puppies. You can take some out for a car picnic. ☞ From I-95 Exit 138, take Rte 64 East for 3.4 mi. to the US 301 Exit, which is N. Wesleyan Blvd. Turn left and continue for 1.4 mi. to 1331 N. Wesleyan Blvd. on your right. ☎ 252-446-2983.

Exit 107: Tobacco Farm Life Museum – Here's an opportunity to walk around some restored historic buildings. Iredell Lueazer Brown's farmhouse, kitchen, smokehouse and tobacco barn are furnished with period artifacts to re-create farmstead life revolving around the Golden Leaf of tobacco. Start with the video "Year in the Life of a Farmer", and then get a glimpse into the social and community life of tobacco farmers and their families in the exhibition area, which showcases a typical kitchen, toys, home remedies, school life, rural doctors, a store, a 1920s tractor and other farming implements, and a kid's hands-on gallery. ◑ Mon-Sat 9:30-5, Sun 2-5. ☞ From I-95 Exit 107 take Rte 301 North through the town toward Lucama/Wilson. Museum is about 1 1/4 mi. on the left at 709 Church St. www.tobacco farmlifemuseum.org ☎ 919-284-3431.

Exit 97: JR's Tobacco & Fragrance Outlet – Much more than a tobacco outlet, this store is a whole city block of bargains in perfume, books, makeup, garden ornaments, housewares, jewelry, toys, Western wear, junk food, towels, dolls, casual clothes, etc. Across the back of the store is one of the largest cigar emporiums you'll ever see. You can only exit the store from one door so make sure to park near there. ◑ Daily 8-9. www.jrtobacco.com ☎ 800-JRCIGAR or 919-965-5055.

And to think it all started with a kiss...

Exit 95: Ava Gardner Museum – What a lovely way to spend an hour stretching your legs. This pretty little museum has film-worn costumes, 33 of Bert Pfeiffer's incredible paintings (hunt for little fun oddities - mouse, bird etc.), MGM publicity photos, movie posters, original scripts and a movie short all about one of our most famous movie stars born right here near Smithfield.

    The museum's collections were preserved due to a fan, Tom Banks, who at 12 was kissed on the cheek by a young secretarial school girl in Wilson, NC. Two years later, in 1941, Banks saw a photo of Ava and learned her identity for the first time. In the years following, he and his wife began collecting Ava memorabilia from every imaginable source. In the early 80's Dr. Banks bought the house where Ava lived from age 2 to 13 to exhibit his collection, and finally the museum moved to this location. ◑ Mon-Sat 9-5, Sun 2-5. ☞ From I-95 Exit 95, head West on E. Market St (Rt 70) for about 1 1/4 miles to 325 E. Market St. on your right. www.avagardner.org ☎ 919-934-5830.

Courtesy: Ava Gardner Museum

Exit 95: Carolina Premium Outlets – Eighty stores should be enough to keep you happy. Some names to help empty your bank account might be: Oneida Home, SAS Factory Shoe Store, Pepperidge Farm, Brooks Brothers Factory Store, Banana Republic Factory Store, OshKosh, Croscill and KB Toy Outlet. ☞ From I-95 Exit 95 head West on E. Market St (Rt 70) for one block to the West service road, called Industrial Park Drive. Turn right and follow it for 1 mile to the outlets. ☀ Mon-Sat 10-9, Sun 10-6 www.carolinaoutletcenter.com ☎ 919-989-8757.

Exit 95: Johnston County NC Visitors' Bureau – This is one of the prettiest Visitors' Bureaus on the Interstate, since it is located in an old home. It covers Exits 79-107. Stop in for the FREE advice and clean restrooms as well as the flyers and coupon booklets. If you go to their website, you will find some coupons to print right there. ☀ Mon-Fri 8:30-5. 1115 Industrial Park Dr. just beside the Carolina Premium Outlet Center. www.johnstonco-cvb.org ☎ 800-441-7829 or 919-989-8687.

Exit 73: Simply Divine B & B – It is rare that you find an Inn where the host is as charming as the Inn. Miss Ellington was an architect in Washington DC (ask her about her work on the Pentagon before 9/11). You will feel like royalty sleeping on hand pressed sheets in the spacious rooms. Breakfast was gourmet - creamy scrambled eggs with bacon alongside the best home fries with caramelized onions and tomatoes and a poached pear filled with sweet cream and laden with raspberry coulis. Hey, there's even an in-ground swimming pool in the warm months! Pets are okay. www.bbonline.com/nc/simplydivine/rooms. html ☎ 910-891-1103.

Courtesy Simply Divine B&B

Exit 73: Major General William C. Lee Airborne Museum – This house was the home of the "Father of the Army Airborne", so the museum charts his personal life as well as the growth of Army airborne divisions for which he was a relentless lobbyist in order to make them a formidable part of our military might.

At tank school in Versailles, France in the '30's he observed German military training and Kurt Student's airborne experiment. He saw the promise of this, and started with test platoons doing parachute jumps (and practiced from parachute towers in Hightstown, NJ). By August 1942, in 26 months, he shepherded the airborne from a test platoon of 50 men to 2 divisions of 8,300 men, and was in charge of the sky: parachutes, air landing battalions and eventually the glider units.

He suffered a major heart attack on the eve of D-Day and missed his chance to lead it. You might have heard of his famous saying "this division has no history, but it has a rendezvous with destiny". ☀ Mon-Fri 10-4, Sat 11-4. ☞ See the Simply Divine B&B on this exit. The museum is just 3 blocks East at 209 West Divine St. www.visitdunn.com ☎ 910-892-1947.

Exit 72: Brass Lantern – If you're in the mood for a quiet upscale dining experience, you know the kind that specializes in prime rib, offers steak, shrimps, perhaps a side of ribs and a nice salad bar, then this one will fit the bill. There are interesting diarama windows of the woods. ☎ 910-892-6309.

Mile 54 Northbound: You can't miss this upside down tractor trailer lying on the side of the road looking very much like a big dead bug with its wheels in the air. It's an ad for a truck towing school (www.wreckmaster.com), the towing industry's first hands-on training company.

Take a shower with your car?

Exit 49: Comfort Inn – In order to separate yourself from the pack, it's good to be different. This motel wins for originality. If you stay here, you are offered a free car wash which sits plunk in the middle of the parking lot. If you want to upgrade, there's a more thorough wash or you can add a shine. Not only that, they offer a pet run, and guests with pets stay in a separate building, away from those with allergies. And if that isn't enough, their free breakfast is also hot, with eggs with ham bits, grits, hash browns and waffles. ☎ 910-323-8333.

Exit 46: Airborne & Special Operations Museum – The legends of those who jump into battle are covered through this brand new museum in artifacts and film. The impressive 5-story glass walled lobby sets the stage with 2 fully deployed parachutes: a WWII era T-5 round chute and a modern MC-4 square chute. You learn the story of Lieutenant Bill Ryder, leader of the Test Platoon, who on August 16th, 1940 became the first American soldier to jump and who was followed by Private William King, the first enlisted paratrooper.

You can walk through a section of a C-47, sit on crates in a WWII Army briefing hut, learn about gliders that dropped off jeeps and bulldozers, see a famous UH-iH (Huey) helicopter from 'Nam days and a Desert Storm hide site. Another exhibit traces the development of the Special Forces, or "Green Berets", from the summer of 1952 to today's Operation Enduring Freedom. Admission is FREE to the museum, but there's a charge for the movie or motion simulator (helicopter attack, parachute jump and ATV pursuit). ◐ Tues-Sat 10-5, Sun 12-5 ☞ Northbound: Exit 46 onto route 87 North for 6 miles and exit at Hay St. Turn right and museum is on left at the corner of Bragg Blvd. Southbound: Exit 52B onto route 24, Grove St which becomes Rowan St. and follow it for 5 miles. Turn left on Bragg Blvd. Museum is on left just before Hay St. 100 Bragg Blvd www.asomf.org ☎ 910-483-3003.

Exit 46: Fayetteville Convention & Visitors Bureau – Well, this one is kind of fun and also good for lazy motorists. Since it is located in a former bank, you can still use the drive-thru window to pick up your maps and ask questions about what to do or where to stay. You do have to get out if you want to use the rest room, though. If you want to hear details about the city while driving between exits 65-40, tune the Visitor Information Network at 1680 AM. ◐ Mon-Fri 8-5, Sat 10-4. 245 Person St. www.visitfayettevillenc.com ☎ 910-483-5311 or 888-NC-CHARM.

> The first round of golf in the new world was played in a pasture just east of Fayetteville in 1728.
>
>

Exit 46: Fascinate–U Children's Museum – For fussy 3-12 year olds, take a break from the road and visit this hands-on interactive little museum where the kids can role-play in a fire station, grocery store, TV studio or emergency 911 call center. The museum was started by 2 Moms who know what kids like, so there's a dress-up area, climbing space and health center offering a transparent anatomical mannequin. ◑ Tues, Thurs, Fri 9-5, Wed 9-7 (FREE from 1-7), Sat 10-5, Sun 12-5. 116 Green St. www.fascinate-u.com ☎ 910-433-1573.

Exit 46: 82nd Airborne Division War Memorial Museum and JFK Special Warfare Museum – Two for the price of FREE is what you can discover inside Fort Bragg, where there is a big museum housing 82nd Airborne weapons, uniforms, aircraft, parachutes and more from 1917 to the present. This division "owns the night", and does most of its training and all of its work in the dark. There is an outdoor display of old aircraft where you can get up close and personal with them. ☎ 910-432-3443.

The other smaller museum, JFK Special Warfare Museum, gives a behind-the-scenes look at all sorts of fascinating sneaky unconventional means that have been used to assist war efforts, with emphasis on Special Operations units. There are fascinating weapons, military art and cultural items from around the  world. You will be surprised to find out that the wearing of the Green Berets was illegal from 1952-1961. ◑ Tues-Sat 10-4:30. JFK ◑ Tues-Sun 11-4. ☞ Exit 46 onto route 87 North for 6 miles and exit at Bragg Blvd. Turn left for about 8 miles to the Main gate of the fort, where you can get additional specific directions. ☎ 910-432-1533 or 910-432-4272.

Exit 46: Green (??) Berets – It was in 1952 when Col. Aaron Bank became first commander of the Special Forces which were mandated to organize civilian natives into guerilla forces in enemy-held territories. He wanted berets as a mark of distinction for these troops and suggested purple, wine-red or green, but the Army turned down the idea. The guys seem to wear them anyway but it wasn't until 1962 that Pres. John F. Kennedy authorized them - and Banks later said he "picked the green because he was an Irishman".

Exit 46: Huske Hardware House – Recycling is what you usually do with a beer bottle, but this hardware store recycled itself into an entire brewing company and restaurant. The micro-brewery produces stouts, lagers and ales to accompany scrumptious enormous shareable plates of food, which include a huge salad. Live music on weekends. For directions, see the Radisson Prince Charles at this exit - the restaurant is right across the street at 405 Hay St. ☎ 910-437-9905.

Exit 46: Radisson Prince Charles – If you want to get off the highway and into a small city, this grand old hotel is located in the heart of an easily accessible, not crowded, downtown. For those of you who enjoy the feel of period decorated rooms, this hotel built in 1925 has recently been restored, and is a Member of Historic Hotels of America. Room rates are comparable to some higher end motels. FREE parking. ☞ Northbound: Exit 46 onto route 87 North for 6 miles and exit at Hay St. Turn right and hotel is on left just over the tracks. Southbound: Exit 52B onto route 24, Grove St which becomes Rowan St. and follow it for 5 miles. Turn left on Hillsboro St. to first left turn on Hay St. and cross the tracks. The hotel is on your left at 450 Hay St. www.radisson-princecharles.com ☎ 910-433-4444.

NC 49 – NC 46

Exit 46: Sicily Drop Zone – Just being on a military base is exciting for some, and Fort Bragg is special because not only can you visit 2 military museums but you can, if you are there at the right time in the evening, get to observe the breathtaking sight of paratroopers billowing through the sky during training at the Sicily Drop Zone. See the museum description for directions. For drop schedule ☎ 910-396-6366.

Exit 20: Lumberton Vistors' Bureau – "When you stop here, you're halfway there" is this center's motto, because they are located halfway between New York City and Miami. Even if their office in the strip mall is closed, you can still find flyers and FREE coupon books outside. You can get info for the whole state of NC or local info like this one: motels in this town have alliances with fitness centers, so if you stay in one here, ask which gym you can go to at no charge. There are no bathrooms in the info center - you have to head a few doors down. 3431 Lackey St. (Service road on W side of I-95 between Exits 19 and 20) ◑ Mon-Fri 9-5 www.lumberton-nc.com ☎ 800-359-6971 or 910-739-9999.

Exit 20: Somewhere In Time Antiques – Collectors Ahoy! In this large green house, a longtime family business showcases their own antiques for sale and those by 29 other dealers who may not be on the premises when you come. You can still purchase their small collectibles, dinnerware, crystal dolls (new Madame Alexander dolls too), right up to furniture and fur-

nishings, especially RS Presurre glassware.

◑ Mon-Sat 10-5:30, Sun 1-5:30. 4420 Kahn Dr. (Service road on E side of I-95 between Exits 20 and 21). ☎ 910-671-8666.

Exit 17: Lumberton River Walk/Britt Park – If you want to take an easy 3-mile loop walk through a park and around a lake or take a pit stop to canoe or swim (Wed-Sun 1-6 in season), fish (anytime), throw a frisbee or run the dog, here's a park close to an exit. There's plenty of rest rooms. But remember the to follow the posted park rules: No sagging pants, no jewelry and no bandanas. ☞ From I-95 Exit 17, turn South toward the town and turn left on W. 5th St. for 1 1/4 mi. Then turn left on Branch St. into the park. ◑ 8-5 pm or dusk. ☎ 910-671-3869.

Exit 14: Southeastern North Carolina Farmers Market. Be sure to stop here if you want to taste some fresh fruits and vegetables or buy: British meats, nursery plants, hams, gift baskets, statues, crafts, dolls, quilts and more. ◑ Mon-Sat 8-6, Sun 1-6. 1027 Hwy 74. www.ncagr.com/markets /facilit/farmark/lumberton/index.htm ☎ 910-618-5699.

Mile 5 Northbound: North Carolina Welcome Center – Don't forget to come and and pick up your FREE motel discount coupon booklets which offer great deals along the way. This is a good moment to take advantage of clean bathrooms. ◑ Daily 8-5. www.commerce.state.nc.us/tourism/welcome ☎ 910-422-8314.

Exit 1: South of the Border – You could only have missed the billboards if you are a sight-impaired driver. This tacky Mexican-themed town is famous to every kid who has ever read the road. What you will find, if you dare to get off, is a Pedroland amusement park, 11 souvenir shops, 6 food joints, 2 gas stations, 100 campsites and a 300-room motor inn sporting carports and an indoor heated or outdoor

swimming pool. You can play indoor golf at the Golf of Mexico or view the whole site from the ride in the glass elevator to the top of the 200-foot tall Sombrero Tower. Olé! www.pedroland.com ☎ 800-845-6011 or 843-774-2411.

☆ SOUTH CAROLINA ☆

Mile 195 Southbound: South Carolina Welcome Center – Don't forget to come and pick up your FREE motel discount coupon booklets which offer great deals along the way. Ask the friendly staff about interesting things to do and see. They can make reservations for you, help with car problems and there's a mail drop. Take advantage of the clean restrooms too. ◗ Daily Mar-Oct 9-5:30, Nov-Feb 9-5.

Keep It Beautiful

To enliven the motorists' traveling experience in South Carolina, since 1991 the State has planted wildflowers along the Interstate. The flowers are planted twice, once for a Spring/Summer appearance and then again for the Summer/Fall season. The 258 north and south areas have flowers and blooms ranging from (gloriosa daisy) orange/red (cosmos) pink/white/crimson or yellow/orange, (purple coneflower) lilac purple and (coreopsis) yellow to gold/maroon.

You can catch patches of these between the following mile markers, Southbound: 16-18, 28-39, 71-85, 105-138, 149-160, 180-197 and Northbound: 5-7, 20-26, 30-39, 68-83, 102-128, 149-157,182-194.

By teaming up with Clemson University Extension Services, they incorporate research and educational opportunities into the program as well. The headline above is a motto you will see on some license tags, those of citizens who have chosen to donate to the program. www.dot.state.sc.us

Exit 181: Abingdon Manor – The sensory overload of driving on a highway all day comes to a grinding halt as you pass through this 100-year-old grand columned portico into a world of gracious dining and elegant surroundings rated by AAA as 4-diamonds for both.

You have, for the time you are here, walked back in time to when life was simpler, slower and full of friendly hospitality in a safe small town. What could be better than drifting off to sleep in a four-poster feather bed surrounded by beautiful antiques (but with 21st century amenities), sipping complimentary sherry in the library or taking your evening tea in front of a warming fire? Breakfast and dinner are served on silver, crystal and china, and are in the style of a private dinner party, with one set meal surrounded by fresh flowers and soothing jazz.

Cooking classes are offered, so you can have fun with another couple or a group of friends, cooking and eating your way through a gourmet weekend at this rest stop half way between New York and Miami. www.abingdonmanor.com ☎ 888-752-5090 or 843-752-5090.

NC 46 – SC 181

Exit 164: Mister Mark's Fun Park – Since Mister Mark is a church youth leader, he knows how important it is to find wholesome activities, so he started up this fun center but made sure all the arcade games are G-rated.

Besides the indoor arcade, there's 18-hole miniature golf, an oval sprint car track, go carts for all ages and a restaurant (pizza, hot dogs, Caesar salad, Southern chicken salad). If you haven't tried them yet (a good bribe for the kids to be quiet in the car) stop for the Dippin' Dots ice cream candies in 7 flavors. ◑ Mon-Thurs 10-10, Fri-Sat 10-11, Sun 1-10 (shorter seasonal hours - call first). ☞ North Cashua Drive is 1/4 mi. East on W. Lucas St. (Rte 52) right off Exit 164. Turn right for 200 yds to the park at 1331 North Cashua Dr. www.mistermarksfunpark.com ☎ 843-669-7373.

Exit 160: Florence Visitor's Center – Don't forget to come and pick up your FREE motel discount coupon booklets which offer great deals along the way. Check out some flyers or ask the friendly staff about interesting things to do and see in Florence; they are full of great advice and, of course, offer clean rest rooms. ◑ Daily 9-5. ☞ 3290 West Radio Drive, just off exit 160A in front of Magnolia Mall and adjoining the Florence Civic Center. www.florencesccvb.com ☎ 800-325-9005 or 843-664-0330.

Exit 160: Magnolia Mall – This mall has the basics of a Best Buy, JC Penney and Sears, but also Limited Too for kids, Lane Bryant, Victoria's Secret and Aeropostale for clothes. If you need it, there's a Piercing Pagoda (but only for ears!). ◑ Mon-Sat 10-9, Sun 1:30-6. 2701 David H. McLeod

Blvd. www.shopmagnoliamall.com ☎ 843-669-0725.

Exit 160: Percy & Willie's – First we loved the baked potato soup, then we scoffed down the house salad - mixed greens topped with eggs, tomatoes, bacon, garlic croutons and a warm honey-mustard bacon dressing. The bread, a most interesting flaky croissant drizzled with honey butter, could easily be sold as a dessert.

We should have stopped right there and be satiated, but no, we had to go on to stuff ourselves with a perfectly cooked filet mignon and fluffy baked potato dressed with butter, sour cream, mixed cheeses, chives and more bacon, and some crunchy fried shrimp with mushrooms in a garlic butter sauce. And then there was no room for the chocolate pecan pie, homemade apple pie or a Snickers-like caramel cheesecake filled with chocolate, nuts, and ice cream a la mode nor the real New York cheesecake from the Carnegie Deli. ◑ Mon-Thurs 11-10, Fri & Sat 11-11, Sun 11-9 ☞ 1 mi. East of I-95 Exit 160. 2401 David H. McLeod Blvd. ☎ 843-669-1620.

Exit 160: Redbone Alley – If you ever told me that I would pine for grits, I would say that you are nuts. As travel journalists, we eat them because we are polite when visiting the South - but to love them and want more? The grits here are yummy, made with lots of cheese, and have strips of ham, mushrooms, spicy shrimp or chicken and sausages. They taste like comfort food. And that would make sense for a family restaurant that is named after the owner's dog and daughter (she's Alley).

The decor here is right out of Las Vegas - it's a Charleston street scene placed

Mile 175: As you drive over the Pee Dee River, you should know that it was the original inspiration for the Stephen Foster's song, "Old Folks at Home". That first line was written as "Way down upon the Pee Dee River", but he later liked the sound of "Way down upon the Suwannee River" better and took literary license and shortened it to Swanee.

inside an old JC Penney store, complete with an ice cream truck (help yourself), pigeons on the upper window ledges and Lowcountry landscape murals painted by Charleston artist David Boatwright. The two-story space has a back porch with glowing lanterns, a children's area with patio seating and an upstairs balcony overlooking the alley and sports bar/grill.

```
┌ ─ ─ ─ ─ ─ ─ ─ ┐
    Peachy Keen
│                 │
  It may surprise you
│ to know that South │
  Carolina, and not
│ Georgia, is the │
  biggest peach pro-
│ ducer in the South. │
└ ─ ─ ─ ─ ─ ─ ─ ┘
```

The menu (full of local farm ingredients) is modern Southern cooking, with lots of steaks, chicken, sandwiches and salads. One dinner plate is enough for 2, or even better, ask for 1/2 portions, and then you can taste an appetizer. ◑ Mon-Thurs 11:30-10, Fri & Sat 11:30-11, Sun 11:30-9. ☞ From I-95 exit 160 head east along David H. McLeod Blvd for 2 miles, crossing W Evans St and turn left on W. Palmetto St. to 1903 West Palmetto St. www.rbaonline.com ☎ 843-673-0035. (If you miss this one there is another location in Sumter, Exit 122: 1342 Broad St. ☎ 803-905-7750.)

Exit 160: Sexton Dental Clinic – Who would've ever thought to combine a vacation with dental work? Obviously many people do, because this clinic has been open for 78 years and has been attracting travelers from all over the U.S. and Canada for their speed and especially their fair prices - complete upper and lower dentures start at $165.00 (acrylic).

With 7 dentists on staff and an in-house lab, one day service for dentures is their goal, and they are open 24 hours a day for emergencies. If multiple extractions are done, an overnight stay (also for unforeseen circumstances, adjustments, remakes) for follow-up is suggested. Appointments

are preferred, so please call or write three weeks in advance. 377 W. Palmetto St. Florence, SC 29501. www.sextondental.com ☎ 843-662-2543. There are two other clinics (Shealy Dental Clinic ☎ 843-667-0286 and Griffin, Watford, Tepper ☎ 800-982-1843), but Sexton is the one most people have heard of.

Mile 139 Southbound: Sumter County Welcome Center – Don't forget to come and and pick up your FREE motel discount coupon booklets which offer great deals along the way. Pick up some flyers or ask the friendly staff about interesting things to do and see in the nearby counties. They can call for reservations for you. Welcome Centers always have clean rest rooms, and this one has picnic tables and vending machines. ◑ Mon-Fri 9-5. ☎ 803-453-5029.

THE ONE THAT GOT AWAY

Between Exits 132 & 122, Mile 129-128: General Francis Marion was one of the most skilled guerrilla fighters of the Revolutionary War, undermining the British and keeping them in a constant state of confusion. He and his men knew the secret Indian and hunters' trails and the murky paths through the cypress mazes. Like phantoms they moved in for quick surprise attacks against much larger forces, and then would melt away to hide in the swamps. Finally Maj. Gen. Cornwallis ordered Lt. Col. Banastre Tarleton to find him. Tarleton tried for days to track Marion through bogs, swamps, and woods but finally gave up, saying, "Come on, my boys, let's go back. As for this damned old fox, the devil himself could not catch him." After that Marion came to be known as the Swamp Fox. The British never did catch him, and his operations were some of the most successful of the war.

Exit 108: Summerton Diner – You won't find this in guidebooks, because this is where the locals have been eating since 1967. They don't cotton much to change, so the same cook has been here for most of those years. Owners John and Lois Hughes (remarried to Rolfe Files) passed this l'il bit of real America down to daughter Lynelle Blackwell, who knows everyone's name and makes you feel welcome too.

Your basics of fried chicken, catfish, calves liver, baked ham, beef stew and chicken pot pie are served with veggie sides that are good enough to make you become a vegetarian: squash and carrot casserole or sweet potato souffle with pineapple and pecans, but also collard greens, lima beans, stewed apples or squash fritters. Try not to fill up with the fresh-from-the-oven biscuits and corn bread, because you will need room for desserts: perhaps home-made coconut cake, pecan pie or banana pudding.

If their vegetable soup is on the menu, we loved the fat chunks of tomatoes, turnips, pole beans, carrots, potatoes and peas in a sweet/spicy tomato broth, and the chile

If you keep your eyes peeled you will notice cotton fields lining the roads. In mid-summer, the flowers are white and look something like a hibiscus. As they mature, they turn to yellow, then pink and lastly to dark red. After 3 days, they fall and leave green pods called cotton bolls, which begin to grow moist fibers inside. As the boll ripens, it turns brown and the fibers continue to expand in the warm sun until they split the boll open and fluffy cotton bursts out. After machine harvesting, cotton is turned into mounds called modules, and then it is trucked to the gin. The raw cotton is cleaned, removing the trash such as burrs, dirt, stems and leaves, and then it moves over to the gin stand where sharp-toothed circular saws pull the fiber from the seed.

The ginned fiber or lint is pressed into 500-lb. bales, and sample fibers are taken to be classified as to fiber length (staple), strength, width, color and cleanliness. Now it moves on to the textile mills, where the bales are opened and the lint is mixed and cleaned further by blowing and beating. Short lint that comes out is sold for use in other industries.

The mixed and fluffed cotton is cleaned, and the fibers are then straightened and turned into a soft, untwisted rope called a sliver. The sliver is pulled through machines to make it thinner, and then the fiber is twisted and wound on bobbins as cotton yarn. The yarn can be woven on looms into fabrics which are called "gray goods" and must be bleached, pre-shrunk, dyed, printed and finished before being wound onto a bolt for clothing or products. If you are interested in learning more about the SC Cotton Trail, try the Marlboro County Historical Museum, ◑ Mon-Fri 9-5. 123 South Marlboro St., Bennettsville. www.sccottontrail.org ☎ 843-479-5624.

was great too. All this for the same price as a fast food trio! ◑ Mon-Wed 7am-9 pm, closed Thurs, Fri-Sun 6 am-9:30 pm. ☞ From I-95 Exit 108 drive west up Buff Blvd for 3/4 mile and turn right on US 15 & 301, which is Church St. The diner is on your left at 32 Church St. ☎ 803-485-6835.

Mile 99 Southbound: South Carolina Welcome Center – Don't forget to stop and ask your questions about the State, pick up flyers, FREE motel coupon booklets and use the clean restrooms. They can make reservations for you, help with car problems and there's a mail drop. There are vending machines here and a picnic area. ◑ Daily Mar-Oct 9-5:30, Nov-Feb 9-5.

Exit 98: Clark's Inn and Restaurant – Fried Green Tomatoes, Really! Enjoy Southern family cooking ratcheted up a few notches, as in "slow food": the fall off the bone baked chicken or mango pecan roast pork. The deep fryer is busy with real southern fried chicken, fried catfish and crunchy fried green tomatoes with apricot/pineapple chutney. For the less brave, there are pastas, roast beef, steaks and seafood, and even stir fries, but the one called lowcountry (sausage, shrimp, chicken, veggies on savory rice) is high on our list.

In 1946 Bubba Clark, fresh from WWII, "temporarily" set up his first restaurant near here in an old bus station, and now, 56 years later, his kids are running this high falutin' dining experience in a large gracious old Inn-like atmosphere, with Momma Helena still around to check the recipes. Don't forget to leave room for her apple crisp and homemade pecan pie. ◑ Daily 6am-9pm. ☞ Head West up the old number 6 highway about 1/4 mile, and the Inn is on your left at 114 Bradford Blvd. www.clarksinnandrestaurant.com ☎ 803-854-2101.

Exit 98: Santee State Park Cabins – This is not your Hansel and Gretel little cabin in the woods, by any stretch of the imagination. If you or your kids pine for the pines, just 5 minutes off the exit, you can rent the heated, air-conditioned 2-bedroom (sleeps 6) polygon-shaped cabins (in the woods or on the pier!) with a full kitchen, TV and living room.

The peace and silence are astounding - so close to all the action at the exit, yet tucked in the woods and sitting on Lake Marion. If you have a bit of time to hang out, there's 25 acres of fun with fishing (striped bass, catfish to catch with free fishing gear), boating (2 boat ramps), tennis, swimming, nature trails, pedal boats and... raccoons, possums, wild turkeys, cormorants, foxes, ospreys, bald eagles, alligators and deer for neighbors. For campers, there's 161 sites too. ☞ From I-95 Exit 98, head West up Route 6 for 1 1/4 miles and turn right on State Park Rd. Keep going straight for about 4 1/2 miles until you see the ranger's cabin to register. Watch out for deer on the road. www.southcarolina parks.com ☎ 803-854-2408.

Exit 98: Smith's Pecans – This is for those of you who need a bit of stimulation after being in the car all day. Here's a gas station (Chevron) minimart/pecan outlet/souvenir shop. You can get your pecan fix here: sugar 'n orange, sugar free chocolate, butter roasted and the ubiquitous pecan log rolls, but you'll also find tacky souvenirs, bottles of cider (black cherry, peach, cherry flavored apple, muscadine, etc), flags, chow chow relish, cherry or apple butter, motor oil, invisible ink drawing

SC 108 – SC 98

books, dried flowers, beer, cigarettes and, of course, your fireworks. ◑ Open 24 hours for you night owls. East side of I-95 right on Route 6.

Exit 68: Edisto River Canoe and Kayak Trail – Here's a great break from long days of driving, and perhaps a treat to dangle in front of the kids to keep them quiet. Right here you cross the Edisto River, part of the ACE Basin consisting of 3 rivers (Ashepoo, Combahee and South Edisto) with 350,000 acres of forested wetlands, fresh, brackish and salt water tidal marshes, barrier islands, finfish, shellfish, bald eagles, wood storks, ospreys, short nose sturgeon and loggerhead sea turtles.

The Canoe and Kayak trail is 60 miles long and follows the same routes used extensively by the early colonists and Native Americans, and is still as wild and undeveloped with live oaks dripping with Spanish moss framing the banks. A handful of outfitters (by Colleton State Park) can take you on guided paddles lasting from 2 hours to overnight. www.southcarolinaparks.com ☎ 843-538-8206. Carolina Heritage Outfitters offers short trips ☎ 843-563-5051.

Exit 53 Northbound or 57 Southbound: The South Carolina Artisans Center – Here's the state's official folk art and craft center, showcasing hand-made creations (blown glass, sweetgrass baskets, carvings, pottery, jewelry, quilts, tatting, folk art, metalwork) by over 280 artists who live and work in South Carolina. Each artist was carefully chosen by an independent jury for his or her fine craftsmanship, unique style and professionalism. Their mission is to interpret, market, preserve and perpetuate the folk art and fine craftsmanship of the state.

The Center is located in a white house with a wrap-around porch containing a handful of rooms choc-a-bloc with one of a kind items, and is definitely worth the 2-mile detour off the road for anyone who loves beautiful arts and crafts. ◑ Mon-Sat 10-5:30, Sun 1-5. ☞ Southbound: from I-95 Exit 57, take Rte 64 South (Bell's Highway) towards Walterboro for 1 3/4 miles until just after it curves right and becomes N. Jefferies Blvd. Turn left on Wichman St to the Center. Northbound: from I-95 Exit 53, take Route 63 East (Sniders Highway) towards Walterboro

for 3 1/2 miles until it becomes S. Jefferies Blvd. and curves to the left in town. Turn right at Wichman St. to the Center at 334 Wichman St. www.southcarolinaartisans.org ☎ 843-549-0011.

Voulez-vous Creuset avec moi?

Exit 38: Le Creuset Factory Store – In 1925 in Fresnoy-le-Grand, France, artisans began producing pots by hand-casting molten cast iron in sand molds, which were polished and sanded by hand and then sprayed with two separate coats of enamel, and fired after each process. The enamel then becomes extremely hard and durable, making it quite resistant to damage during daily use. These pots are impervious to acids and other chemicals, and are popular for their even cooking temperatures and heat retaining blanket, so they can be used on the table keeping food hot for a long time.

Le Creuset is the world's leading manufacturer using this method, and it is the choice cookware of leading chefs and people who just love to cook. The pots have lids that seal in steam to braise food in its own juices, they can be used on any kind of stove top or oven, and have a lifetime guarantee. This factory store carries firsts, seconds and exclusive colors of the pots and then tea kettles, wooden spoons, pitchers, copper bowls, graters, Screwpull wine accessories, Riedel wine glasses and kitchen gadgets. ◑ Mon-Fri 9-6, Sat 8-6, Sun 9-6. ☞ From I-95 Exit 38 go west along Route 68 towards Hampton and turn right at the first street - you'll see the store at the end of the street. www.lecreuset.com ☎ 843-589-6650.

Exit 33: The Lowcountry Visitors Center & Museum – This is one if the most interesting Visitors' Centers along I-95, since it is housed in the Frampton House, built in 1868, and is one of the only plantation homes in the area open to the public. The property was part of an original King's grant to the Frampton family in the 1700s. In 1865, General Sherman's troops burned down the first plantation house and all the farm buildings.

Civil War earthworks, erected by Robert E. Lee's troops in defence of the important railroad supply line for the Confederacy from Savannah to Charleston, lie under the 250 year old live oak trees (covered in Spanish moss) in the back yard.

Besides the friendly advice and visitor information from Jim and Lois, in the recreated 1900's plantation house parlor there are objects from the 10 museums in the Lowcountry, including artwork from Walterboro's South Carolina Artisans Center (see Exit 53), and things to buy like: Jim Beam steak sauce, bird sculptures, painted boxes, dog & cat pens and syrup buckets. If you are lucky (or unlucky?) you will chance upon one of the house ghosts. ◑ Daily 9-5:30 ☞ Route 17 Frontage road just East of I-95 to Lowcountry Lane on your right. 1 Lowcountry Lane. www.South CarolinaLowcountry.com ☎ 800-528-6870 or 843-717-3090.

RELIEVING STRESS, LOWCOUNTRY STYLE

Exit 33: Joggling boards like the one placed at the front of the Lowcountry Vis-

itors Center and Museum look like a long, long bench, and have graced Southern lawns and porches for years. Folklore has it that sometime in the 1800's a "lady of the house" in a rice plantation in South Carolina suffered from an arthritis-like ailment. When writing back home to her relatives in Europe, she complained of her pain and inability to exercise. Supposedly, their reply included complete plans for a joggling board, and it was constructed on her plantation.

The gentle side-to-side and back and forth rocking motions allowed her some degree of exercise (obviously not up to today's standards) while being able to sit and enjoy the beauty of her land. Their popularity with children helped spread the concept all over Lowcountry South Carolina, and they are still constructed using similar materials (yellow pine) and methods (hardwood dowel or more pricey mortise and tendon). You can see one, try it out and order it at the Lowcountry Visitor Center and Museum. ◑ Daily 9-5:30. See the write-up below for directions. 1 Lowcountry Lane. www.SouthCarolinaLowcountry.com ☎ 800-528-6870.

Photo taken by Jim Wescott

Exit 33: KOA Point South – Even if you are not a camper, you just may want to think about this sleeping option. At this park, you can stay overnight in a converted caboose, a trolley car or in a little Hansel and Gretel cabin. The caboose is actually

SC 68 – SC 33

sitting on train tracks and has a front and back platform, the pine cottage has a porch and wooden swing and just enough room for the beds. The trolley came here all the way from Charleston and is glass windowed, so you have the whole outside inside during the day but can close the blinds at night.

The facilities are sparse - bring your own sheets, pillows or sleeping bags to put on the double bed for the folks and 2 singles for the kids. They have heat and AC but NO bathrooms. For those, and showers, there's the main shower building nearby. Take advantage of the whole RV park with lakes, forests, picnic grounds, etc. for your enjoyment. See our Campground pages at back for directions. ☎ 800-726-5733.

Exit 33: Sabatier Factory Outlet –

In 1834 Bonnet Sabatier, at the age of 29, registered the "Sabatier" trademark, and began what has become a cutlery benchmark for excellence. For centuries his village, Thiers in south central France, has been the center of the art of French knife making.

This outlet shop is a family owned business, and the only one in the U.S. which has been authorized by K Sabatier (there are other Sabatier brands/factories) in Thiers to sell the "K" knives. The outlet sells directly to the public, bypassing all the middlemen and thus allowing better prices.

Ask about the different lines, as the forged and stamped, full or partial tang knives are of different qualities. Each series has about three dozen different knives, for everything from slicing salmon to boning a pheasant. Our Sabatier knives, which we've used since we married, are the favorite tools in our kitchen. ◑ Daily 8-6. ☞ Rte 17 Frontage road just East of I-95. www.sabatier.com ☎ 800-525-6399 or 843-726-6444.

Exit 21: Blue Heron Nature Trail –

If it's time for just a little stretch or you want to run the kids (there's a swing, a fountain, observation platform and more), here's an easy half mile loop around a pond constructed of a combination of recycled tires, boardwalk, and brick.

The 3-acre lake is the home for fish, turtles, ducks, wading herons and several assorted alligators up to 4' long. Depending on the season, you should come across butterflies which are attracted to flowers chosen to entice them in a butterfly shaped

> ## Order! Order!
>
> **Exit 21:** Henry Martyn Robert was born in 1837 on a plantation near Robertville. Don't know the name? Ever hear of Robert's Rules of Order? Henry's ancestor Pierre Robert was pastor of the first Huguenot colony in South Carolina, and since the Reverend was against slavery, he moved his family to the midwest when Henry was a child. Henry Robert was appointed to West Point, and was an inspired engineer who was involved with most of the major river and harbor improvement and fortification projects undertaken all over the U.S. Robert's Rules, the authoritative reference work on parliamentary procedures, was first published in February 1876.

garden. They have placed feeders in a back-yard habitat to attract birds, and food dispensers on the banks of the pond to tempt ducks and turtles.

The trail is FREE and is lighted to be enjoyed any time. If you arrive between 9 and 5, visit the log cabin at the end of the trail which has wildlife exhibits (alligator, bobcat, fox, duck, owl, squirrel) and, when closed, a container on the porch with brochures. ☞ From I-95 Exit 21 go West on Rte 336 and turn right at the first gas station (BP). Go down the road a bit toward Jasper's Porch Restaurant, and park in the paved area at the end of the restaurant parking lot next to the grassy knoll. www.sctrails.net or www.angelfire.com/sc/blueheron ☎ 843-726-7611.

Exit 18: Switzerland – Early in the 1700's, immigrants from Switzerland tried to set up a silk colony in the new world. There were fortunes to be made for suppliers, as it was a precious commodity in Europe. They cleared the land and planted the necessary mulberry trees for the worms. More were lured here by their pamphlet called "The Contented and Homesickless Swiss Settler in the New World".

Jean Pierry Purry managed to get the British Government to subsidize the settlement, so by 1733 about 170 French and German Swiss Protestants founded Purrysburg on the Savannah River. Alas, they had not counted on the sweltering summers, swamps and malaria. In 1772, they did manage to export 144 lbs. of raw silk, but they died by the scores. The survivors, who moved to higher ground, were more successful with cattle, and named their new village Switzerland, which is why you see that sign going southbound at exit 18.

HONEY THE MONEY DOG

Exit 5: Crazy D's All American Fireworks at the El Cheapo Gas Station – Getting gas can't get much more fun than this. When Joyce Rogers' husband, Don, picked up a cocker spaniel named Honey 6 years ago at the pound, he could never have anticipated the fame she would bring his gas station. This being a family business, Honey came to work with them (as does their daughter and grandkid) each day, and was very friendly with all the customers.

One slow day, Don decided to teach her to take money (bills only) and bring it to his wife at the cash. He would command, "Honey go get the money!". Soon everyone in the town wanted to gas up at Don's pumps to watch Honey come grab their money between her teeth and run back to Joyce at the cash. Honey can tell real money from fake Monopoly money or even foreign currency - if it's not real, she'll just drop it on the floor.

Honey gets a treat every time she comes back to the cash, so now Honey is on diet treats. The family has a real sense of humor, because the gas mart itself has a 4-foot chicken outside, a player piano and an animated figure which talks back to customers as they come in. Oh yes, and they sell snacks, fireworks, offer a smoothie bar for fruit drinks and sell novelty size 100 underwear! 15967 Whyte Hardee Bld (Rte 17 South). ☎ 843-784-5086.

SC 33 – SC 5

Exit 5: Jasper's – Home cooking just doesn't get much tastier than this. For 25 years, Betty and Lori Taylor, a mother and daughter team, have been churning out daily lunch and dinner buffets of crunchy southern fried chicken, savory pot roast and potatoes, BBQ pork, lasagna, etc. along with the healthy collard greens, black-eyed peas, brussels sprouts, lima beans, mashed potatoes, gravy and a cold salad bar which might include: spiced apples, macaroni salad, bean salad and beets. All this and homemade pies and cakes (could be coconut cream, chocolate cake) for only $8 for dinner! You could also just order char-grilled steaks, chicken, etc. off the menu at dinner time. ◗ Lunch Mon-Fri 11-2, Dinner daily 5-9. 18226 Whyte Hardee Blvd. on the North side of I-95. ☎ 800-229-1301 or 843-784-5800.

Mile 0: As you pass the bottom of South Carolina or especially as you enter it from Georgia, you can't help but notice the palmetto trees planted in the median. The South Carolina flag has the unusual symbol of a palmetto tree smack in the center of it. Why?

Back on June 28, 1776 the British fleet, with 9 warships and 270 heavy guns, atta-cked the fort on Sullivan Island. The fort had been built with sand and logs from the palmetto tree, whose insides contain thick elastic fibers which smothered the bombs before they could explode, frus-trating the British. The Americans were so low on ammunition that they could only fire 1 shot for every 6 they received.

The tide of the battle turned, literally, that day when the tide went out, since some of the British ships ran aground on the shoal where Fort Sumter now stands. The British abandoned the ship, Actaeon, and when it exploded, it sent up an infer-no which seemed to Col. Moultrie "a grand pillar of smoke, which soon expanded itself at the top, and to appearance, formed the figure of a palmetto tree". After a day of heavy fighting and the loss of a ship, the Brits gave up and sailed away, giving the States their first major victory of the Revolutionary War.

Within days came the signing of the Dec-laration of Independence, as the victory was a favorable sign of the Americans' capacity to oppose the British. The tough palmetto tree was then given the place of honor in the middle of the South Carolina flag, and the State's nickname eventually became the Palmetto State.

Caution: Men Working

If you are complaining about the slowdown of traffic as you watch people working on the highway, think about how roads were constructed in the olden days. In South Carolina, it was compulsory that all men helped to clear roads in their neck of the woods (literally!). They com-plained that they had better things to do and didn't want to dig up tree stumps and shovel dirt just so strangers could pass through their town. So in 1788, the state passed a law limiting road duty to 12 days a year. There was a $2 fine for a white man if he missed the work and slave owners were fined $1 a day if slaves failed to show.

Mile 4 Northbound: South Carolina Welcome Center – Here's a beautifully landscaped center, and it is very inviting to stop and ask your questions about the State, pick up flyers and FREE motel coupon booklets and use the clean restrooms. They can make reservations for you or help with car problems, and there's a mail drop There are vending machines here and a picnic area. ◗ Daily Mar-Oct 9-5:30, Nov-Feb 9-5.

☆ GEORGIA ☆

Mile 111 Southbound: Georgia Visitor Information Center – Don't forget to come and and pick up your FREE motel discount coupon booklets which offer great deals along the way. Pick up some flyers or ask the friendly staff about interesting things to do and see in Georgia. They are full of great advice and can make reservations for you. There are clean rest rooms, a dog walk and covered picnic tables. ◗ Daily 8:30-5:30, restrooms 7-11. ☎ 912 963 2546.

Exit 109: Eli Whitney wound up in Port Wentworth to work for Catharine Greene, the widow of General Nathaniel Greene (who was 2nd in command to General George Washington), perhaps as a tutor for her orphaned children. General Greene had been given The Mulberry Grove Plantation here as a gift from the spoils of the Revolutionary War.

Whitney was no average tutor. A Yale graduate, he tinkered with inventions, and Phineas Miller, the plantation manager, and Mrs Greene challenged Whitney to create a machine that would solve the problem of separating cotton. He came up with the idea of the cotton gin (shortened form of the word "engine") in 1793.

This invention revolutionized the South, making it possible to process cotton on a grand scale. The farmers that he had helped cheated him out of any royalties for the invention, so Whitney went back to New Haven, where he did even better for the North by reinventing the system of production by introducing interchangeable parts and mass production.

Exit 104: Sonic – If you or your kids have never experienced a fast food drive-in restaurant with car hops (tray toters, curb girls), this chain still has them. Hickory smoke-flavored burgers or chicken "toaster sandwiches" and coney hot dogs with chile and cheese can be washed down with cherry limeades, cream pie shakes (strawberry, banana, chocolate) or real malts. Any of the following flavors can be added to personalize your drink: vanilla, chocolate, cherry, grape, orange, blue coconut, watermelon, strawberry, pineapple or green apple, and you can have a fresh lemon or lime twist. All are ordered via an intercom, brought to you and hung on your car window, sometimes by kids on wheels.

The term "car hops" originated back when cars still had running boards. Servers would hop onto the boards and direct the car to a spot, thus the nickname "car hop". In 1940 Life Magazine's cover photo featured one and gave them national attention. In the 50's and 60's, when Americans fell in love with their cars, this type of restaurant flourished, because they could stay and eat in them and show them off.

SC 5 – GA 104

Sonic, which was started by Troy Smith in Oklahoma, has been around for 51 years and is the largest employer of car hops in the U.S. You can cop an "ADD-itude" by adding cheese, chili, bacon or jalapeños to your sandwich or you can even ask for chocolate syrup on your fries! www.sonicdrivein.com

Exit 99: Savannah is a unique city, for it was the first planned city in the US, and is now the largest (1,600 restored structures within a 2.5 sq. mile area) national Historic Landmark District. Savannah is full of history, architecture, historic inns (43) and ghosts, with a reputation as one of America's most haunted cities. You can take tours by foot, by car, horse-drawn carriage, hearse, riverboat or in the popular continuous trolleys, which will take you through Savannah's canopy of live oaks and around many of its grid of 24 original squares (21 remain) called greens.

James Edward Oglethorpe arrived in these parts in February 1733, and named Georgia after England's King George II, with Savannah becoming its first city. Its citizens were given the freedom to worship as they pleased, but laws forbade rum, slaves, Catholics and lawyers (how did they know?). The town flourished without Native American warfare or hardship because Oglethorpe pledged only friendship and good will towards the Yamacraw chief, Tomo-chi-chi.

The economy boomed with the exportation of cotton, allowing the building of the lavish homes and churches that we can still see today. The cotton warehouses on River St. are still there (sitting on the cobblestones made from the ballast left by the old sailing ships), and world cotton prices were set in the halls of Savannah's Cotton Exchange (built in 1887), which you can still see today at Drayton and Bay St.

If you choose to drive into Savannah, ask at the tourist office or a hotel about the Visitor DayPass, which for $8 allows you 2 days of FREE parking at meters (over 1 hr), city lots and parking garages. Main Visitor Center: ◗ Mon-Fri 8:30-5, Sat, Sun & Holidays 9-5. ☞ From I-95 Exit 99, take I-16 East, past I-516 to exit 167, which leaves you on Martin Luther King Blvd. Turn left to 301 Martin Luther King Blvd. www.savannahvisit.com ☎ 912-944-0455. Trolleys leave from the parking lot here. Other locations: Hospitality Center, ◗ Daily 10-10, Jan 10-6, Feb & Mar 10-8. 1A W. River St. ☎ 912-651-6662. Convention and Visitor's Bureau ◗ M-F 8:30-5, 101 E. Bay St. ☎ 877-SAVANNAH or 912-644-6401.

Exit 99: First African Baptist Church – Oldest in America, this Congregation was established in 1775 and the building was built in 1859 by slaves and free blacks who built it brick by brick by lantern light in their meager time off. One of the first ministers, Andrew Cox Marshall, asked blacks who were saving up to buy their freedom ($1,500) to put the money towards buying the land.

To build this structure, men made the bricks down by the river in the overnight hours and women carried them up to this spot. Many of the church's original pews bear the tribal markings of the African slaves. If you get to see the basement, you might notice air holes in the floorboards - this was for the Underground Railroad. The Sunday school started here in 1826 is supposed to be the oldest in N. America. See Visitor Center for directions. 23 Montgomery St. ☎ 912-233-6597.

Mile 99: Sherman's famous March to the Sea passed across the highway in the middle of December in 1864. The March started back in Atlanta on November 15 as the Union Army blazed a 50-mile path eastward, burning everything in its sight. As they reached the Port of Savannah, the citizens and Southern Army were nowhere to be found. About 10,000 people and troops had fled to safety by using their flat bottomed rice boats (padded with rice and straw) to make a long, long pontoon all the way to SC - quite a clever feat. So on Christmas Day, Sherman sent the famous telegram to President Lincoln, "I beg to present you as a Christmas gift the city of Savannah". The gift, of course, wasn't the city itself nor the guns, the ammunition or the cotton, but the end-in-sight of the Civil War.

Exit 99: Ships of the Sea Maritime Museum – This museum is worth seeing, if just for the building itself - Scarbrough House, a Greek Revival manor built in 1819. The magnificently reconditioned rooms are filled with ship models and paintings of ships, but also plotting instruments, shipbuilding tools, compasses, sextants, crossstaff, ring dial and sand glass. Learn about the cats in the brothel windows in English ports in the 18th and 19th centuries: green eyes = open, red eyes= full or cops are around, cat's back to window = closed. See if you can find all the ships named "Savannah" (gunboat, paddleboat, frigate, steamship, nuclear ship, Navy cruiser, etc.).

If you think its hard laying computer cable, learn about the laying of the transatlantic cable. ◐ Tues- Sun 10-5 41 Martin. Luther King Blvd. www.shipsofthe sea.org ☎ 912-232-1511.

Exit 99: River Street's Waving Girl Statue – Romantics amongst you will love this legend which recounts the story of Florence Martus's and of her sweetheart who left town on a ship. She promised to greet and wave to every ship that sailed into port until he came home. Sailors all over the world knew about her, but he never did show up.

Between Exits 94 & 90, Mile 92-91: In the evening of October 1, 1779, Col. John White, Captains George Melvin and A.G.C. Elholm, a sergeant and 3 privates snared 141 British troops and 4 ships without firing a single bullet! What they did was very clever. The 7 of them built campfires scattered through the woods around the Ogeechee River bank, where the enemy had settled for the night. They then walked back and forth from fire to fire yelling orders to imaginary troops, and even going so far as challenging each other as sentinels, leading the British to believe they were surrounded.

Then, with ultimate nerve, they put into motion the second part of their plan. White rode into the British camp and asked them to surrender without casualties. Captain French did so gladly, thanking them for their mercy. At that point, Captain Elholm rode in briskly asking where to place the artillery. White answered, "Keep them back, Keep them back, sir... Move your men off, and send me 3 guides to conduct them to The American post in Sunbury." He then promised he himself would go constrain his impatient "army".

The Smallest Church in America (Well, Almost)

Exit 67: Christ Chapel was a vision of Mrs. Agnes Harper, a rural grocer who dreamed of a quiet sanctuary for travelers passing through Georgia for meditation and inter-denominational worship. With limited funds, she managed to have erected a 10' x 15' building which seats 12 with foldaway kneelers. Mrs Harper imported the stained glass windows from England and placed a glass star in the roof to permit the midday sun to light the interior.

Prior to her death, she named the site Memory Park and deeded the church to Jesus Christ to prevent it from ever being sold. In 1983, the McIntosh Chamber of Commerce adopted the little Church and now makes the needed repairs. Though it goes by the "Smallest" billing around here, that designation probably fits the one in Oneida, New York at 3.5' x 6'.

Nestled in live oaks near the headwaters of the South Newport River, travelers continue to stop for a moment of rest, peace and tranquility. Mrs Harper once said, "It is not the dimensions of the church which is important - it is the extent of the faith.". Local ministers lead worship services at the little Church every  3rd Sunday, and it is open 24 hours a day. ☞ From I-95 take highway 17 South for about 1 mile. The church is on the left.

Exit 49: McIntosh County Chamber of Commerce – For information on local attractions from Exit 49 to Exit 67, this waterfront Visitors' Center can answer any questions. Pick up flyers and take advantage of a clean bathroom. ☞ From I-95 Exit 49, take highway 251 East for a mile to its end at Rte 17. Turn right for 1 mile to where Rte 25 makes a left onto Fort King George Dr - don't cross the bridge. Turn left and the building is on your right. 105 Fort King George Dr. ◑ Mon-Sat 9-5. www.mcintoshcounty.com ☎ 912-437-6684.

Exit 49: Altamaha Outposts Coastal Adventures – If you want a break in the middle of your trip, why not go out in a canoe or kayak on a river, cypress swamp or salt marsh? Rentals and tours (2-6 hours) might have you getting up close and personal with  dolphins, aligators, otters, manatees, bald eagles, ospreys, herons or egrets. Overnight camping trips are possible. Call ahead, since the tides determine the day's events. www.altamaha.com ☎ 912-437-6010.

Exit 49: Fort King George – If you want a quick stop to stretch your legs and glean a bit of history, pop over to this fort, which was first constructed in 1721 by scouts led by Colonel John "Tuscarora Jack" Barnwell, a prominent planter and Indian fighter. At the time, it was the southernmost outpost of the British Empire in North America, but it was abandoned in 1732.

The French, who had settled in Canada, came down the Mississippi all the way to the Gulf of Mexico, and were considered a threat from the north and west, while Spain posed a threat from Florida. This left the British colonies along the coast with the possibility of being surrounded, and thus the need for this fort.

This reconstruction has a three-storied gabled blockhouse, with a supply magazine on the lower level, a gun room on the second floor, with cannon ports on the walls to fire at enemy boats in the river, and a third floor gun room with lookout posts. Also on the site are barracks, officers' quarters, the guardhouse, house of office (bathroom), a scout boat, indigenous huts (for scouts, sawyers, slaves), a blacksmith shop, bakery and molasses beer brewery, 4 sentry boxes, a 360 degree swivel gun and 9 cannon emplacements.

In addition to the Fort, there's a short film, a small museum, Scottish pioneer village, British cemetery, sawmill ruins, a nature trail and a great view of the marshlands. ◑ Tues-Sat 9-5, Sun 2-5:30. ☞ See the instructions above for the McIntosh County building, but keep following Rte 25 as it turns left onto Fort King George Dr before you cross the bridge. Follow the Drive for about 1 mile to the fort. www.gastateparks.org ☎ 912-437-4770.

Exit 49: Georgia Island Factory Shoppes – With a Book Warehouse to pick up some vacation reading and some regular and outlet stores to empty your purse, this mall tempts you with Coach, Woolrich, Mikasa Outlet, Quiksilver, KB Toy Outlet, Nautica Factory Store, Springmaid/Wamsutta, Rockport Outlet and more. Seniors over 55 get 10% off on Tuesdays. Ask Customer Service about special coupons offered by center merchants. ◑ Mon-Sat 10-9, Sun 11-6. www.horizongroup.com ☎ 888-545-7224 or 912-437-2700.

Exit 49: Open Gates B & B - Why stay at a noisy I-95 exit motel when you can drive 2 minutes off the exit and sleep in the spacious quiet of a 128-year-old white frame Victorian house? Built by a wealthy timber baron in 1876, it overlooks historic Vernon Square and is one block from the shrimp boaters on the waterfront. You can sit on rocking chairs on the front porch under the shade of a live oak tree, enjoy the large cypress library perusing the owners' extensive collection of field guides and books on local natural history and dine in the morning surrounded by antiques and a friendly proprietor.

Kelly Spratt and her husband Jeff are biologists by trade (he commutes to work by boat!) and offer, besides their gracious hospitality, birding tours, river tours, or kayak, boating and fishing adventures or the opportunity to visit Sapelo Island to learn about the unique Gullah language

and culture. Don't be surprised if you are greeted with wine & cheese when you arrive. www.opengatesbnb.com ☎ 912-437-6985.

Courtesy: Open Gates B&B

Exit 49: Skippers' Fish Camp – "Just caught" flounder or shrimp should have you driving off this exit. In a glass and wood decor with a water view location, the menu here takes your from an oyster bar to crab cakes and South Georgia catfish, or for landlubbers, steaks, ribs and BBQ, of course. Make sure to order some of the sides: sweet potato souffle or cheddar cheese grits and the peach cobbler for dessert. See the McIntosh County C of C for directions. 85 Screven St. ☎ 912-437-3474.

Exit 49: Walter's Caviar – Howell Boone's family has been in the seafood business for 3 generations, and they have shrimp boats and process their own catches. He started Walter's Caviar in 1980, farming the caviar from sturgeon, a bony plated fish which can live up to 50 years and weigh 1,000 pounds. The fish are netted by fishermen working in pairs out of small open boats, often at night.

A sturgeon spends a major portion of its life in the lower reaches of rivers, but swims up to freshwater streams in order to spawn. Sturgeon roe is caviar. The best caviar is made when the sturgeon is processed immediately after being caught.

Boone learned the techniques used by the most advanced Russian caviar processors, and is thus able to produce excellent

GA 49 – GA 49

caviar made only from true sturgeon roe, comparable to that of Russia and Iran. Caviar contains 47 vitamins and minerals, has 68 grams of fat per pound and 74 calories per ounce.

Famous Georgians who have shopped here: President Jimmy Carter and Rosalyn, Ted and Jane Turner and billionairess Ann Cox Chambers. You can order the caviar or fresh Georgia shrimp online from their web site. www.georgiaseafood.com ☎ 912-437-6560.

Exit 42: Hofwyl-Broadfield Plantation – Once you cross the pasture, the same one the Dent family strode for 167 years, pass the bottling house, dairy barn, commissary, pay shed, and servants' quarters, please do ring the bell on the porch for entrance. Notice the 696 acres of marsh and try to imagine it as a cypress swamp that hundreds of slaves cleared by hand, levelled for proper drainage and constructed miles of ditches and dikes and floodgates for rice farming.

William Brailsford and his son-in-law James M. Troup ran it as a rice plantation, living in the pinnacle of coastal society until the Civil War. The slaves were the foundation of rice culture, as well as the cotton industry; slaves were chosen by "task orientation" for

this work, since they had the experience and tools that they brought with them from the Windward Rice Coast of West Africa, along with the ability to withstand the heat, humidity and malarial environment. After the War, much of the estate was sold off for taxes, and by the 1880's most of the wealth was gone. Without the cheap slave labor, and with competition from the West and with the hurricanes, the East coast rice empire was gone by the early 20th century.

The property was turned into a dairy farm until 1942 and run by sisters Miriam and Ophelia Dent, who were the first to

Spanish Moss is neither Spanish nor Moss

It's an "epiphyte", a type of plant that lives off moisture in the atmosphere and has no roots. Other names for it are long moss (stems can grow up to 25') or vegetable horsehair, and it is a distant cousin to the pineapple! It sometimes produces tiny yellow flowers.

You see the silvery green veils covering trees from North Carolina right down to South America. The plant is fed by mineral-rich cells that wash off the host tree. The more cells the tree exudes, the more for the Spanish Moss to live on, so old trees and decaying trees are a veritable feast.

Rainwater is captured by scales on its small tendrils which also keep internal moisture from evaporating. There was quite an industry in the South using Spanish moss as mattress stuffing until synthetic materials came along. Henry Ford used it for stuffing the seats of Model T's. The moss picked directly from the trees is relatively bug-free. However, picked up from the ground, it can harbor chiggers (mites) that burrow into the skin and cause intense itching. Treating the moss with bleach diluted with water for a minute or so in a microwave oven takes care of the critters.

free it from debt. The wonder of this old house is that Miss Ophelia Troup Dent left it as a scrapbook of generations of an entire family. All of the family furnishings, photos and mementos are still there, as if they've just left for the day. If you are lucky, Andy Beckman will be offering your tour and giving you insights into a family he knew. ◑ Tues-Sat 9-5, Sun 2-5:30. ☞ From I-95 take Rte 99 East for 1 mile to Rte 17 & 25. Turn left on US 17 for about 1 mile. www.hofwylplantation.org ☎ 912-264-7333.

Mile 40 Southbound: Brunswick & Golden Isles Welcome Center – Don't forget to come and and get some FREE motel discount coupon booklets or request that reservations be made for you in the Brunswick area. Pick up some flyers or ask the friendly staff about interesting things to do and see in Brunswick or Georgia. There are clean rest rooms, an RV dump and picnic tables. ◑ Daily 9-5, rest rooms 24 hours. www.bgivb.com ☎ 800-933-COAST or 912-264-0202.

Exit 36: Futura 2000 Touchless Car Wash – Going West off this exit, behind the Amoco gas station, we found a super duper car wash which has everything you could need to clean your car in one spot. There are 3 bays in which to wash it yourself or you can use the touchless automatic one ($3-$6). On a wall in front is a mini-mart of vending machines selling: dri-foaming carpet shampoo, a jumbo blue sham, a super truck towel, all purpose window cleaner, Armor-all and 5 flavors of hanging air fresheners. You can have auto fragrances sprayed in the car, use a wheel cleaner or undercarriage spray, and use a wet-vac or a dry one.

Exit 36: The Factory that Never was – Notice on the west side of the highway, just south of the exit, the huge crumbling red brick chimney. In April of 1917, while the U.S. was in the midst of WWI, Glynn Coun-

ty was selected as the site for an enormous picric acid factory. This was needed for the manufacture of explosives. The Butterworth-Judson Corporation of NY built the $7,000,000 plant on a 1,400 acre site which would also become a company town.

Plans included 13 miles of railroad track and 5 artesian wells to supply the plant's daily need of 30,000,000 gallons of water. Building required 5,000 laborers, and an additional 6,000 workers were needed to man the facility, so a national and international (most locals were serving in the war or already working on other nearby war efforts) campaign was mounted to fill the spots. The then governor of Georgia, Hugh M. Dorsey, issued a "Work or Fight" proclamation to rally support.

On November 11, 1918, just thirty days from scheduled completion, the war in Europe ended. It was thought that after the war, the facility could be converted to manufacture chemicals or dyes, but its peacetime use never materialized. Over the years, most of the factory structures were demolished, including the twin of the chimney you see. The remaining buildings still in use have incredibly thick walls and huge oak beams. Some ruins can be seen behind the Sleep Inn.

A HUNDRED BOTTLES OF CHAMPAGNE ON THE HULL

Exit 36: By 1942, during WWII, over 500 million tons of ships and cargo had already been lost to enemy U-boats. The U.S. Marine Commission ordered stronger 447-foot cargo vessels to be built at 16 sites, and they came to be known as Liberty Ships. Though each of them was christened with a name when launched, each operated at sea anonymously, so that the enemy could not guess its mission or cargo.

The Brunswick shipyard, manned by 16,000 people, was able to produce 4 a month, taking an amazing average of only 89 days to construct each one, reaching a grand total of 99 ships. Receiving word that they must produce 6 ships for the month of December 1944, the J.A. Jones shipyard workers showed their dedication by guaranteeing and delivering 7! They then requested to receive no pay for the extra work done on Christmas Day, and each worker endorsed their time-and-a-half pay check back to the U.S. Government.

At the end of the war, the employee training ship, a cut-away model, was placed on display. After 20 years, it was badly rusted and was scrapped, and in 1991, after 4 years of fund-raising, a 23-foot scale model was built, which can now be seen on the grounds of the Mary Ross Waterfront Park in downtown Brunswick. It was christened, like all the others, with a bottle of champagne, and this, their 100th Liberty Ship, was duly named "City of Brunswick".

The park also has an outdoor musical playscape (see story and directions at Exit 36), a Saturday farmers market, the shrimp fleet and huge ocean-going freighters.

Exit 36: Musical playscape – Kids young and old will get a hoot out of this fun area in Mary Ross Waterfront Park, which is a collection of outdoor musical instruments constructed of wood, metal and PVC pipe. It was designed by Bond Anderson, who owns Sound Play in Parrott, GA.

Anderson, a classically trained flutist who plays with the Albany Symphony Orchestra, decided to create wind-generated outdoor instruments. He has designed and built similar musical playscapes throughout the U.S. The instruments, aside from their attractive art forms, foster an appreciation of the ingenuity of many different cultures, since they are inspired by instruments from around the world.

Interestingly, the instruments are tuned to pitch, and local bands have used them as part of their performances. While you are in the park, you might also take in the Liberty Ship on display and the shrimp boats in the harbor. ☞ From I-95 take Rte 25 & 341 East for about 5 miles to Gloucester Street and turn right to Bay St and the Mary Ross Waterfront Park. www.soundplay.com

Exit 3: Ramada Inn & Suites – Sometimes even chain motels can stand out from their cookie cutter peers, and this one does it with a hot breakfast. You get scrambled eggs, bacon, grits, biscuits, juice and coffee, or you can have cold cereal if you prefer. Also, for golfing nuts, there is a 5-hole putting green to practice on. 930 Highway 40 E. ☎ 912-729-3000.

Mile 1 Northbound: Georgia Visitor Information Center – Don't forget to come and and get some FREE motel discount coupon booklets or request that reservations be made for you. Pick up some flyers or ask the friendly staff about interesting things to do and see in Georgia. There are clean rest rooms, an RV dump, and this one has a dog walk area and picnic tables. ◑ Daily 8:30-5:30, restrooms 7-11. ☎ 912-729-3253.

Exit 1: Lang's Marina Restaurant – It doesn't get much fresher than this, since Calvin Lang owns the marina, a fleet of fishing boats and the restaurant too. When you can eat shrimp caught the same day, you'll be so spoiled it will be hard to go back to the frozen ones at home.

The dinner menu offers you fish or seafood simply prepared: fried, blackened or grilled. If

they have them, try the rock shrimp (fished from around the Gulf), very tender and a different taste - perhaps a cross between a shrimp and a langoustine. Expect a line-up of locals, a really good sign that this is good food. If this interests you, please note it's about 10 miles in from the exit. ◑ Lunch Tues-Fri 11-2, Dinner Wed-Sat 5-9. ☞ Take Saint Marys Rd East from I-95 about 3 1/4 mi. to Rte 40. Turn right and follow it as it turns into Osborne Rd and then as it curves right to become Osborne St. to the end on Saint Marys St. Turn right for 1/4 mile. Restaurant is on the left. 307 W. St. Marys St. ☎ 912-882-4432.

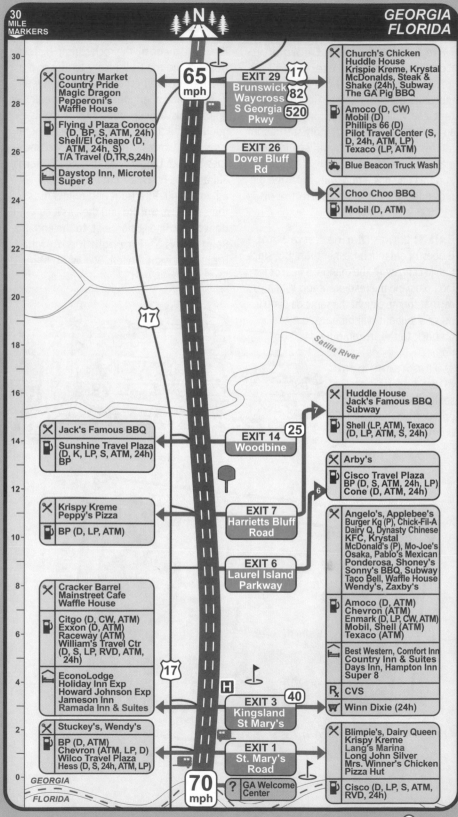

30 MILE MARKERS

GEORGIA
FLORIDA

N

65 mph

EXIT 29
Brunswick
Waycross
S Georgia
Pkwy

17
82
520

Country Market
Country Pride
Magic Dragon
Pepperoni's
Waffle House

Flying J Plaza Conoco
(D, BP, S, ATM, 24h)
Shell/El Cheapo (D,
ATM, 24h, S)
T/A Travel (D,TR,S,24h)

Daystop Inn, Microtel
Super 8

Church's Chicken
Huddle House
Krispie Kreme, Krystal
McDonalds, Steak &
Shake (24h), Subway
The GA Pig BBQ

Amoco (D, CW)
Mobil (D)
Phillips 66 (D)
Pilot Travel Center (S,
D, 24h, ATM, LP)
Texaco (LP, ATM)

Blue Beacon Truck Wash

EXIT 26
Dover Bluff
Rd

Choo Choo BBQ

Mobil (D, ATM)

17

Satilla River

Jack's Famous BBQ

Sunshine Travel Plaza
(D, K, LP, S, ATM, 24h)
BP

EXIT 14
Woodbine

25

7

Huddle House
Jack's Famous BBQ
Subway

Shell (LP, ATM), Texaco
(D, LP, ATM, S, 24h)

Arby's

Cisco Travel Plaza
BP (D, S, ATM, 24h, LP)
Cone (D, ATM, 24h)

6

Krispy Kreme
Peppy's Pizza

BP (D, LP, ATM)

EXIT 7
Harrietts Bluff
Road

EXIT 6
Laurel Island
Parkway

Angelo's, Applebee's
Burger Kg (P), Chick-Fil-A
Dairy Q, Dynasty Chinese
KFC, Krystal
McDonald's (P), Mo-Joe's
Osaka, Pablo's Mexican
Ponderosa, Shoney's
Sonny's BBQ, Subway
Taco Bell, Waffle House
Wendy's, Zaxby's

Amoco (D, ATM)
Chevron (ATM)
Enmark (D, LP, CW, ATM)
Mobil, Shell (ATM)
Texaco (ATM)

Cracker Barrel
Mainstreet Cafe
Waffle House

Citgo (D, CW, ATM)
Exxon (D, ATM)
Raceway (ATM)
William's Travel Ctr
(D, S, LP, RVD, ATM,
24h)

EconoLodge
Holiday Inn Exp
Howard Johnson Exp
Jameson Inn
Ramada Inn & Suites

17

H

Best Western, Comfort Inn
Country Inn & Suites
Days Inn, Hampton Inn
Super 8

CVS

Winn Dixie (24h)

EXIT 3
Kingsland
St Mary's

40

Stuckey's, Wendy's

BP (D, ATM)
Chevron (ATM, LP, D)
Wilco Travel Plaza
Hess (D, S, 24h, ATM, LP)

EXIT 1
St. Mary's
Road

Blimpie's, Dairy Queen
Krispy Kreme
Lang's Marina
Long John Silver
Mrs. Winner's Chicken
Pizza Hut

GEORGIA
FLORIDA

70 mph

?
GA Welcome
Center

Cisco (D, LP, S, ATM,
RVD, 24h)

© 2004

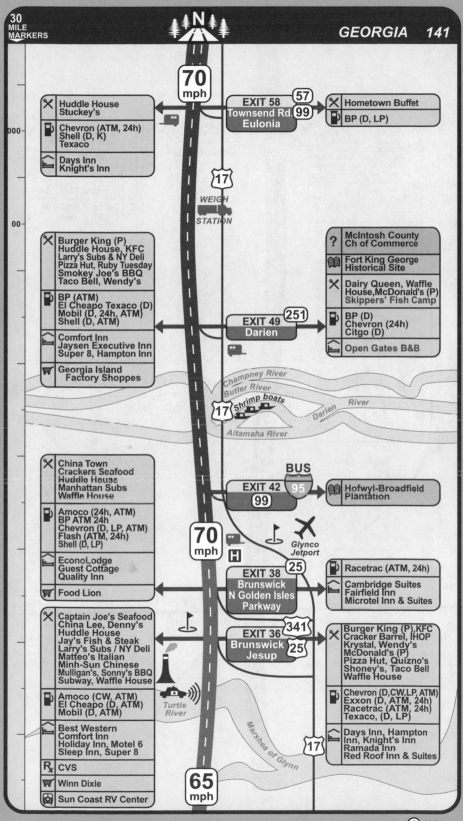

70 mph

EXIT 58 57 99
Townsend Rd.
Eulonia

✕	Huddle House Stuckey's
⛽	Chevron (ATM, 24h) Shell (D, K) Texaco
🛏	Days Inn Knight's Inn

| ✕ | Hometown Buffet |
| ⛽ | BP (D, LP) |

17 US

WEIGH STATION

✕	Burger King (P) Huddle House, KFC Larry's Subs & NY Deli Pizza Hut, Ruby Tuesday Smokey Joe's BBQ Taco Bell, Wendy's
⛽	BP (ATM) El Cheapo Texaco (D) Mobil (D, 24h, ATM) Shell (D, ATM)
🛏	Comfort Inn Jaysen Executive Inn Super 8, Hampton Inn
🛒	Georgia Island Factory Shoppes

EXIT 49 251
Darien

?	McIntosh County Ch of Commerce
📖	Fort King George Historical Site
✕	Dairy Queen, Waffle House, McDonald's (P) Skippers' Fish Camp
⛽	BP (D) Chevron (24h) Citgo (D)
🛏	Open Gates B&B

Champney River
Butler River
Shrimp boats
17 US
Darien River
Altamaha River

✕	China Town Crackers Seafood Huddle House Manhattan Subs Waffle House
⛽	Amoco (24h, ATM) BP ATM 24h Chevron (D, LP, ATM) Flash (ATM, 24h) Shell (D, LP)
🛏	EconoLodge Guest Cottage Quality Inn
🛒	Food Lion

EXIT 42 BUS 95 99

| 📖 | Hofwyl-Broadfield
Plantation |

70 mph

H

Glynco Jetport

EXIT 38 25
Brunswick
N Golden Isles
Parkway

| ⛽ | Racetrac (ATM, 24h) |
| 🛏 | Cambridge Suites
Fairfield Inn
Microtel Inn & Suites |

EXIT 36 341 25
Brunswick
Jesup

✕	Captain Joe's Seafood China Lee, Denny's Huddle House Jay's Fish & Steak Larry's Subs / NY Deli Matteo's Italian Minh-Sun Chinese Mulligan's, Sonny's BBQ Subway, Waffle House
⛽	Amoco (CW, ATM) El Cheapo (D, ATM) Mobil (D, ATM)
🛏	Best Western Comfort Inn Holiday Inn, Motel 6 Sleep Inn, Super 8
℞	CVS
🛒	Winn Dixie
🚐	Sun Coast RV Center

Turtle River

✕	Burger King (P), KFC Cracker Barrel, IHOP Krystal, Wendy's McDonald's (P) Pizza Hut, Quizno's Shoney's, Taco Bell Waffle House
⛽	Chevron (D, CW, LP, ATM) Exxon (D, ATM, 24h) Racetrac (ATM, 24h) Texaco, (D, LP)
🛏	Days Inn, Hampton Inn, Knight's Inn Ramada Inn Red Roof Inn & Suites

Marshes of Glynn

17 US

65 mph

© 2004

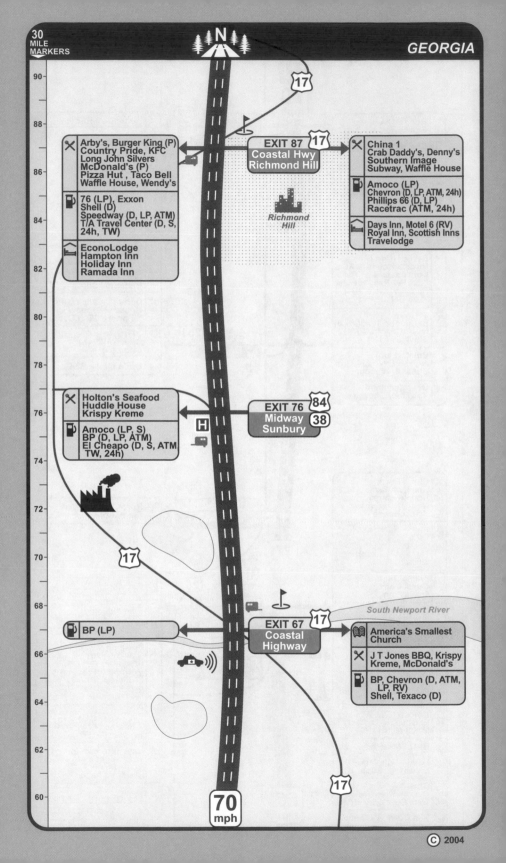

N

90
88
86
84
82
80
78
76
74
72
70
68
66
64
62
60

17

EXIT 87 **17**
Coastal Hwy
Richmond Hill

Richmond Hill

× Arby's, Burger King (P)
Country Pride, KFC
Long John Silvers
McDonald's (P)
Pizza Hut , Taco Bell
Waffle House, Wendy's

⛽ 76 (LP), Exxon
Shell (D)
Speedway (D, LP, ATM)
T/A Travel Center (D, S,
24h, TW)

🛏 EconoLodge
Hampton Inn
Holiday Inn
Ramada Inn

× China 1
Crab Daddy's, Denny's
Southern Image
Subway, Waffle House

⛽ Amoco (LP)
Chevron (D, LP, ATM, 24h)
Phillips 66 (D, LP)
Racetrac (ATM, 24h)

🛏 Days Inn, Motel 6 (RV)
Royal Inn, Scottish Inns
Travelodge

EXIT 76 **84**
Midway **38**
Sunbury

× Holton's Seafood
Huddle House
Krispy Kreme

⛽ Amoco (LP, S)
BP (D, LP, ATM)
El Cheapo (D, S, ATM
TW, 24h)

H

17

South Newport River

EXIT 67 **17**
Coastal
Highway

⛽ BP (LP)

📖 America's Smallest
Church

× J T Jones BBQ, Krispy
Kreme, McDonald's

⛽ BP, Chevron (D, ATM,
LP, RV)
Shell, Texaco (D)

17

70 mph

© 2004

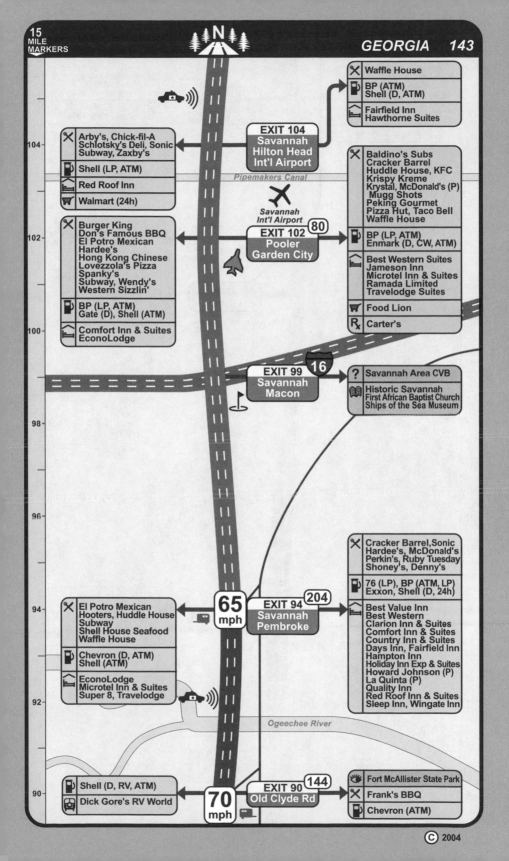

✕	Waffle House
⛽	BP (ATM) Shell (D, ATM)
🏨	Fairfield Inn Hawthorne Suites

EXIT 104
Savannah Hilton Head Int'l Airport

✕	Arby's, Chick-fil-A Schlotsky's Deli, Sonic Subway, Zaxby's
⛽	Shell (LP, ATM)
🏨	Red Roof Inn
🛒	Walmart (24h)

Pipemakers Canal

✈ *Savannah Int'l Airport*

✕	Baldino's Subs Cracker Barrel Huddle House, KFC Krispy Kreme Krystal, McDonald's (P) Mugg Shots Peking Gourmet Pizza Hut, Taco Bell Waffle House

EXIT 102 **80**
Pooler Garden City

✕	Burger King Don's Famous BBQ El Potro Mexican Hardee's Hong Kong Chinese Lovezzola's Pizza Spanky's Subway, Wendy's Western Sizzlin'
⛽	BP (LP, ATM) Gate (D), Shell (ATM)
🏨	Comfort Inn & Suites EconoLodge

⛽	BP (LP, ATM) Enmark (D, CW, ATM)
🏨	Best Western Suites Jameson Inn Microtel Inn & Suites Ramada Limited Travelodge Suites
🛒	Food Lion
℞	Carter's

EXIT 99 **16**
Savannah Macon

?	Savannah Area CVB
📖	Historic Savannah First African Baptist Church Ships of the Sea Museum

✕	Cracker Barrel, Sonic Hardee's, McDonald's Perkin's, Ruby Tuesday Shoney's, Denny's
⛽	76 (LP), BP (ATM, LP) Exxon, Shell (D, 24h)

65 mph

EXIT 94 **204**
Savannah Pembroke

✕	El Potro Mexican Hooters, Huddle House Subway Shell House Seafood Waffle House
⛽	Chevron (D, ATM) Shell (ATM)
🏨	EconoLodge Microtel Inn & Suites Super 8, Travelodge

🏨	Best Value Inn Best Western Clarion Inn & Suites Comfort Inn & Suites Country Inn & Suites Days Inn, Fairfield Inn Hampton Inn Holiday Inn Exp & Suites Howard Johnson (P) La Quinta (P) Quality Inn Red Roof Inn & Suites Sleep Inn, Wingate Inn

Ogeechee River

70 mph

EXIT 90 **144**
Old Clyde Rd

⛽	Shell (D, RV, ATM)
🚌	Dick Gore's RV World

🖐	Fort McAllister State Park
✕	Frank's BBQ
⛽	Chevron (ATM)

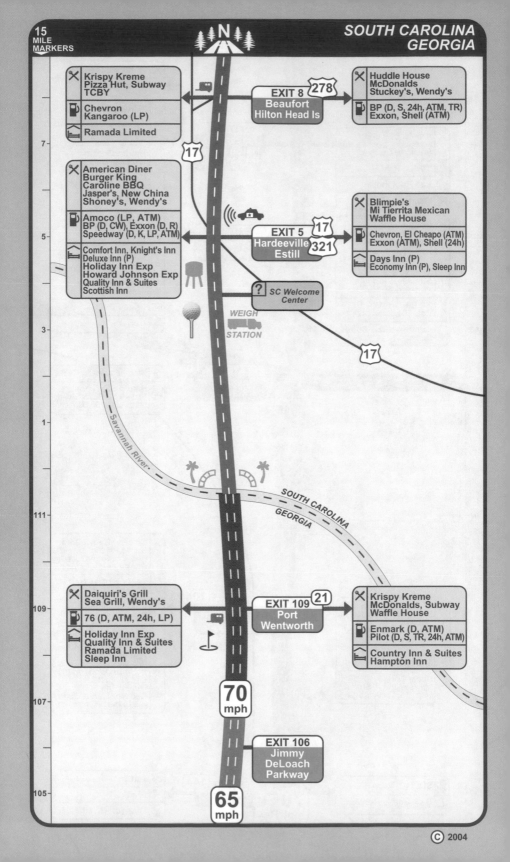

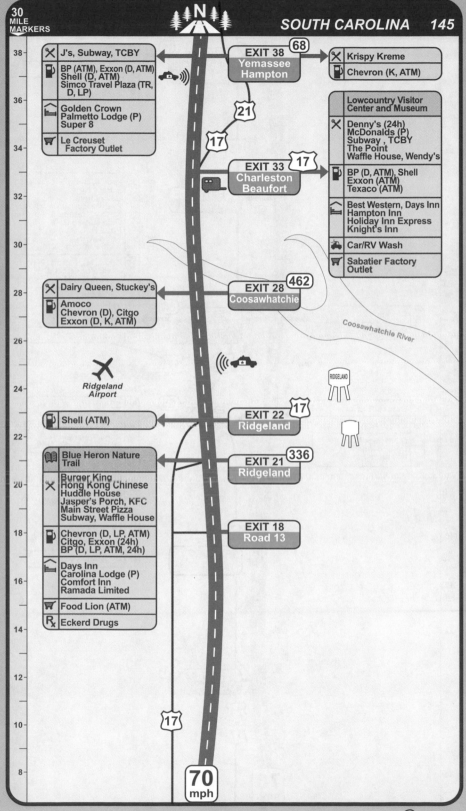

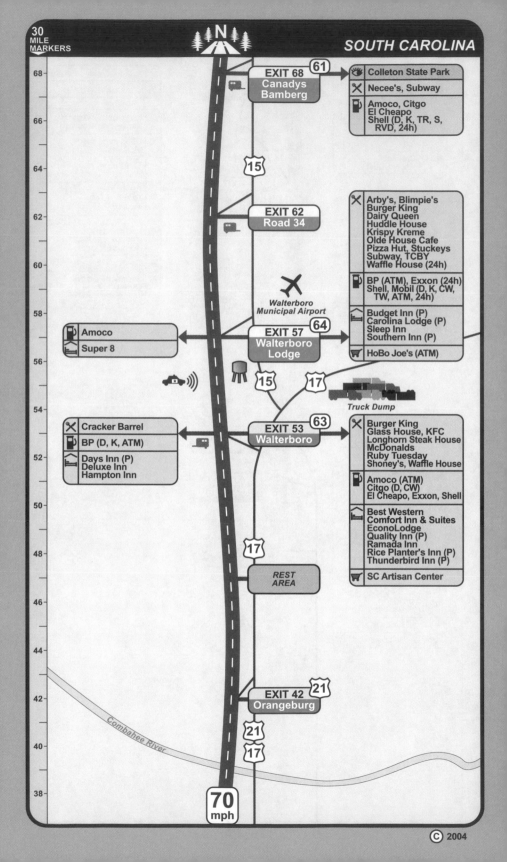

68

EXIT 68 `61`
Canadys
Bamberg

✋ Colleton State Park

✕ Necee's, Subway

⛽ Amoco, Citgo
El Cheapo
Shell (D, K, TR, S,
    RVD, 24h)

66

`15`

64

EXIT 62
Road 34

62

✕ Arby's, Blimpie's
Burger King
Dairy Queen
Huddle House
Krispy Kreme
Olde House Cafe
Pizza Hut, Stuckeys
Subway, TCBY
Waffle House (24h)

60

✈
Walterboro
Municipal Airport

⛽ BP (ATM), Exxon (24h)
Shell, Mobil (D, K, CW,
    TW, ATM, 24h)

58

⛽ Amoco

🛏 Super 8

EXIT 57 `64`
Walterboro
Lodge

🛏 Budget Inn (P)
Carolina Lodge (P)
Sleep Inn
Southern Inn (P)

🛒 HoBo Joe's (ATM)

56

`15`   `17`

54

🚗)))

Truck Dump

✕ Cracker Barrel

⛽ BP (D, K, ATM)

🛏 Days Inn (P)
Deluxe Inn
Hampton Inn

EXIT 53 `63`
Walterboro

52

✕ Burger King
Glass House, KFC
Longhorn Steak House
McDonalds
Ruby Tuesday
Shoney's, Waffle House

⛽ Amoco (ATM)
Citgo (D, CW)
El Cheapo, Exxon, Shell

50

🛏 Best Western
Comfort Inn & Suites
EconoLodge
Quality Inn (P)
Ramada Inn
Rice Planter's Inn (P)
Thunderbird Inn (P)

48

`17`

🛒 SC Artisan Center

REST
AREA

46

44

42

EXIT 42 `21`
Orangeburg

Combahee River

`21`

40

`17`

38

70
mph

© 2004

N

EXIT 98 — 6
Eutawville
Santee

210

Santee State Park

Burger King
Clark's Family Rest.
Cracker Barrel
Krispy Kreme
Maurice's BBQ
McDonald's (P)
Peking Chinese
Pizza Hut, TCBY
Waffle House, Wendy's

Citgo (K), Exxon (LP)
Hess (ATM, D, K)
Horizon (D, K, ATM)
Shell (ATM, D, R, 24h)

Budget Motel
Clark's Inn, Comfort Inn
Country Inn & Suites
Mansion Park
Quality Inn & Suites
Santee Economy Inn
State Park Cabins

Bojangles, El Pueblo
Huddle House
KFC, Pizza Hut
Santee Seafood
Shoney's, Thai House
Theo's Italian
Verandah Seafood

BP Amoco (ATM)
Chevron (BP, K, 24h, ATM)
Citgo (K)
Texaco (D, LP, CW)

Best Western
Days Inn (P)
Hampton Inn (P)
Howard Johnson Exp
Ramada (P), Super 8
Travelodge

EXIT 93 — 15
Santee
Elloree

15

Piggly-Wiggly
Russell Stover Outlet
Santee Outlets
Smith's Pecans

EXIT 90 — 176
Holly Hill
Cameron

Exxon (D, ATM)

210

26

EXIT 86 — 26
Charleston
Columbia

EXIT 82 — 178
Harleyville
Bowman

Shell (D)

Dairy Queen
Stuckey's
Wendy's

Amoco
Hess (D, LP, 24h)
Wilco Trvl Ctr (D, S, 24h)

Peachtree Inn (P)

15

Huddle House
Taco Bell

BP (ATM)
Shell (D, ATM, 24h)

Best Western
Days Inn
Southern Inn (P)
Super 8

EXIT 77 — 78
St. George
Branchville

Empire Chinese
Giorgio's Pizza
Hardee's, KFC
McDonald's (P)
Pizza Hut, Subway
TCBY, Waffle House
Western Sizzlin' Steak

Exxon (ATM)
Shell (K, ATM)

American Inn (P)
Comfort Inn
EconoLodge
Quality Inn (P)

CVS

Food Lion (ATM)

PARKING AREA
(No Services)

Edisto river

15

70 mph

© 2004

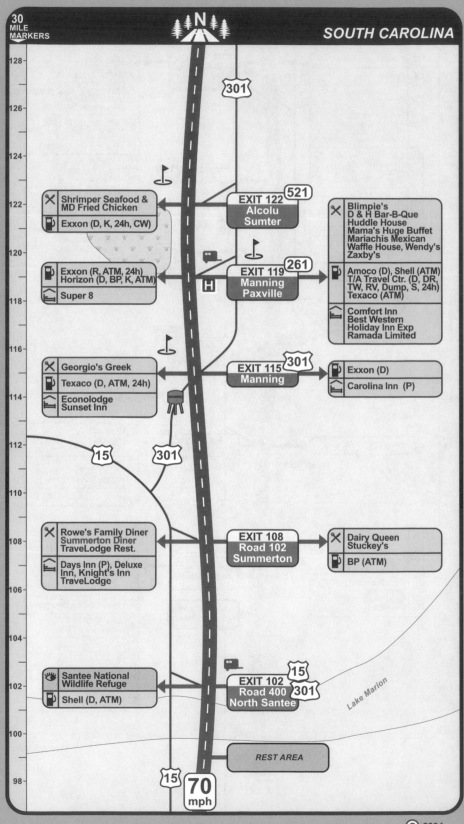

N

301

128
126
124
122

Shrimper Seafood &
MD Fried Chicken

Exxon (D, K, 24h, CW)

EXIT 122 **521**
Alcolu
Sumter

Blimpie's
D & H Bar-B-Que
Huddle House
Mama's Huge Buffet
Mariachis Mexican
Waffle House, Wendy's
Zaxby's

120

Exxon (R, ATM, 24h)
Horizon (D, BP, K, ATM)

Super 8

EXIT 119 **261**
Manning
Paxville

Amoco (D), Shell (ATM)
T/A Travel Ctr. (D, DR,
TW, RV, Dump, S, 24h)
Texaco (ATM)

Comfort Inn
Best Western
Holiday Inn Exp
Ramada Limited

118
116

Georgio's Greek

Texaco (D, ATM, 24h)

Econolodge
Sunset Inn

EXIT 115 **301**
Manning

Exxon (D)

Carolina Inn (P)

114

112

15   **301**

110

108

Rowe's Family Diner
Summerton Diner
TraveLodge Rest.

Days Inn (P), Deluxe
Inn, Knight's Inn
TraveLodge

EXIT 108
Road 102
Summerton

Dairy Queen
Stuckey's

BP (ATM)

106
104
102

Santee National
Wildlife Refuge

Shell (D, ATM)

EXIT 102 **15**
Road 400 **301**
North Santee

Lake Marion

100

REST AREA

98

15 **70**
mph

© 2004

N

55 mph

158

156

154

152

150

148

146

144

142

140

138

136

134

132

130

128

| Carol's / Young's Plantation Inn |
| Sunoco |
| Tree Top Inn / Young's Plantation Inn |

76

HONDA

EXIT 157 76
Florence
Timmonsville

| McDonald's / Swamp Fox Diner / Waffle House |
| Amoco (R,LP,Tow/24h) / Exxon (ATM), Philips 66 / Texaco (D,LP,24h,ATM) |
| Days Inn / Howard Johnson Exp / & Suites, Swampfox / Inn, Villager Lodge |

Florence

EXIT 153
Honda Way

| Darrell's Diner |
| Exxon (D) |

EXIT 150 403
Sardis
Timmonsville

| BP (D, 24h) |
| Budget Inn |

403

76

EXIT 146 341
Olanta
Lynchburg

| Relax Inn |

53

301

| Shell (K) |

EXIT 141 53
Shiloh 58

| Exxon (D, K) |
| Don Mar RV Sales & / Sevice |

REST AREA

53

| Exxon (D, ATM) |

EXIT 135 378
Sumter
Turbeville

| Compass / Eagle's Nest |
| BP (D) / Citgo (24h) |
| Days Inn / Knight's Inn |

378

EXIT 132 527
Sardinia
Bishopville

Black River

301

70 mph

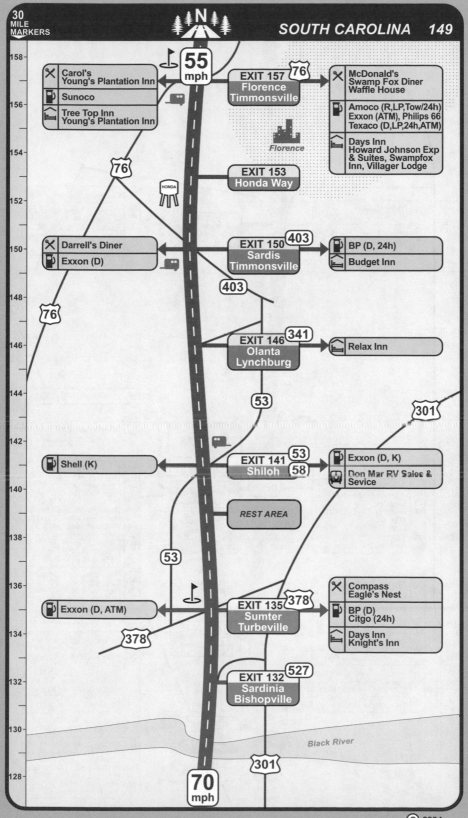

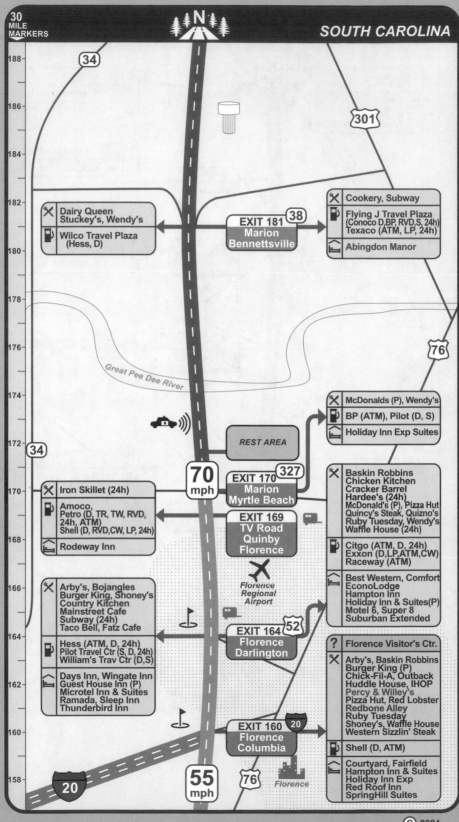

188 —
186 —
184 —

34

301

182 —

✗ Dairy Queen
Stuckey's, Wendy's

⛽ Wilco Travel Plaza
(Hess, D)

EXIT 181
Marion
Bennettsville
38

✗ Cookery, Subway

⛽ Flying J Travel Plaza
(Conoco D,BP, RVD,S, 24h)
Texaco (ATM, LP, 24h)

🏨 Abingdon Manor

180 —
178 —
176 —

76

Great Pee Dee River

174 —
172 —

✗ McDonalds (P), Wendy's

⛽ BP (ATM), Pilot (D, S)

🏨 Holiday Inn Exp Suites

34

REST AREA

170 —

70
mph

EXIT 170
Marion
Myrtle Beach
327

✗ Iron Skillet (24h)

⛽ Amoco,
Petro (D, TR, TW, RVD,
24h, ATM)
Shell (D, RVD,CW, LP, 24h)

🏨 Rodeway Inn

EXIT 169
TV Road
Quinby
Florence

✗ Baskin Robbins
Chicken Kitchen
Cracker Barrel
Hardee's (24h)
McDonald's (P), Pizza Hut
Quincy's Steak, Quizno's
Ruby Tuesday, Wendy's
Waffle House (24h)

⛽ Citgo (ATM, D, 24h)
Exxon (D,LP,ATM,CW)
Raceway (ATM)

168 —

Florence
Regional
Airport

🏨 Best Western, Comfort
EconoLodge
Hampton Inn
Holiday Inn & Suites(P)
Motel 6, Super 8
Suburban Extended

166 —

✗ Arby's, Bojangles
Burger King, Shoney's
Country Kitchen
Mainstreet Cafe
Subway (24h)
Taco Bell, Fatz Cafe

EXIT 164
Florence
Darlington
52

? Florence Visitor's Ctr.

164 —

⛽ Hess (ATM, D, 24h)
Pilot Travel Ctr (S, D, 24h)
William's Trav Ctr (D,S)

✗ Arby's, Baskin Robbins
Burger King (P)
Chick-Fil-A, Outback
Huddle House, IHOP
Percy & Willey's
Pizza Hut, Red Lobster
Redbone Alley
Ruby Tuesday
Shoney's, Waffle House
Western Sizzlin' Steak

162 —

🏨 Days Inn, Wingate Inn
Guest House Inn (P)
Microtel Inn & Suites
Ramada, Sleep Inn
Thunderbird Inn

160 —

EXIT 160
Florence
Columbia
20

⛽ Shell (D, ATM)

🏨 Courtyard, Fairfield
Hampton Inn & Suites
Holiday Inn Exp
Red Roof Inn
SpringHill Suites

158 —

20

55
mph

76

Florence

© 2004

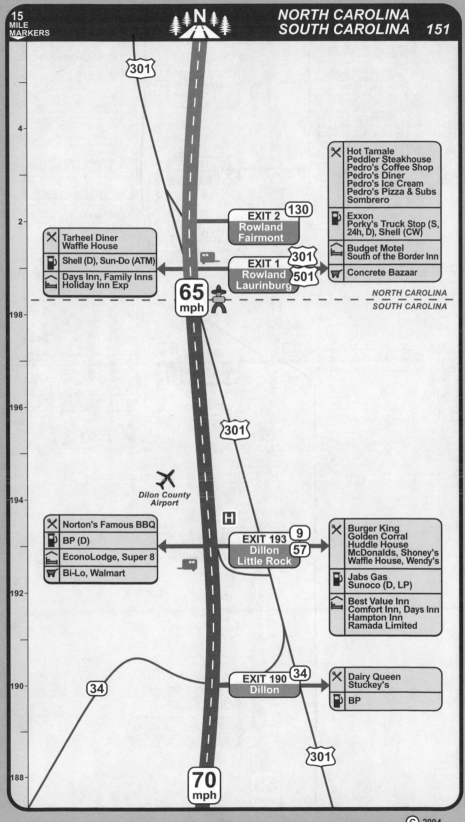

301

EXIT 2 130
Rowland
Fairmont

✕ Hot Tamale
Peddler Steakhouse
Pedro's Coffee Shop
Pedro's Diner
Pedro's Ice Cream
Pedro's Pizza & Subs
Sombrero

⛽ Exxon
Porky's Truck Stop (S, 24h, D), Shell (CW)

🛏 Budget Motel
South of the Border Inn

🛒 Concrete Bazaar

✕ Tarheel Diner
Waffle House

⛽ Shell (D), Sun-Do (ATM)

🛏 Days Inn, Family Inns
Holiday Inn Exp

EXIT 1 301
Rowland 501
Laurinburg

65 mph

NORTH CAROLINA
SOUTH CAROLINA

198

196

301

194

Dilon County
Airport

H

✕ Norton's Famous BBQ
⛽ BP (D)
🛏 EconoLodge, Super 8
🛒 Bi-Lo, Walmart

EXIT 193 9
Dillon 57
Little Rock

✕ Burger King
Golden Corral
Huddle House
McDonalds, Shoney's
Waffle House, Wendy's

⛽ Jabs Gas
Sunoco (D, LP)

🛏 Best Value Inn
Comfort Inn, Days Inn
Hampton Inn
Ramada Limited

192

34

190

EXIT 190 34
Dillon

✕ Dairy Queen
Stuckey's

⛽ BP

301

188

70 mph

© 2004

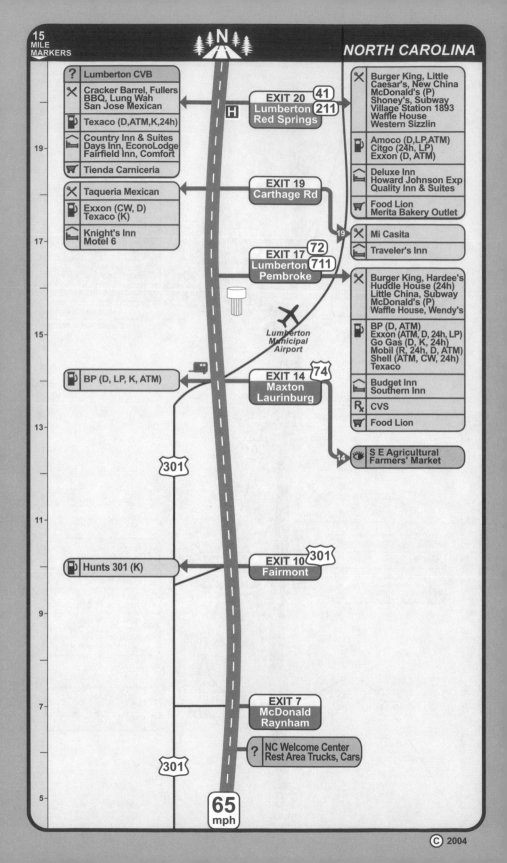

North

? Lumberton CVB

✕ Cracker Barrel, Fullers BBQ, Lung Wah San Jose Mexican

⛽ Texaco (D, ATM, K, 24h)

🛏 Country Inn & Suites Days Inn, EconoLodge Fairfield Inn, Comfort

🛒 Tienda Carniceria

EXIT 20 (41) (211)
Lumberton Red Springs

H

✕ Burger King, Little Caesar's, New China McDonald's (P) Shoney's, Subway Village Station 1893 Waffle House Western Sizzlin

⛽ Amoco (D, LP, ATM) Citgo (24h, LP) Exxon (D, ATM)

🛏 Deluxe Inn Howard Johnson Exp Quality Inn & Suites

🛒 Food Lion Merita Bakery Outlet

✕ Taqueria Mexican

⛽ Exxon (CW, D) Texaco (K)

🛏 Knight's Inn Motel 6

EXIT 19
Carthage Rd

19 **✕ Mi Casita**

🛏 Traveler's Inn

EXIT 17 (72) (711)
Lumberton Pembroke

✕ Burger King, Hardee's Huddle House (24h) Little China, Subway McDonald's (P) Waffle House, Wendy's

⛽ BP (D, ATM) Exxon (ATM, D, 24h, LP) Go Gas (D, K, 24h) Mobil (R, 24h, D, ATM) Shell (ATM, CW, 24h) Texaco

🛏 Budget Inn Southern Inn

Rx CVS

🛒 Food Lion

Lumberton Municipal Airport

⛽ BP (D, LP, K, ATM)

EXIT 14 (74)
Maxton Laurinburg

14 **👁 S E Agricultural Farmers' Market**

301

⛽ Hunts 301 (K)

EXIT 10 (301)
Fairmont

EXIT 7
McDonald Raynham

? NC Welcome Center Rest Area Trucks, Cars

301

65 mph

© 2004

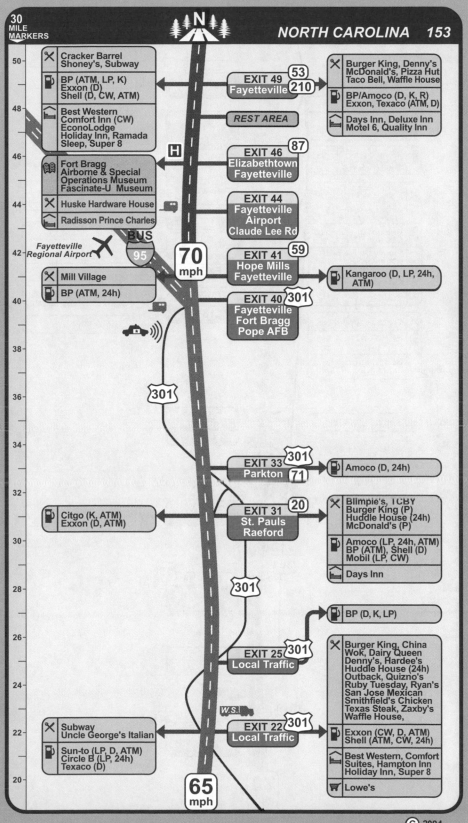

- 50
- 48
- 46
- 44
- 42
- 40
- 38
- 36
- 34
- 32
- 30
- 28
- 26
- 24
- 22
- 20

Cracker Barrel Shoney's, Subway

BP (ATM, LP, K) Exxon (D) Shell (D, CW, ATM)

Best Western Comfort Inn (CW) EconoLodge Holiday Inn, Ramada Sleep, Super 8

Fort Bragg Airborne & Special Operations Museum Fascinate-U Museum

Huske Hardware House

Radisson Prince Charles

Fayetteville Regional Airport

Mill Village

BP (ATM, 24h)

Citgo (K, ATM) Exxon (D, ATM)

Subway Uncle George's Italian

Sun-to (LP, D, ATM) Circle B (LP, 24h) Texaco (D)

EXIT 49 Fayetteville **53 210**

REST AREA

H

EXIT 46 Elizabethtown Fayetteville **87**

EXIT 44 Fayetteville Airport Claude Lee Rd

EXIT 41 Hope Mills Fayetteville **59**

EXIT 40 Fayetteville Fort Bragg Pope AFB **US 301**

BUS 95

70 mph

301

EXIT 33 Parkton **301 71**

EXIT 31 St. Pauls Raeford **20**

301

EXIT 25 Local Traffic **US 301**

301

W.S.

EXIT 22 Local Traffic **US 301**

65 mph

Burger King, Denny's McDonald's, Pizza Hut Taco Bell, Waffle House

BP/Amoco (D, K, R) Exxon, Texaco (ATM, D)

Days Inn, Deluxe Inn Motel 6, Quality Inn

Kangaroo (D, LP, 24h, ATM)

Amoco (D, 24h)

Blimpie's, TCBY Burger King (P) Huddle House (24h) McDonald's (P)

Amoco (LP, 24h, ATM) BP (ATM), Shell (D) Mobil (LP, CW)

Days Inn

BP (D, K, LP)

Burger King, China Wok, Dairy Queen Denny's, Hardee's Huddle House (24h) Outback, Quizno's Ruby Tuesday, Ryan's San Jose Mexican Smithfield's Chicken Texas Steak, Zaxby's Waffle House,

Exxon (CW, D, ATM) Shell (ATM, CW, 24h)

Best Western, Comfort Suites, Hampton Inn Holiday Inn, Super 8

Lowe's

© 2004

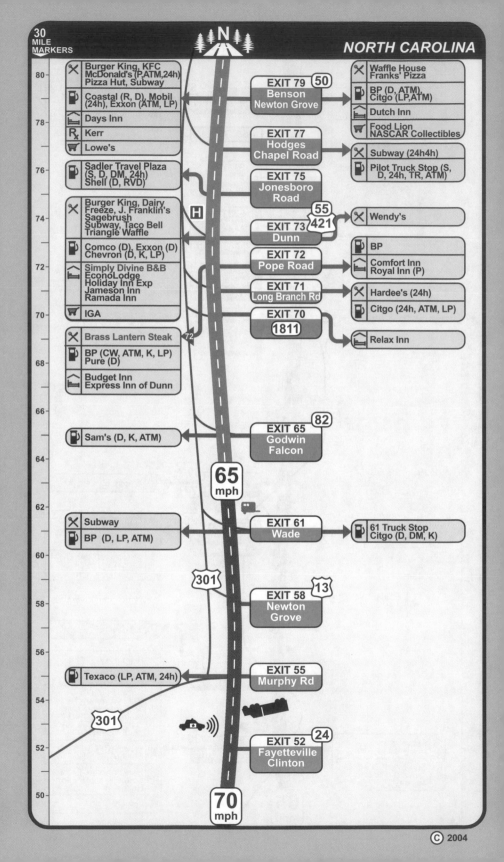

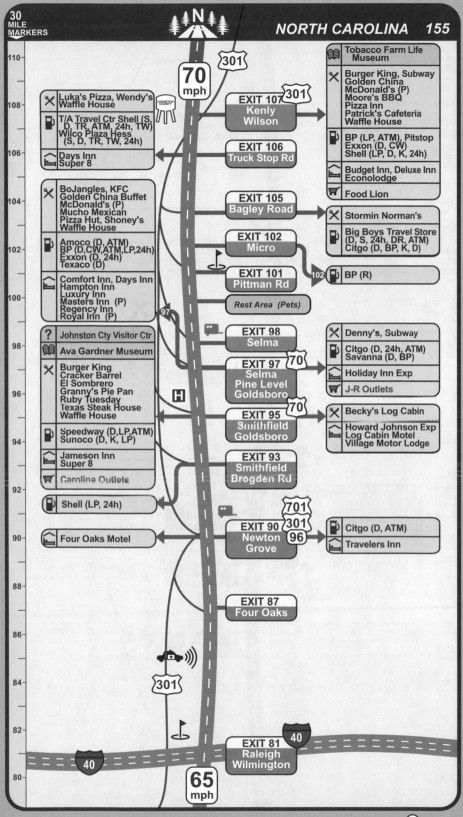

N

301

70 mph

JOHNSTON COUNTY

EXIT 107 — Kenly / Wilson — 301

EXIT 106 — Truck Stop Rd

EXIT 105 — Bagley Road

EXIT 102 — Micro

EXIT 101 — Pittman Rd

Rest Area (Pets)

EXIT 98 — Selma

EXIT 97 — Selma / Pine Level / Goldsboro — 70

EXIT 95 — Smithfield / Goldsboro — 70

EXIT 93 — Smithfield / Brogden Rd

EXIT 90 — Newton Grove — 701 / 301 / 96

EXIT 87 — Four Oaks

301

EXIT 81 — Raleigh / Wilmington — 40

40

65 mph

West side (left):

- ✕ Luka's Pizza, Wendy's, Waffle House
- ⛽ T/A Travel Ctr Shell (S, D, TR, ATM, 24h, TW), Wilco Plaza Hess (S, D, TR, TW, 24h)
- 🛏 Days Inn, Super 8

- ✕ BoJangles, KFC, Golden China Buffet, McDonald's (P), Mucho Mexican, Pizza Hut, Shoney's, Waffle House
- ⛽ Amoco (D, ATM), BP (D,CW,ATM,LP,24h), Exxon (D, 24h), Texaco (D)
- 🛏 Comfort Inn, Days Inn, Hampton Inn, Luxury Inn, Masters Inn (P), Regency Inn (P), Royal Inn (P)

- ? Johnston Cty Visitor Ctr
- 📖 Ava Gardner Museum
- ✕ Burger King, Cracker Barrel, El Sombrero, Granny's Pie Pan, Ruby Tuesday, Texas Steak House, Waffle House
- ⛽ Speedway (D,LP,ATM), Sunoco (D, K, LP)
- 🛏 Jameson Inn, Super 8
- 🛒 Carolina Outlets

- ⛽ Shell (LP, 24h)

- 🛏 Four Oaks Motel

East side (right):

- 📖 Tobacco Farm Life Museum
- ✕ Burger King, Subway, Golden China, McDonald's (P), Moore's BBQ, Pizza Inn, Patrick's Cafeteria, Waffle House
- ⛽ BP (LP, ATM), Pitstop, Exxon (D, CW), Shell (LP, D, K, 24h)
- 🛏 Budget Inn, Deluxe Inn, Econolodge
- 🛒 Food Lion

- ✕ Stormin Norman's
- ⛽ Big Boys Travel Store (D, S, 24h, DR, ATM), Citgo (D, BP, K, D)

- 102 ⛽ BP (R)

- ✕ Denny's, Subway
- ⛽ Citgo (D, 24h, ATM), Savanna (D, BP)
- 🛏 Holiday Inn Exp
- 🛒 J-R Outlets

- ✕ Becky's Log Cabin
- 🛏 Howard Johnson Exp, Log Cabin Motel, Village Motor Lodge

- ⛽ Citgo (D, ATM)
- 🛏 Travelers Inn

© 2004

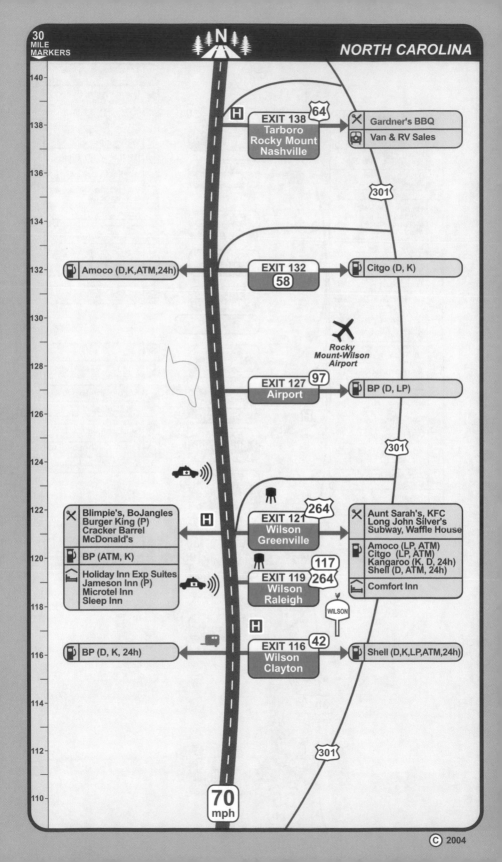

N

EXIT 138 64
Tarboro
Rocky Mount
Nashville

Gardner's BBQ
Van & RV Sales

301

Amoco (D,K,ATM,24h)

EXIT 132
58

Citgo (D, K)

Rocky
Mount-Wilson
Airport

EXIT 127 97
Airport

BP (D, LP)

301

EXIT 121 264
Wilson
Greenville

Aunt Sarah's, KFC
Long John Silver's
Subway, Waffle House

Amoco (LP, ATM)
Citgo (LP, ATM)
Kangaroo (K, D, 24h)
Shell (D, ATM, 24h)

Comfort Inn

Blimpie's, BoJangles
Burger King (P)
Cracker Barrel
McDonald's

BP (ATM, K)

Holiday Inn Exp Suites
Jameson Inn (P)
Microtel Inn
Sleep Inn

EXIT 119 117
264
Wilson
Raleigh

WILSON

EXIT 116 42
Wilson
Clayton

BP (D, K, 24h)

Shell (D,K,LP,ATM,24h)

301

70 mph

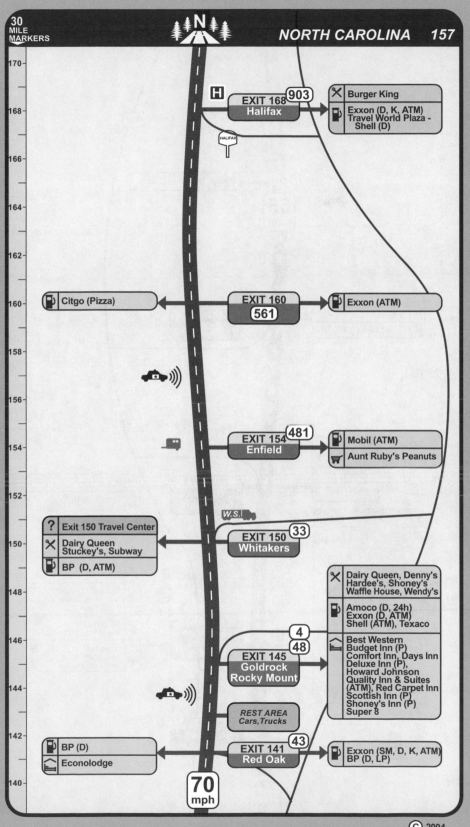

H EXIT 168 ⟨903⟩
Halifax

- ✗ Burger King
- ⛽ Exxon (D, K, ATM)
  Travel World Plaza - Shell (D)

HALIFAX

⛽ Citgo (Pizza)

EXIT 160
⟨561⟩

⛽ Exxon (ATM)

EXIT 154 ⟨481⟩
Enfield

- ⛽ Mobil (ATM)
- 🛒 Aunt Ruby's Peanuts

W.S.

- ❓ Exit 150 Travel Center
- ✗ Dairy Queen
  Stuckey's, Subway
- ⛽ BP (D, ATM)

EXIT 150 ⟨33⟩
Whitakers

- ✗ Dairy Queen, Denny's
  Hardee's, Shoney's
  Waffle House, Wendy's
- ⛽ Amoco (D, 24h)
  Exxon (D, ATM)
  Shell (ATM), Texaco
- 🏠 Best Western
  Budget Inn (P)
  Comfort Inn, Days Inn
  Deluxe Inn (P),
  Howard Johnson
  Quality Inn & Suites
  (ATM), Red Carpet Inn
  Scottish Inn (P)
  Shoney's Inn (P)
  Super 8

⟨4⟩
⟨48⟩
EXIT 145
Goldrock
Rocky Mount

REST AREA
Cars, Trucks

- ⛽ BP (D)
- 🏠 Econolodge

EXIT 141 ⟨43⟩
Red Oak

- ⛽ Exxon (SM, D, K, ATM)
  BP (D, LP)

70
mph

© 2004

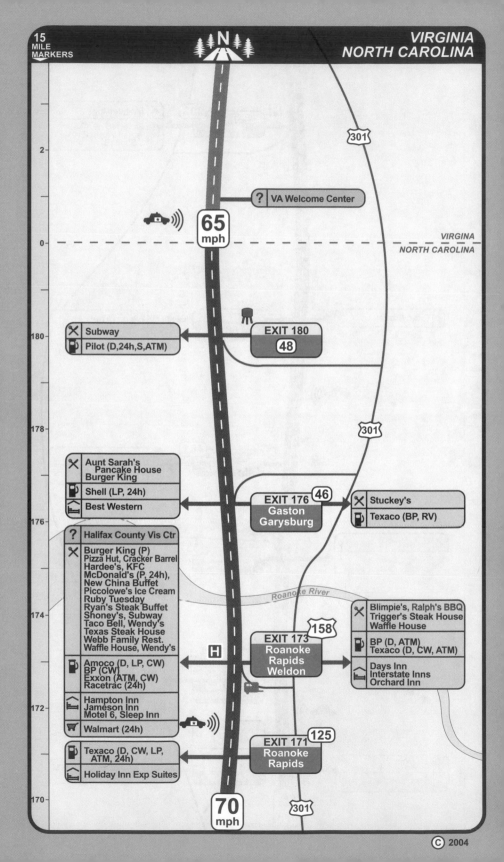

| 301 |

| ? | VA Welcome Center |

65 mph

VIRGINA
NORTH CAROLINA

| 301 |

| Subway |
| Pilot (D,24h,S,ATM) |

EXIT 180
48

| Aunt Sarah's Pancake House Burger King |
| Shell (LP, 24h) |
| Best Western |

EXIT 176 **46**
Gaston
Garysburg

| Stuckey's |
| Texaco (BP, RV) |

| ? | Halifax County Vis Ctr |
| Burger King (P) Pizza Hut, Cracker Barrel Hardee's, KFC McDonald's (P, 24h), New China Buffet Piccolowe's Ice Cream Ruby Tuesday Ryan's Steak Buffet Shoney's, Subway Taco Bell, Wendy's Texas Steak House Webb Family Rest. Waffle House, Wendy's |
| Amoco (D, LP, CW) BP (CW) Exxon (ATM, CW) Racetrac (24h) |
| Hampton Inn Jameson Inn Motel 6, Sleep Inn |
| Walmart (24h) |
| Texaco (D, CW, LP, ATM, 24h) |
| Holiday Inn Exp Suites |

Roanoke River

| Blimpie's, Ralph's BBQ Trigger's Steak House Waffle House |
| BP (D, ATM) Texaco (D, CW, ATM) |
| Days Inn Interstate Inns Orchard Inn |

EXIT 173 **158**
Roanoke
Rapids
Weldon

H

EXIT 171 **125**
Roanoke
Rapids

70 mph

| 301 |

© 2004

N

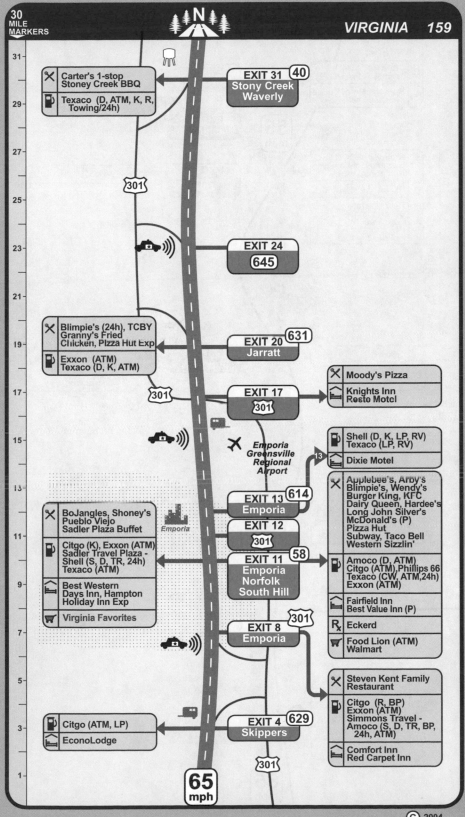

EXIT 31 (40)
Stony Creek Waverly

- Carter's 1-stop Stoney Creek BBQ
- Texaco (D, ATM, K, R, Towing/24h)

301

EXIT 24 (645)

EXIT 20 (631)
Jarratt

- Blimpie's (24h), TCBY Granny's Fried Chicken, Pizza Hut Exp
- Exxon (ATM) Texaco (D, K, ATM)

301

EXIT 17 (301)

- Moody's Pizza
- Knights Inn Resto Motel

Emporia Greensville Regional Airport

(13)
- Shell (D, K, LP, RV) Texaco (LP, RV)
- Dixie Motel

EXIT 13 (614)
Emporia

- Applebee's, Arby's Blimpie's, Wendy's Burger King, KFC Dairy Queen, Hardee's Long John Silver's McDonald's (P) Pizza Hut Subway, Taco Bell Western Sizzlin'

EXIT 12 (301)

- BoJangles, Shoney's Pueblo Viejo Sadler Plaza Buffet
- Citgo (K), Exxon (ATM) Sadler Travel Plaza - Shell (S, D, TR, 24h) Texaco (ATM)
- Best Western Days Inn, Hampton Holiday Inn Exp
- Virginia Favorites

Emporia

EXIT 11 (58)
Emporia Norfolk South Hill

- Amoco (D, ATM) Citgo (ATM), Phillips 66 Texaco (CW, ATM, 24h) Exxon (ATM)
- Fairfield Inn Best Value Inn (P)
- Eckerd
- Food Lion (ATM) Walmart

EXIT 8 (301)
Emporia

- Steven Kent Family Restaurant
- Citgo (R, BP) Exxon (ATM) Simmons Travel - Amoco (S, D, TR, BP, 24h, ATM)
- Comfort Inn Red Carpet Inn

EXIT 4 (629)
Skippers

- Citgo (ATM, LP)
- EconoLodge

301

65 mph

© 2004

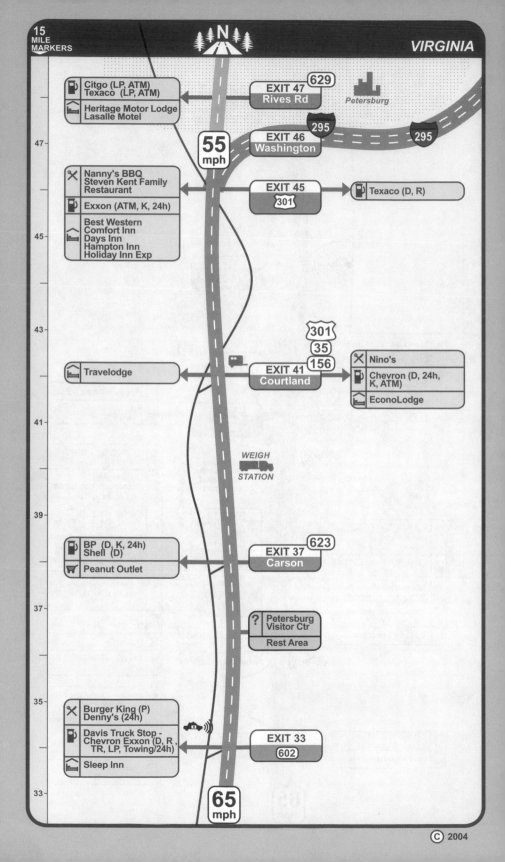

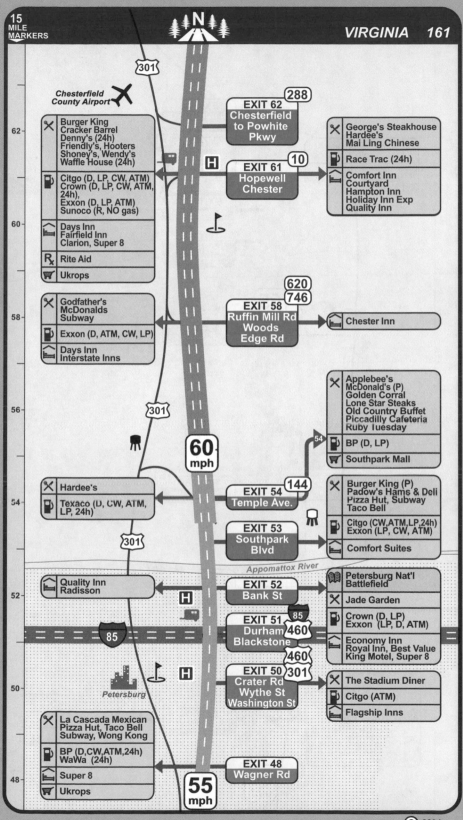

301

Chesterfield
County Airport ✈

62

✗ Burger King
Cracker Barrel
Denny's (24h)
Friendly's, Hooters
Shoney's, Wendy's
Waffle House (24h)

🛢 Citgo (D, LP, CW, ATM)
Crown (D, LP, CW, ATM, 24h),
Exxon (D, LP, ATM)
Sunoco (R, NO gas)

60

🛏 Days Inn
Fairfield Inn
Clarion, Super 8

℞ Rite Aid

🛒 Ukrops

58

✗ Godfather's
McDonalds
Subway

🛢 Exxon (D, ATM, CW, LP)

🛏 Days Inn
Interstate Inns

56

301

60 mph

54

✗ Hardee's

🛢 Texaco (D, CW, ATM, LP, 24h)

301

52

🛏 Quality Inn
Radisson

85

50

Petersburg

✗ La Cascada Mexican
Pizza Hut, Taco Bell
Subway, Wong Kong

🛢 BP (D,CW,ATM,24h)
WaWa (24h)

🛏 Super 8

🛒 Ukrops

48

55 mph

EXIT 62 288
Chesterfield
to Powhite
Pkwy

H

EXIT 61 10
Hopewell
Chester

EXIT 58 620 746
Ruffin Mill Rd
Woods
Edge Rd

54

EXIT 54 144
Temple Ave.

EXIT 53
Southpark
Blvd

Appomattox River

H

EXIT 52
Bank St

EXIT 51 85
Durham 460
Blackstone

460

EXIT 50 301
Crater Rd
Wythe St
Washington St

H

EXIT 48
Wagner Rd

✗ George's Steakhouse
Hardee's
Mai Ling Chinese

🛢 Race Trac (24h)

🛏 Comfort Inn
Courtyard
Hampton Inn
Holiday Inn Exp
Quality Inn

🛏 Chester Inn

✗ Applebee's
McDonald's (P)
Golden Corral
Lone Star Steaks
Old Country Buffet
Piccadilly Cafeteria
Ruby Tuesday

🛢 BP (D, LP)

🛒 Southpark Mall

✗ Burger King (P)
Padow's Hams & Deli
Pizza Hut, Subway
Taco Bell

🛢 Citgo (CW,ATM,LP,24h)
Exxon (LP, CW, ATM)

🛏 Comfort Suites

📖 Petersburg Nat'l
Battlefield

✗ Jade Garden

🛢 Crown (D, LP)
Exxon (LP, D, ATM)

🛏 Economy Inn
Royal Inn, Best Value
King Motel, Super 8

✗ The Stadium Diner

🛢 Citgo (ATM)

🛏 Flagship Inns

© 2004

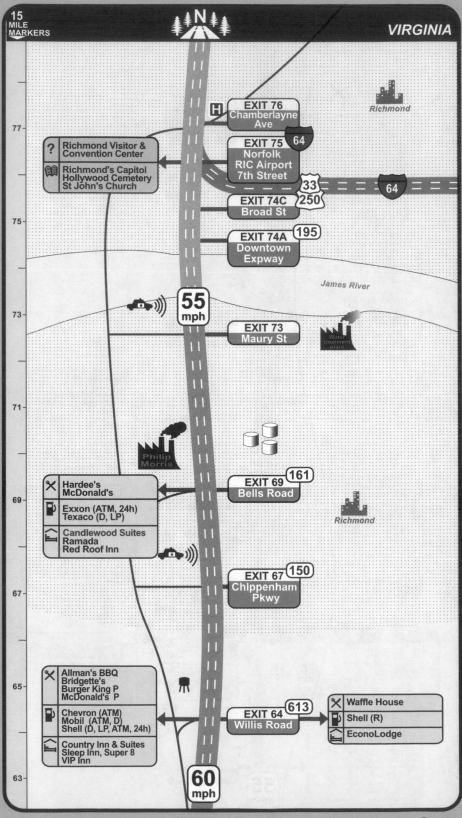

N

77 -

EXIT 76
Chamberlayne Ave

Richmond

? Richmond Visitor & Convention Center

EXIT 75   64
Norfolk
RIC Airport
7th Street

Richmond's Capitol
Hollywood Cemetery
St John's Church

33   64
250

EXIT 74C
Broad St

75 -

EXIT 74A   195
Downtown
Expway

James River

55 mph

73 -

EXIT 73
Maury St

Water treatment plant

71 -

Philip Morris

Hardee's
McDonald's

EXIT 69   161
Bells Road

Richmond

Exxon (ATM, 24h)
Texaco (D, LP)

69 -

Candlewood Suites
Ramada
Red Roof Inn

EXIT 67   150
Chippenham
Pkwy

67 -

65 -

Allman's BBQ
Bridgette's
Burger King P
McDonald's P

Waffle House

Chevron (ATM)
Mobil (ATM, D)
Shell (D, LP, ATM, 24h)

EXIT 64   613
Willis Road

Shell (R)

Country Inn & Suites
Sleep Inn, Super 8
VIP Inn

EconoLodge

63 -

60 mph

N

📖 Historic Ashland

✕ Arby's, Buckhorn
Burger King, KFC
Cracker Barrel
Homemades by Suzanne
Los Amigos Mexican
McDonald's
Ponderosa
Smoking Pig BBQ
Subway, Ruby Tuesday
Waffle House (24h)

⛽ BP (CW, ATM)
Citgo (D, ATM)
Exxon (ATM, 24h)
T/A Travel Ctr (D, 24h, S, TR), Shell (ATM)
Texaco (LP, CW)

🛏 Ashland Inn
Budget Inn, Days Inn
Super 8, EconoLodge
Hampton inn
Henry Clay Inn
Holiday Inn Exp
Microtel Inn & Suites
Travelodge

℞ Rite Aid

EXIT 92 (54)
Hanover Ashland
→ ⛽ Mobil (BP, R)

EXIT 89 (802)
Lewistown Road
→ ✕ Country Pride
Pizza Hut, Taco Bell
Quizno's, Krispy Kreme

⛽ Shell (ATM,LP)
T/A Travel Ctr (D, R, S, ATM, 24h)

65 mph

✕ Mama Mia's, Subway
⛽ Texaco (D, ATM, CW)
🛏 Best Western
🛒 Virginia Center Commons

EXIT 86 (656)
Atlee Elmont
→ ✕ McDonald's
⛽ Amoco

📖 Lewis Ginter Botanical Garden

✕ Dairy Queen, Wendy's
El Paso Mexican
Hardee's
McDonald's (P)
River City Diner
Waffle House

⛽ Citgo (ATM)
Exxon, Texaco (D, 24h)

🛏 Holiday Inn, Sleep Inn

🛒 Lowe's
North Park Mall

60 mph

EXIT 84 (295)
Norfolk
Rocky Mount NC
Charlottesville
295

EXIT 83 (73)
Parham Rd
→ ✕ McDonald's (P)
⛽ Mobil (D, ATM, 24h)

EXIT 82 (301)(2)
Chamberlayne Ave
→ 🛏 Quality Inn & Suites
Ramada Limited
Super 8

✕ Little Caesar's Pizza
Top's China
℞ CVS
🛒 Ukrops

EXIT 81 (1)
→ ✕ Arby's, Friendly's,
Pizza Hut
La Casita Mexican
Red House Chinese
Taco Bell

EXIT 80 (161)
Hermitage Rd
Lakeside Ave
→ ⛽ Chevron (D, K, LP, BP, CW, ATM), BP (K, D)
Exxon (CW, ATM,24h)
Texaco (D, LP)

Diamond Stadium **64**

EXIT 79 (64)(195)
Charlottesville
→ 🛏 Travelodge
Town Motel
℞ Walgreens

📖 Virginia State Capitol
✕ Bill's Virginia BBQ
⛽ Citgo (D,ATM)
🛏 Days Inn

H

EXIT 78 (161)
Boulevard
→ ✕ Zippy's
⛽ Texaco (D,LP,K,R,ATM)
🛏 Holiday Inn

55 mph

© 2004

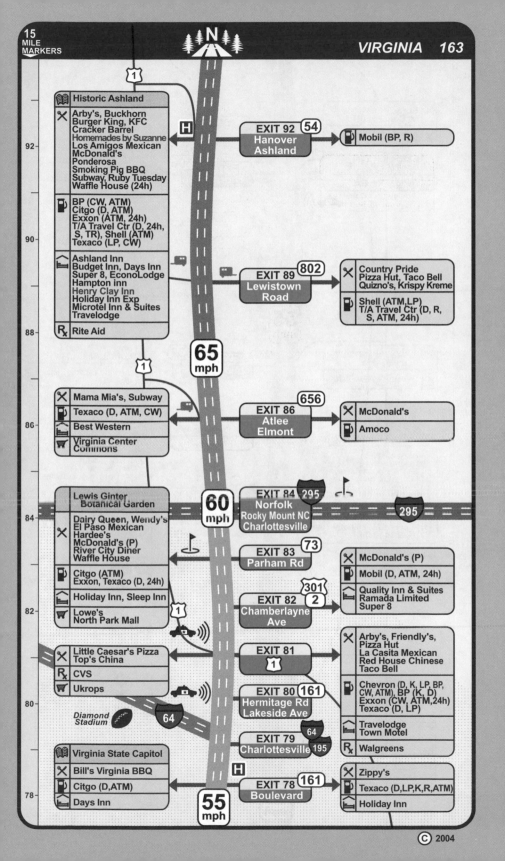

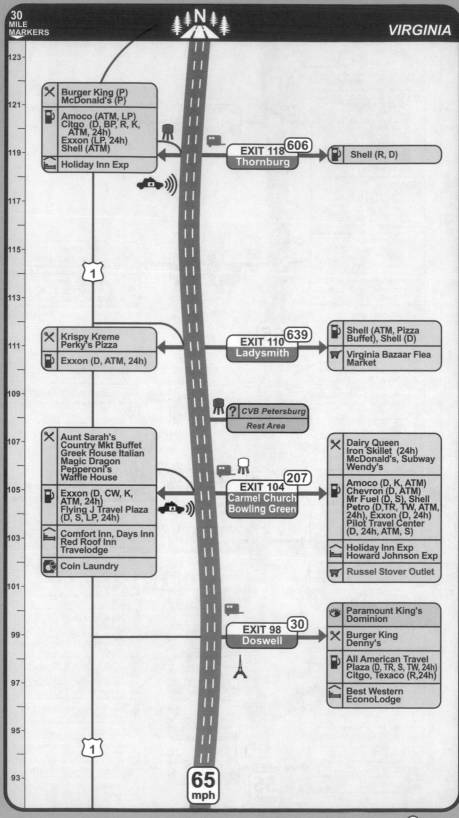

VIRGINIA

N

123
121
119
117
115
113
111
109
107
105
103
101
99
97
95
93

1

Burger King (P)
McDonald's (P)

Amoco (ATM, LP)
Citgo (D, BP, R, K,
ATM, 24h)
Exxon (LP, 24h)
Shell (ATM)

Holiday Inn Exp

EXIT 118 606
Thornburg

Shell (R, D)

Krispy Kreme
Perky's Pizza

Exxon (D, ATM, 24h)

EXIT 110 639
Ladysmith

Shell (ATM, Pizza
Buffet), Shell (D)

Virginia Bazaar Flea
Market

? CVB Petersburg
Rest Area

Aunt Sarah's
Country Mkt Buffet
Greek House Italian
Magic Dragon
Pepperoni's
Waffle House

Exxon (D, CW, K,
ATM, 24h)
Flying J Travel Plaza
(D, S, LP, 24h)

Comfort Inn, Days Inn
Red Roof Inn
Travelodge

Coin Laundry

EXIT 104 207
Carmel Church
Bowling Green

Dairy Queen
Iron Skillet (24h)
McDonald's, Subway
Wendy's

Amoco (D, K, ATM)
Chevron (D, ATM)
Mr Fuel (D, S), Shell
Petro (D,TR, TW, ATM,
24h), Exxon (D, 24h)
Pilot Travel Center
(D, 24h, ATM, S)

Holiday Inn Exp
Howard Johnson Exp

Russel Stover Outlet

EXIT 98 30
Doswell

Paramount King's
Dominion

Burger King
Denny's

All American Travel
Plaza (D, TR, S, TW, 24h)
Citgo, Texaco (R,24h)

Best Western
EconoLodge

1

65
mph

© 2004

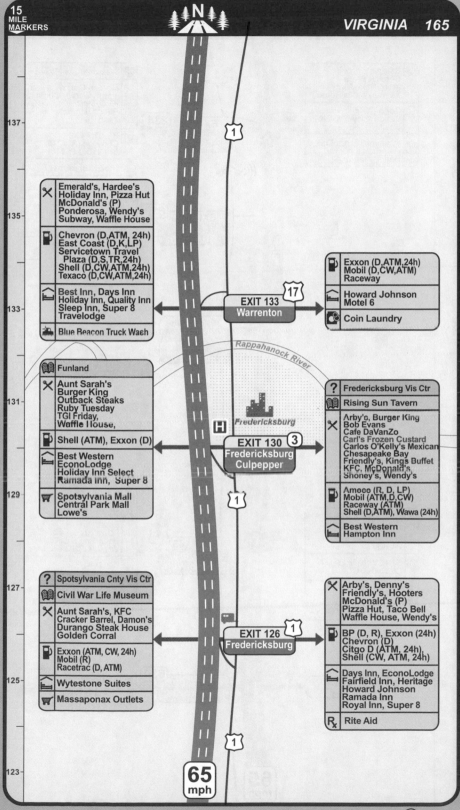

137

1

135
Emerald's, Hardee's
Holiday Inn, Pizza Hut
McDonald's (P)
Ponderosa, Wendy's
Subway, Waffle House

Chevron (D,ATM, 24h)
East Coast (D,K,LP)
Servicetown Travel
  Plaza (D,S,TR,24h)
Shell (D,CW,ATM,24h)
Texaco (D,CW,ATM,24h)

133
Best Inn, Days Inn
Holiday Inn, Quality Inn
Sleep Inn, Super 8
Travelodge

Blue Beacon Truck Wash

EXIT 133
Warrenton

17

Exxon (D,ATM,24h)
Mobil (D,CW,ATM)
Raceway

Howard Johnson
Motel 6

Coin Laundry

Rappahanock River

131
Funland

Aunt Sarah's
Burger King
Outback Steaks
Ruby Tuesday
TGI Friday,
Waffle House,

Shell (ATM), Exxon (D)

Best Western
EconoLodge
Holiday Inn Select
Ramada Inn, Super 8

129
Spotsylvania Mall
Central Park Mall
Lowe's

H

Fredericksburg

EXIT 130
Fredericksburg
Culpepper

3

Fredericksburg Vis Ctr

Rising Sun Tavern

Arby's, Burger King
Bob Evans
Cafe DaVanZo
Carl's Frozen Custard
Carlos O'Kelly's Mexican
Chesapeake Bay
Friendly's, Kings Buffet
KFC, McDonald's,
Shoney's, Wendy's

Amoco (R, D, LP)
Mobil (ATM,D,CW)
Raceway (ATM)
Shell (D,ATM), Wawa (24h)

Best Western
Hampton Inn

127
Spotsylvania Cnty Vis Ctr

Civil War Life Museum

Aunt Sarah's, KFC
Cracker Barrel, Damon's
Durango Steak House
Golden Corral

Exxon (ATM, CW, 24h)
Mobil (R)
Racetrac (D, ATM)

125
Wytestone Suites

Massaponax Outlets

EXIT 126
Fredericksburg

1

Arby's, Denny's
Friendly's, Hooters
McDonald's (P)
Pizza Hut, Taco Bell
Waffle House, Wendy's

BP (D, R), Exxon (24h)
Chevron (D)
Citgo D (ATM, 24h),
Shell (CW, ATM, 24h)

Days Inn, EconoLodge
Fairfield Inn, Heritage
Howard Johnson
Ramada Inn
Royal Inn, Super 8

Rite Aid

1

123

65
mph

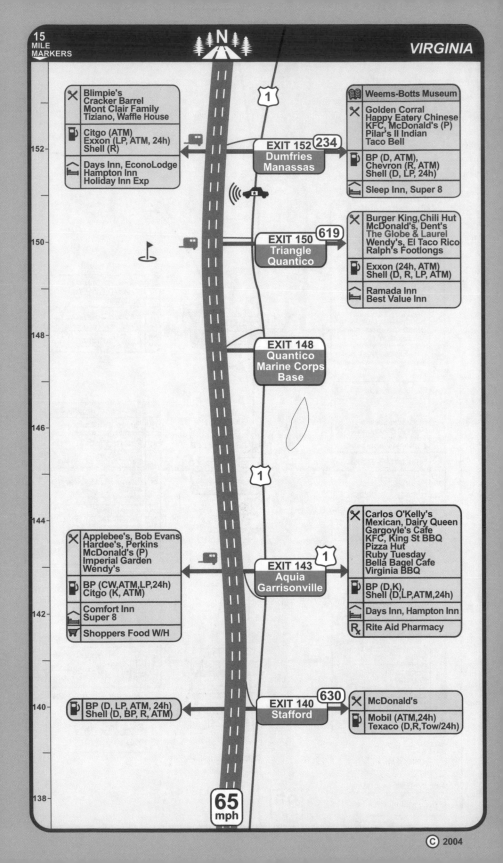

N

1

EXIT 152 (234)
Dumfries
Manassas

Blimpie's
Cracker Barrel
Mont Clair Family
Tiziano, Waffle House

Citgo (ATM)
Exxon (LP, ATM, 24h)
Shell (R)

Days Inn, EconoLodge
Hampton Inn
Holiday Inn Exp

Weems-Botts Museum

Golden Corral
Happy Eatery Chinese
KFC, McDonald's (P)
Pilar's II Indian
Taco Bell

BP (D, ATM),
Chevron (R, ATM)
Shell (D, LP, 24h)

Sleep Inn, Super 8

EXIT 150 (619)
Triangle
Quantico

Burger King,Chili Hut
McDonald's, Dent's
The Globe & Laurel
Wendy's, El Taco Rico
Ralph's Footlongs

Exxon (24h, ATM)
Shell (D, R, LP, ATM)

Ramada Inn
Best Value Inn

EXIT 148
Quantico
Marine Corps
Base

1

EXIT 143
Aquia
Garrisonville

1

Applebee's, Bob Evans
Hardee's, Perkins
McDonald's (P)
Imperial Garden
Wendy's

BP (CW,ATM,LP,24h)
Citgo (K, ATM)

Comfort Inn
Super 8

Shoppers Food W/H

Carlos O'Kelly's
Mexican, Dairy Queen
Gargoyle's Cafe
KFC, King St BBQ
Pizza Hut
Ruby Tuesday
Bella Bagel Cafe
Virginia BBQ

BP (D,K),
Shell (D,LP,ATM,24h)

Days Inn, Hampton Inn

Rite Aid Pharmacy

EXIT 140 (630)
Stafford

BP (D, LP, ATM, 24h)
Shell (D, BP, R, ATM)

McDonald's

Mobil (ATM,24h)
Texaco (D,R,Tow/24h)

65 mph

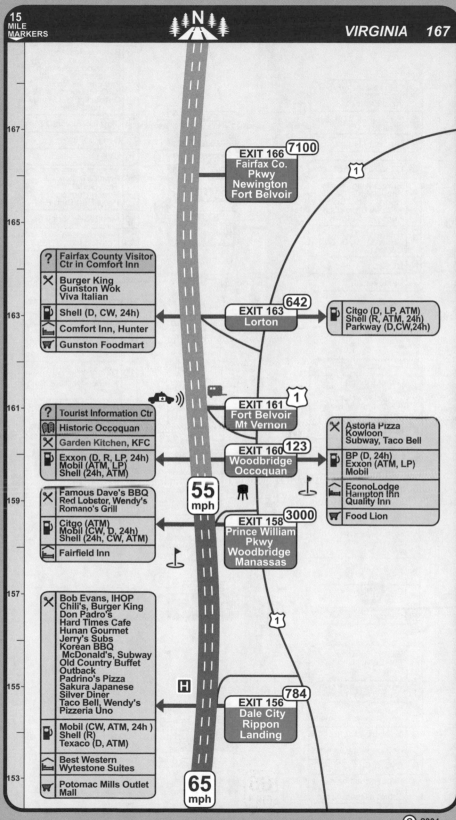

N

EXIT 166 7100
Fairfax Co. Pkwy
Newington
Fort Belvoir

1

?	Fairfax County Visitor Ctr in Comfort Inn
✕	Burger King Gunston Wok Viva Italian
⛽	Shell (D, CW, 24h)
🛏	Comfort Inn, Hunter
🛒	Gunston Foodmart

EXIT 163 642
Lorton

⛽	Citgo (D, LP, ATM) Shell (R, ATM, 24h) Parkway (D,CW,24h)

EXIT 161 1
Fort Belvoir
Mt Vernon

?	Tourist Information Ctr
📖	Historic Occoquan
✕	Garden Kitchen, KFC
⛽	Exxon (D, R, LP, 24h) Mobil (ATM, LP) Shell (24h, ATM)

EXIT 160 123
Woodbridge
Occoquan

✕	Astoria Pizza Kowloon Subway, Taco Bell
⛽	BP (D, 24h) Exxon (ATM, LP) Mobil
🛏	EconoLodge Hampton Inn Quality Inn
🛒	Food Lion

✕	Famous Dave's BBQ Red Lobster, Wendy's Romano's Grill
⛽	Citgo (ATM) Mobil (CW, D, 24h) Shell (24h, CW, ATM)
🛏	Fairfield Inn

55 mph

EXIT 158 3000
Prince William
Pkwy
Woodbridge
Manassas

✕	Bob Evans, IHOP Chili's, Burger King Don Padro's Hard Times Cafe Hunan Gourmet Jerry's Subs Korean BBQ McDonald's, Subway Old Country Buffet Outback Padrino's Pizza Sakura Japanese Silver Diner Taco Bell, Wendy's Pizzeria Uno
⛽	Mobil (CW, ATM, 24h) Shell (R) Texaco (D, ATM)
🛏	Best Western Wytestone Suites
🛒	Potomac Mills Outlet Mall

H

EXIT 156 784
Dale City
Rippon
Landing

65 mph

© 2004

China Best Carryout
McDonald's (P)
Pizza Express

Exxon (CW, ATM, 24h)
Shell (R, 24h)

Import Int'l Food

H

Beijing, Bo Jangles
Burger King, Subway
Cameron's Seafood
Checkers, Cici's all
you can eat Pizza
KFC, McDonald's (P)
Outback, PW's Wings
Quizno's, Wendy's

Citgo(D), Exxon(D,24h)

Red Roof Inn

CVS

EXIT 4 (414)
St Barnabas Rd
Oxon Hill

4

H

Oxon Hill Farm

Burger King, Yum's
Papa John's, Deli
Henry's Soul Cafe
KFC, McDonald's (P)
Popeyes, Subway

BP (R, TR, D, 24h)
Chevron (R, D, 24h)
Crown (24h)

CVS

Eastover

EXIT 3 (210)
India
Head Hwy
Forest Heights

Frank's Italian
East Buffet
Ranch House
Pizza Hut, Taco Bell

Mobil (CW), Shell (R)

Best Western
Comfort Inn

EXIT 2 (295)
Indian Head
Washington

2

WOODROW
WILSON
MEMORIAL
BRIDGE

POTOMAC
RIVER

178

MARYLAND
DRAWBRIDGE   VIRGINIA

Alexandria

Alexandria CVB

Christ Church
Carlyle House
Torpedo Factory
Apothecary Museum

Exxon (24h, R/24h)
Hess (D, K)

H

H

Holiday Inn

Collingwood Library
and Museum

Mount Vernon

Alexandria Diner
Great American Stks

Amoco (D, 24h)
Mobil (D, R, 24h)
Sunoco (R, ATM, CW)
Texaco (D, R)

Hampton Inn, Relax Inn
Travelers Motel
Red Roof Inn
Carriage House B&B

EXIT 177 (1)
Fort Belvoir
Alexandria

176

EXIT 176 (241)
Telegraph Rd
Alexandria

Janet's Java
Pilar's Restaurant

Amoco (R)
Exxon (D, LP)
Hess (D), Citgo (R)

Pearl's Discount Arts
& Crafts

174

EXIT 174
Eisenhower Ave
Connector
Alexandria

172

395

EXIT 173 (613)
Van Dorn St
Franconia

Comfort Inn

495

170

Baskin Robbins
Bob Evans, Quizno's
Canton Cafe, KFC
Chicken Out
Ding How Carry Out
Dragon Sea Buffet
Hard Times Cafe
McDonald's
Roadhouse, Popeyes

Mobil (R, 24h)

Holiday Inn, Red Roof

CVS (24h)

Pepperidge Farm
Le Latino Mkt
Talbot's Outlet Store

KEEP RIGHT HERE

EXIT 170 (495)
Tyson's
Corner

Bennigan's, Thai Cafe
Pizza King

Courtyard, Days Inn
Hampton Inn, Hilton

Springfield Mall

EXIT 169 (644)
Franconia
Springfield

168

55
mph

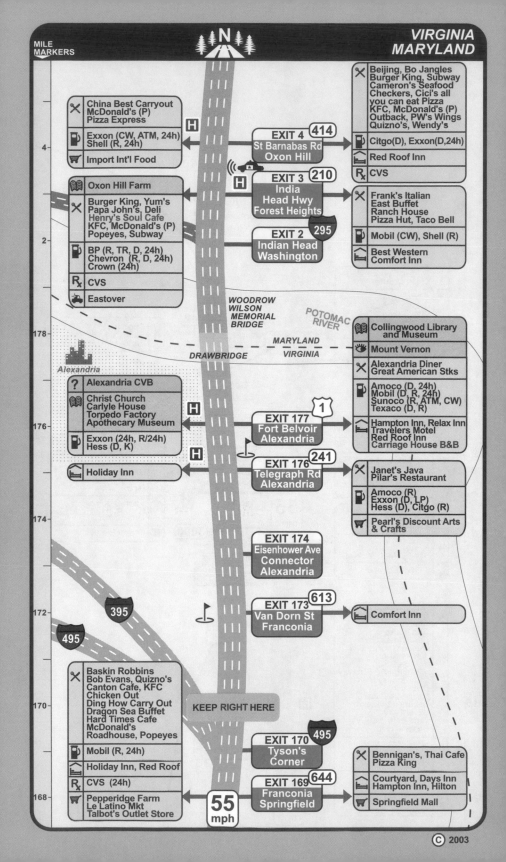

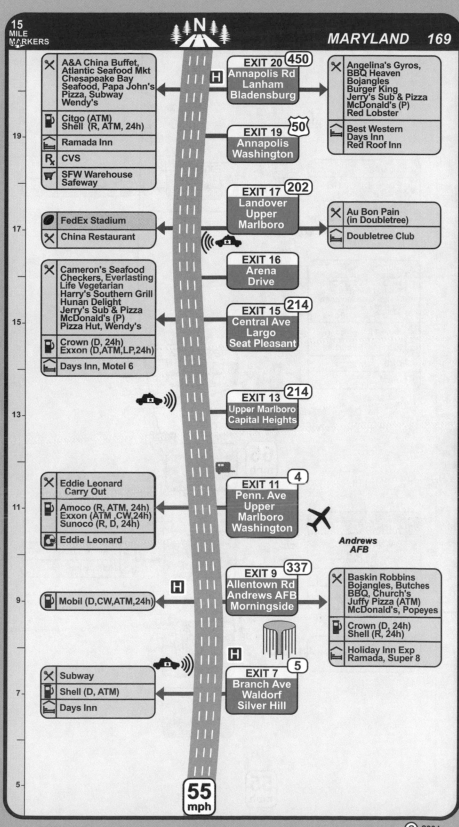

EXIT 20 450
Annapolis Rd
Lanham
Bladensburg

A&A China Buffet, Atlantic Seafood Mkt, Chesapeake Bay Seafood, Papa John's Pizza, Subway, Wendy's

Angelina's Gyros, BBQ Heaven, Bojangles, Burger King, Jerry's Sub & Pizza, McDonald's (P), Red Lobster

EXIT 19 50
Annapolis
Washington

Citgo (ATM), Shell (R, ATM, 24h)

Ramada Inn

CVS

SFW Warehouse, Safeway

Best Western, Days Inn, Red Roof Inn

EXIT 17 202
Landover
Upper
Marlboro

FedEx Stadium

China Restaurant

Au Bon Pain (in Doubletree)

Doubletree Club

EXIT 16
Arena
Drive

Cameron's Seafood, Checkers, Everlasting Life Vegetarian, Harry's Southern Grill, Hunan Delight, Jerry's Sub & Pizza, McDonald's (P), Pizza Hut, Wendy's

Crown (D, 24h), Exxon (D, ATM, LP, 24h)

Days Inn, Motel 6

EXIT 15 214
Central Ave
Largo
Seat Pleasant

EXIT 13 214
Upper Marlboro
Capital Heights

Eddie Leonard Carry Out

Amoco (R, ATM, 24h), Exxon (ATM, CW, 24h), Sunoco (R, D, 24h)

Eddie Leonard

EXIT 11 4
Penn. Ave
Upper
Marlboro
Washington

Andrews AFB

EXIT 9 337
Allentown Rd
Andrews AFB
Morningside

Mobil (D, CW, ATM, 24h)

Baskin Robbins, Bojangles, Butches BBQ, Church's, Juffy Pizza (ATM), McDonald's, Popeyes

Crown (D, 24h), Shell (R, 24h)

Holiday Inn Exp, Ramada, Super 8

EXIT 7 5
Branch Ave
Waldorf
Silver Hill

Subway

Shell (D, ATM)

Days Inn

55 mph

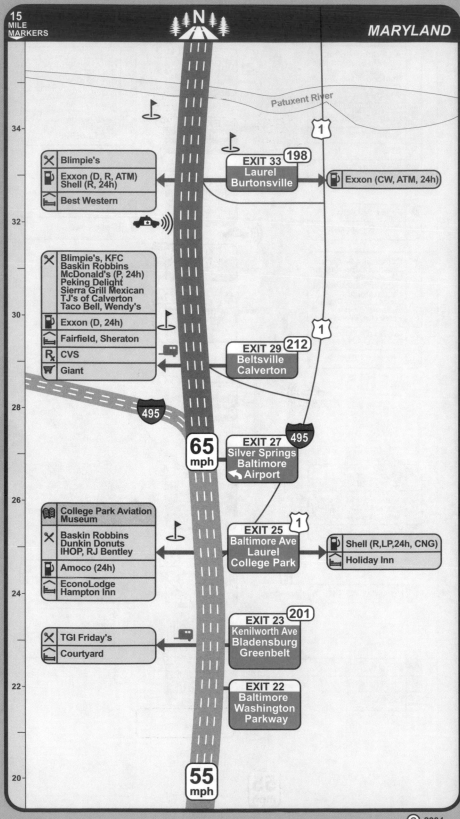

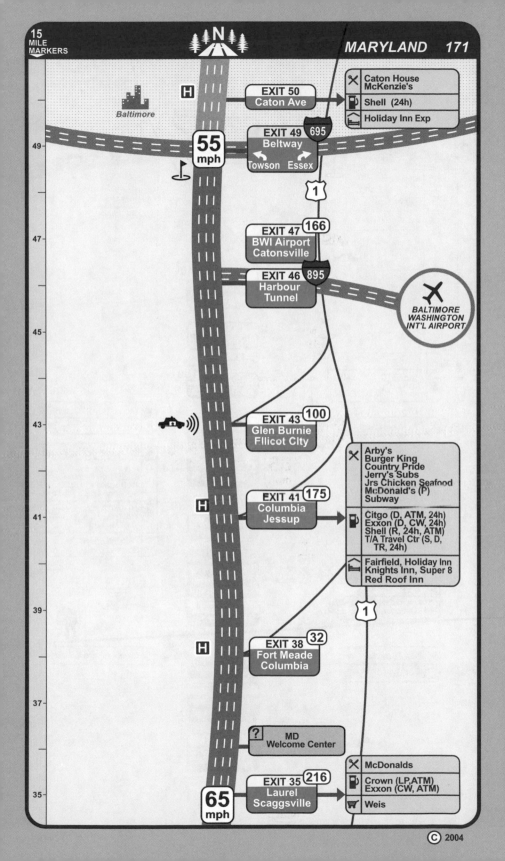

N

Baltimore

H

EXIT 50
Caton Ave

✕ Caton House
McKenzie's

⛽ Shell (24h)

🏨 Holiday Inn Exp

EXIT 49   695
Beltway
Towson   Essex

55 mph

1

EXIT 47   166
BWI Airport
Catonsville

EXIT 46   895
Harbour
Tunnel

✈ BALTIMORE
WASHINGTON
INT'L AIRPORT

EXIT 43   100
Glen Burnie
Fllicot Clty

✕ Arby's
Burger King
Country Pride
Jerry's Subs
Jrs Chicken Seafood
McDonald's (P)
Subway

H

EXIT 41   175
Columbia
Jessup

⛽ Citgo (D, ATM, 24h)
Exxon (D, CW, 24h)
Shell (R, 24h, ATM)
T/A Travel Ctr (S, D,
TR, 24h)

🏨 Fairfield, Holiday Inn
Knights Inn, Super 8
Red Roof Inn

1

H

EXIT 38   32
Fort Meade
Columbia

? MD
Welcome Center

✕ McDonalds

⛽ Crown (LP,ATM)
Exxon (CW, ATM)

🛒 Weis

EXIT 35   216
Laurel
Scaggsville

65 mph

© 2004

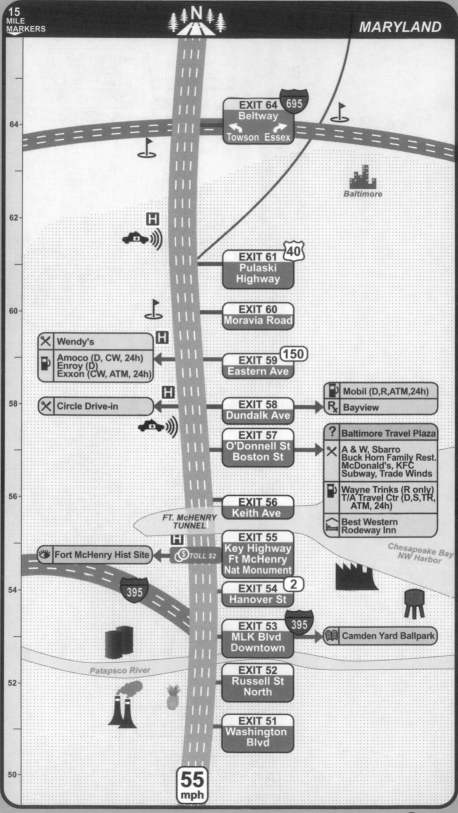

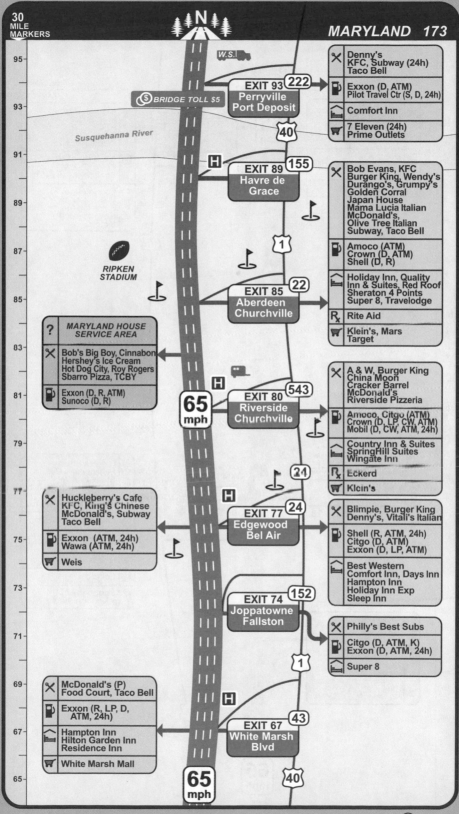

N

95

93

W.S.

$ BRIDGE TOLL $5

EXIT 93 222
Perryville
Port Deposit

✕	Denny's KFC, Subway (24h) Taco Bell
🗋	Exxon (D, ATM) Pilot Travel Ctr (S, D, 24h)
🛏	Comfort Inn
🛒	7 Eleven (24h) Prime Outlets

Susquehanna River

40

91

H

EXIT 89 155
Havre de
Grace

89

1

| ✕ | Bob Evans, KFC
Burger King, Wendy's
Durango's, Grumpy's
Golden Corral
Japan House
Mama Lucia Italian
McDonald's,
Olive Tree Italian
Subway, Taco Bell |
| 🗋 | Amoco (ATM)
Crown (D, ATM)
Shell (D, R) |

87

RIPKEN STADIUM

| 🛏 | Holiday Inn, Quality
Inn & Suites, Red Roof
Sheraton 4 Points
Super 8, Travelodge |

85

EXIT 85 22
Aberdeen
Churchville

| Rx | Rite Aid |
| 🛒 | Klein's, Mars
Target |

83

?	MARYLAND HOUSE SERVICE AREA
✕	Bob's Big Boy, Cinnabon Hershey's Ice Cream Hot Dog City, Roy Rogers Sbarro Pizza, TCBY
🗋	Exxon (D, R, ATM) Sunoco (D, R)

81

H

65 mph

EXIT 80 543
Riverside
Churchville

| ✕ | A & W, Burger King
China Moon
Cracker Barrel
McDonald's
Riverside Pizzeria |
| 🗋 | Amoco, Citgo (ATM)
Crown (D, LP, CW, ATM)
Mobil (D, CW, ATM, 24h) |

79

| 🛏 | Country Inn & Suites
SpringHill Suites
Wingate Inn |

24

| Rx | Eckerd |
| 🛒 | Klein's |

77

✕	Huckleberry's Cafe KFC, King's Chinese McDonald's, Subway Taco Bell
🗋	Exxon (ATM, 24h) Wawa (ATM, 24h)
🛒	Weis

H

EXIT 77 24
Edgewood
Bel Air

75

| ✕ | Blimpie, Burger King
Denny's, Vitali's Italian |
| 🗋 | Shell (R, ATM, 24h)
Citgo (D, ATM)
Exxon (D, LP, ATM) |

73

| 🛏 | Best Western
Comfort Inn, Days Inn
Hampton Inn
Holiday Inn Exp
Sleep Inn |

EXIT 74 152
Joppatowne
Fallston

71

✕	Philly's Best Subs
🗋	Citgo (D, ATM, K) Exxon (D, ATM, 24h)
🛏	Super 8

1

69

✕	McDonald's (P) Food Court, Taco Bell
🗋	Exxon (R, LP, D, ATM, 24h)
🛏	Hampton Inn Hilton Garden Inn Residence Inn
🛒	White Marsh Mall

H

EXIT 67 43
White Marsh
Blvd

67

65 mph

40

65

© 2004

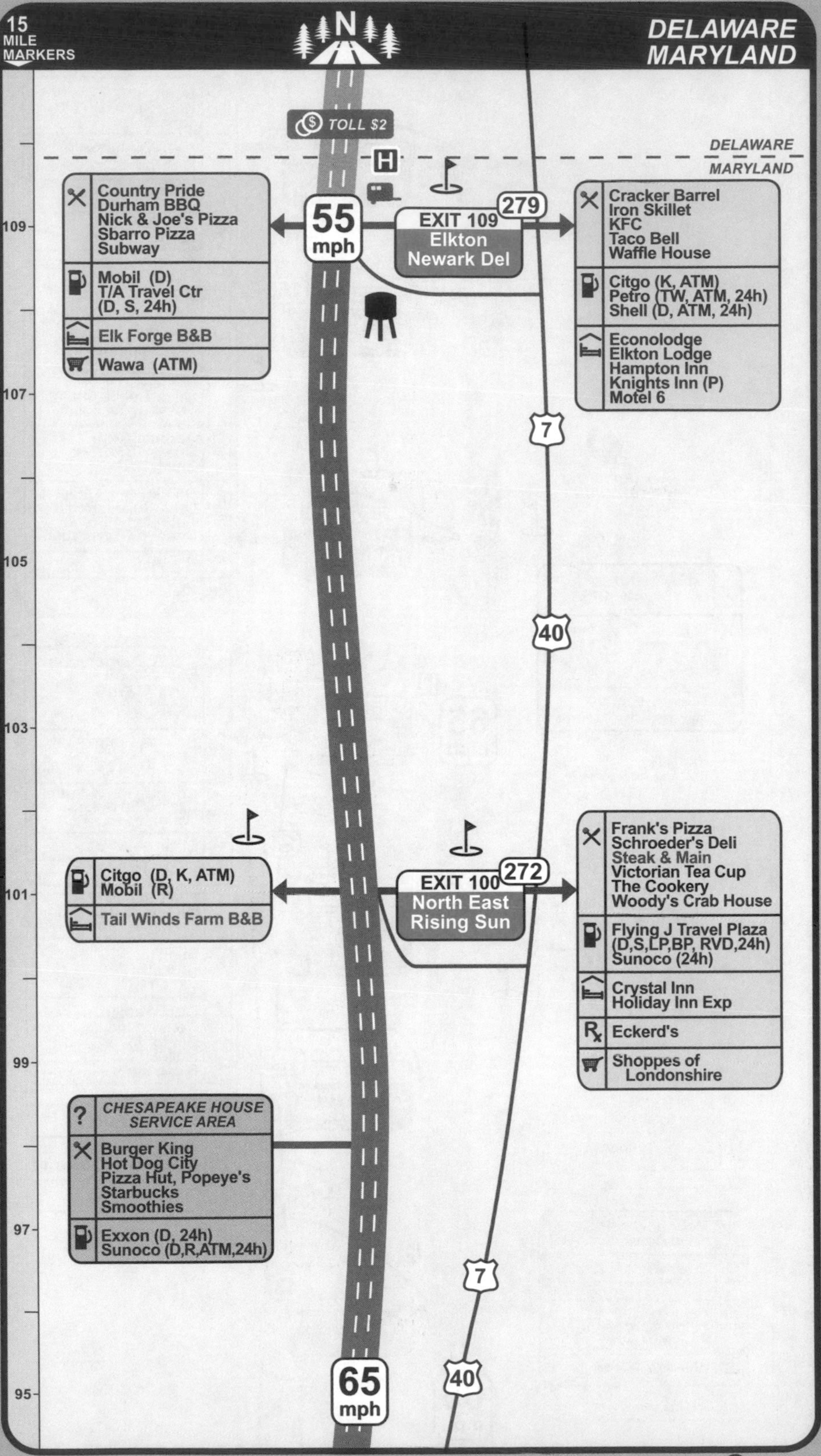

N

TOLL $2

H

DELAWARE
MARYLAND

55 mph

EXIT 109
Elkton
Newark Del

279

109

× Country Pride
Durham BBQ
Nick & Joe's Pizza
Sbarro Pizza
Subway

⛽ Mobil (D)
T/A Travel Ctr
(D, S, 24h)

🛏 Elk Forge B&B

🛒 Wawa (ATM)

× Cracker Barrel
Iron Skillet
KFC
Taco Bell
Waffle House

⛽ Citgo (K, ATM)
Petro (TW, ATM, 24h)
Shell (D, ATM, 24h)

🛏 Econolodge
Elkton Lodge
Hampton Inn
Knights Inn (P)
Motel 6

7

107

40

105

103

⛽ Citgo (D, K, ATM)
Mobil (R)

🛏 Tail Winds Farm B&B

EXIT 100
North East
Rising Sun

272

× Frank's Pizza
Schroeder's Deli
Steak & Main
Victorian Tea Cup
The Cookery
Woody's Crab House

⛽ Flying J Travel Plaza
(D,S,LP,BP, RVD,24h)
Sunoco (24h)

🛏 Crystal Inn
Holiday Inn Exp

℞ Eckerd's

🛒 Shoppes of
Londonshire

101

99

? *CHESAPEAKE HOUSE*
SERVICE AREA

× Burger King
Hot Dog City
Pizza Hut, Popeye's
Starbucks
Smoothies

⛽ Exxon (D, 24h)
Sunoco (D,R,ATM,24h)

7

97

40

65 mph

95

© 2004

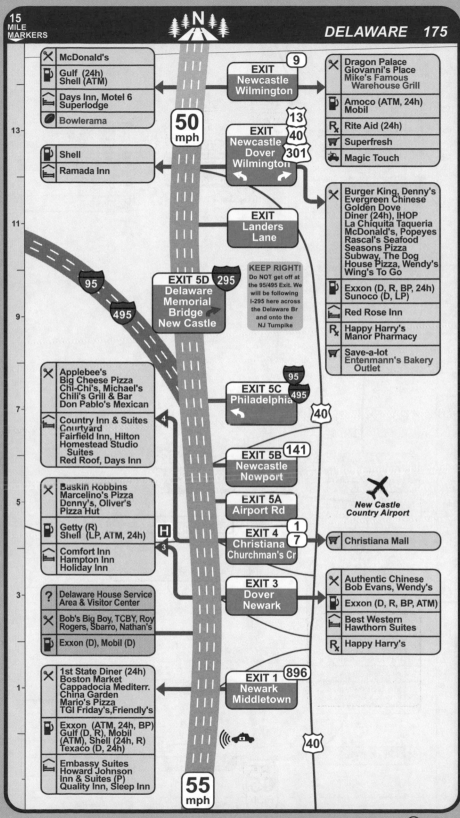

Exits and Services

50 mph

EXIT 9 — Newcastle, Wilmington

(westbound)
- McDonald's
- Gulf (24h), Shell (ATM)
- Days Inn, Motel 6, Superlodge
- Bowlerama

(eastbound)
- Dragon Palace, Giovanni's Place, Mike's Famous Warehouse Grill
- Amoco (ATM, 24h), Mobil
- Rite Aid (24h)
- Superfresh
- Magic Touch

EXIT 13 / 40 / 301 — Newcastle, Dover, Wilmington

(westbound)
- Shell
- Ramada Inn

EXIT — Landers Lane

(eastbound)
- Burger King, Denny's, Evergreen Chinese, Golden Dove Diner (24h), IHOP, La Chiquita Taqueria, McDonald's, Popeyes, Rascal's Seafood, Seasons Pizza, Subway, The Dog House Pizza, Wendy's, Wing's To Go
- Exxon (D, R, BP, 24h), Sunoco (D, LP)
- Red Rose Inn
- Happy Harry's, Manor Pharmacy
- Save-a-lot, Entenmann's Bakery Outlet

EXIT 5D — 295 — Delaware Memorial Bridge, New Castle

KEEP RIGHT! Do NOT get off at the 95/495 Exit. We will be following I-295 here across the Delaware Br and onto the NJ Turnpike

EXIT 5C — 95 / 495 — Philadelphia

(westbound, 4)
- Applebee's, Big Cheese Pizza, Chi-Chi's, Michael's, Chili's Grill & Bar, Don Pablo's Mexican
- Country Inn & Suites, Courtyard, Fairfield Inn, Hilton, Homestead Studio Suites, Red Roof, Days Inn

40

EXIT 5B — 141 — Newcastle, Newport

EXIT 5A — Airport Rd

(westbound)
- Baskin Robbins, Marcelino's Pizza, Denny's, Oliver's, Pizza Hut
- Getty (R), Shell (LP, ATM, 24h)
- Comfort Inn, Hampton Inn, Holiday Inn

H

New Castle Country Airport

EXIT 4 — 1 / 7 — Christiana, Churchman's Cr

(eastbound)
- Christiana Mall

3

EXIT 3 — Dover, Newark

(eastbound)
- Authentic Chinese, Bob Evans, Wendy's
- Exxon (D, R, BP, ATM)
- Best Western, Hawthorn Suites
- Happy Harry's

(westbound)
- Delaware House Service Area & Visitor Center
- Bob's Big Boy, TCBY, Roy Rogers, Sbarro, Nathan's
- Exxon (D), Mobil (D)

EXIT 1 — 896 — Newark, Middletown

(westbound)
- 1st State Diner (24h), Boston Market, Cappadocia Mediterr., China Garden, Mario's Pizza, TGI Friday's, Friendly's
- Exxon (ATM, 24h, BP), Gulf (D, R), Mobil (ATM), Shell (24h, R), Texaco (D, 24h)
- Embassy Suites, Howard Johnson Inn & Suites (P), Quality Inn, Sleep Inn

40

55 mph

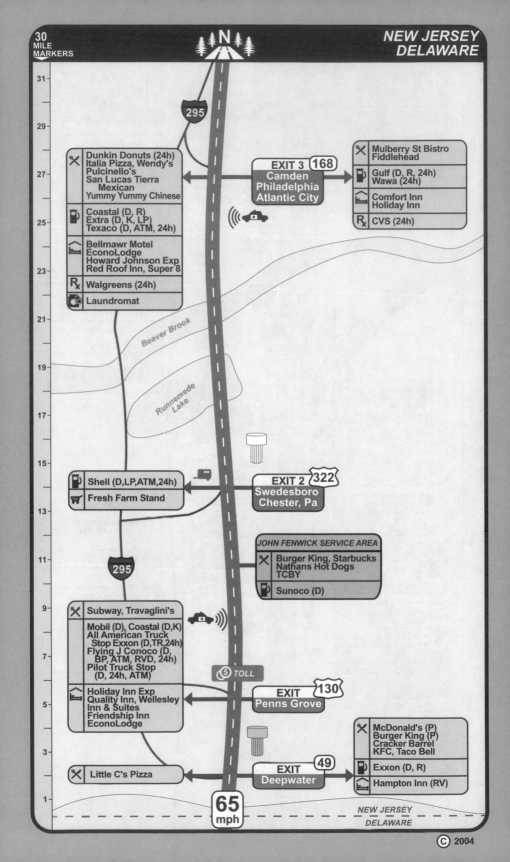

N

295

31

29

27
EXIT 3 168
Camden
Philadelphia
Atlantic City

✕ Dunkin Donuts (24h)
Italia Pizza, Wendy's
Pulcinello's
San Lucas Tierra
Mexican
Yummy Yummy Chinese

✕ Mulberry St Bistro
Fiddlehead

🅿 Gulf (D, R, 24h)
Wawa (24h)

🛏 Comfort Inn
Holiday Inn

℞ CVS (24h)

25
🅿 Coastal (D, R)
Extra (D, K, LP)
Texaco (D, ATM, 24h)

🛏 Bellmawr Motel
EconoLodge
Howard Johnson Exp
Red Roof Inn, Super 8

23
℞ Walgreens (24h)

🧺 Laundromat

21
Beaver Brook

19

Runnemede
Lake
17

15
EXIT 2 322
Swedesboro
Chester, Pa

🅿 Shell (D,LP,ATM,24h)

🛒 Fresh Farm Stand

13

JOHN FENWICK SERVICE AREA

11
295
✕ Burger King, Starbucks
Nathans Hot Dogs
TCBY

🅿 Sunoco (D)

9
✕ Subway, Travaglini's

Mobil (D), Coastal (D,K)
All American Truck
Stop Exxon (D,TR,24h)
Flying J Conoco (D,
BP, ATM, RVD, 24h)
Pilot Truck Stop
(D, 24h, ATM)
7

💲 TOLL

5
EXIT 130
Penns Grove

🛏 Holiday Inn Exp
Quality Inn, Wellesley
Inn & Suites
Friendship Inn
EconoLodge

✕ McDonald's (P)
Burger King (P)
Cracker Barrel
KFC, Taco Bell
3

🅿 Exxon (D, R)

1
EXIT 49
Deepwater

✕ Little C's Pizza

🛏 Hampton Inn (RV)

65
mph

NEW JERSEY
DELAWARE

© 2004

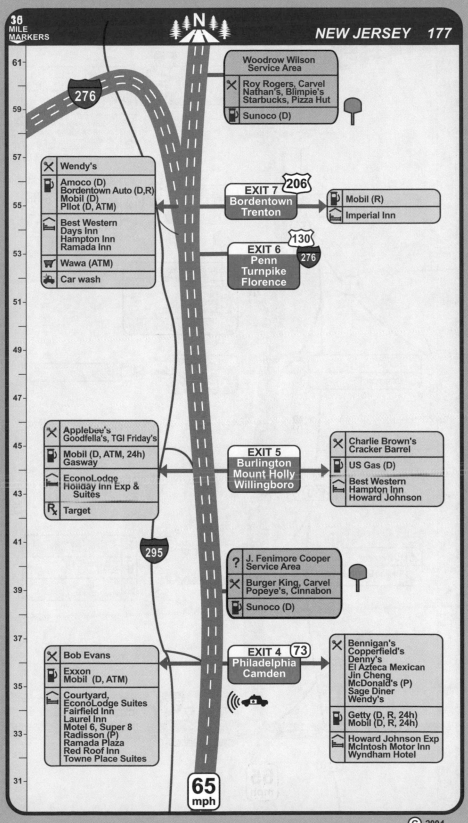

Woodrow Wilson Service Area
✕ Roy Rogers, Carvel Nathan's, Blimpie's Starbucks, Pizza Hut
⛽ Sunoco (D)

276

✕ Wendy's
⛽ Amoco (D)
Bordentown Auto (D,R)
Mobil (D)
Pilot (D, ATM)
🛏 Best Western
Days Inn
Hampton Inn
Ramada Inn
🛒 Wawa (ATM)
🚗 Car wash

EXIT 7 206
Bordentown
Trenton
⛽ Mobil (R)
🛏 Imperial Inn

EXIT 6 130 276
Penn
Turnpike
Florence

✕ Applebee's
Goodfella's, TGI Friday's
⛽ Mobil (D, ATM, 24h)
Gasway
🛏 EconoLodge
Holiday Inn Exp & Suites
Rx Target

EXIT 5
Burlington
Mount Holly
Willingboro
✕ Charlie Brown's
Cracker Barrel
⛽ US Gas (D)
🛏 Best Western
Hampton Inn
Howard Johnson

295

? J. Fenimore Cooper
Service Area
✕ Burger King, Carvel
Popeye's, Cinnabon
⛽ Sunoco (D)

✕ Bob Evans
⛽ Exxon
Mobil (D, ATM)
🛏 Courtyard,
EconoLodge Suites
Fairfield Inn
Laurel Inn
Motel 6, Super 8
Radisson (P)
Ramada Plaza
Red Roof Inn
Towne Place Suites

EXIT 4 73
Philadelphia
Camden
✕ Bennigan's
Copperfield's
Denny's
El Azteca Mexican
Jin Cheng
McDonald's (P)
Sage Diner
Wendy's
⛽ Getty (D, R, 24h)
Mobil (D, R, 24h)
🛏 Howard Johnson Exp
McIntosh Motor Inn
Wyndham Hotel

65 mph

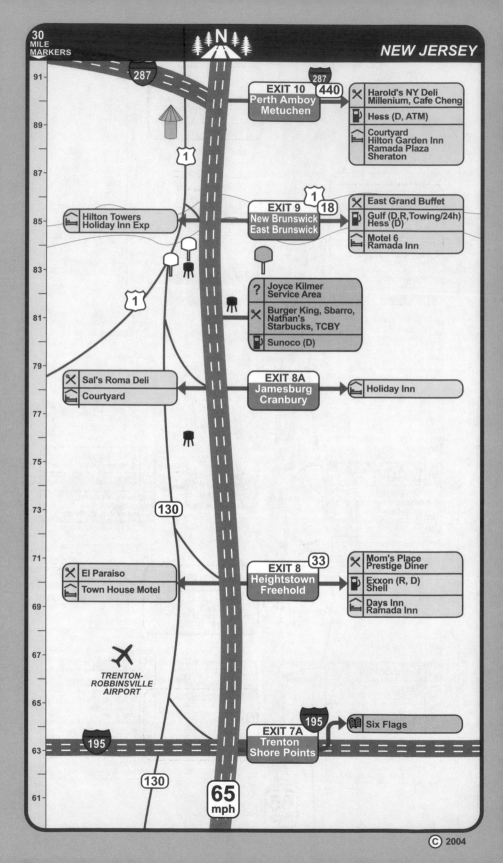

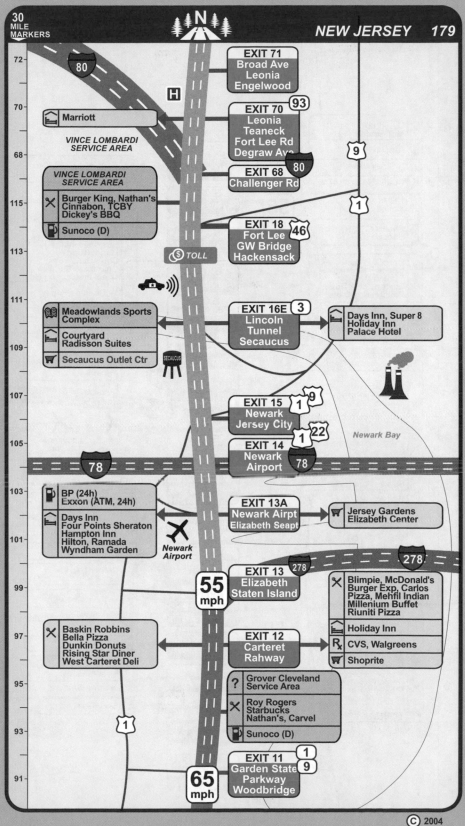

72 —

80

H

EXIT 71
Broad Ave
Leonia
Engelwood

70 —

Marriott

VINCE LOMBARDI SERVICE AREA

EXIT 70 **93**
Leonia
Teaneck
Fort Lee Rd
Degraw Ave
80

68 —

VINCE LOMBARDI SERVICE AREA

EXIT 68
Challenger Rd

9

115 —

Burger King, Nathan's
Cinnabon, TCBY
Dickey's BBQ

Sunoco (D)

1

EXIT 18 **46**
Fort Lee
GW Bridge
Hackensack

113 —

$ TOLL

111 —

Meadowlands Sports
Complex

Courtyard
Radisson Suites

Secaucus Outlet Ctr

EXIT 16E **3**
Lincoln
Tunnel
Secaucus

Days Inn, Super 8
Holiday Inn
Palace Hotel

109 —

SECAUCUS

107 —

EXIT 15 **1** **9**
Newark
Jersey City

105 —

EXIT 14 **1** **22**
Newark
Airport

Newark Bay

78

78

103 —

BP (24h)
Exxon (ATM, 24h)

Days Inn
Four Points Sheraton
Hampton Inn
Hilton, Ramada
Wyndham Garden

EXIT 13A
Newark Airpt
Elizabeth Seapt

Jersey Gardens
Elizabeth Center

101 —

Newark
Airport

278

99 —

55 mph

EXIT 13 **278**
Elizabeth
Staten Island

Blimpie, McDonald's
Burger Exp, Carlos
Pizza, Mehfil Indian
Millenium Buffet
Riuniti Pizza

97 —

Baskin Robbins
Bella Pizza
Dunkin Donuts
Rising Star Diner
West Carteret Deli

EXIT 12
Carteret
Rahway

Holiday Inn

CVS, Walgreens

Shoprite

95 —

? Grover Cleveland
Service Area

Roy Rogers
Starbucks
Nathan's, Carvel

Sunoco (D)

93 —

1

91 —

65 mph

EXIT 11 **1** **9**
Garden State
Parkway
Woodbridge

© 2004

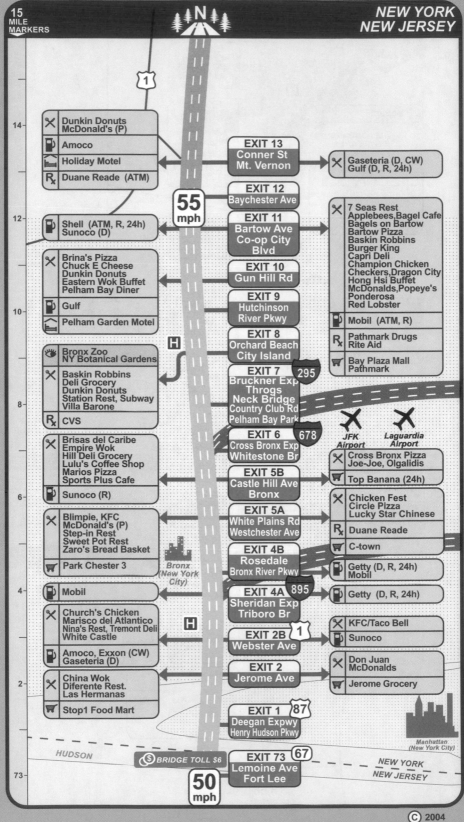

N

U.S. 1

EXIT 13
Conner St
Mt. Vernon

Dunkin Donuts
McDonald's (P)
Amoco
Holiday Motel
Duane Reade (ATM)

Gaseteria (D, CW)
Gulf (D, R, 24h)

55 mph

EXIT 12
Baychester Ave

EXIT 11
Bartow Ave
Co-op City
Blvd

Shell (ATM, R, 24h)
Sunoco (D)

7 Seas Rest
Applebees, Bagel Cafe
Bagels on Bartow
Bartow Pizza
Baskin Robbins
Burger King
Capri Deli
Champion Chicken
Checkers, Dragon City
Hong Hsi Buffet
McDonalds, Popeye's
Ponderosa
Red Lobster

EXIT 10
Gun Hill Rd

Brina's Pizza
Chuck E Cheese
Dunkin Donuts
Eastern Wok Buffet
Pelham Bay Diner
Gulf
Pelham Garden Motel

EXIT 9
Hutchinson
River Pkwy

Mobil (ATM, R)

EXIT 8
Orchard Beach
City Island

Pathmark Drugs
Rite Aid

Bay Plaza Mall
Pathmark

H

Bronx Zoo
NY Botanical Gardens
Baskin Robbins
Deli Grocery
Dunkin Donuts
Station Rest, Subway
Villa Barone
CVS

EXIT 7   295
Bruckner Exp
Throgs
Neck Bridge
Country Club Rd
Pelham Bay Park

JFK
Airport

Laguardia
Airport

EXIT 6   678
Cross Bronx Exp
Whitestone Br

Brisas del Caribe
Empire Wok
Hill Deli Grocery
Lulu's Coffee Shop
Marios Pizza
Sports Plus Cafe
Sunoco (R)

Cross Bronx Pizza
Joe-Joe, Olgalidis
Top Banana (24h)

EXIT 5B
Castle Hill Ave
Bronx

EXIT 5A
White Plains Rd
Westchester Ave

Chicken Fest
Circle Pizza
Lucky Star Chinese
Duane Reade
C-town

Blimpie, KFC
McDonald's (P)
Step-in Rest
Sweet Pot Rest
Zaro's Bread Basket
Park Chester 3

EXIT 4B
Rosedale
Bronx River Pkwy

Getty (D, R, 24h)
Mobil

Bronx
(New York
City)

Mobil

EXIT 4A   895
Sheridan Exp
Triboro Br

Getty (D, R, 24h)

H

Church's Chicken
Marisco del Atlantico
Nina's Rest, Tremont Deli
White Castle
Amoco, Exxon (CW)
Gaseteria (D)

EXIT 2B   1
Webster Ave

KFC/Taco Bell
Sunoco

China Wok
Diferente Rest.
Las Hermanas
Stop1 Food Mart

EXIT 2
Jerome Ave

Don Juan
McDonalds
Jerome Grocery

EXIT 1   87
Deegan Expwy
Henry Hudson Pkwy

Manhattan
(New York City)

HUDSON

BRIDGE TOLL $6

EXIT 73   67
Lemoine Ave
Fort Lee

NEW YORK
NEW JERSEY

50 mph

73

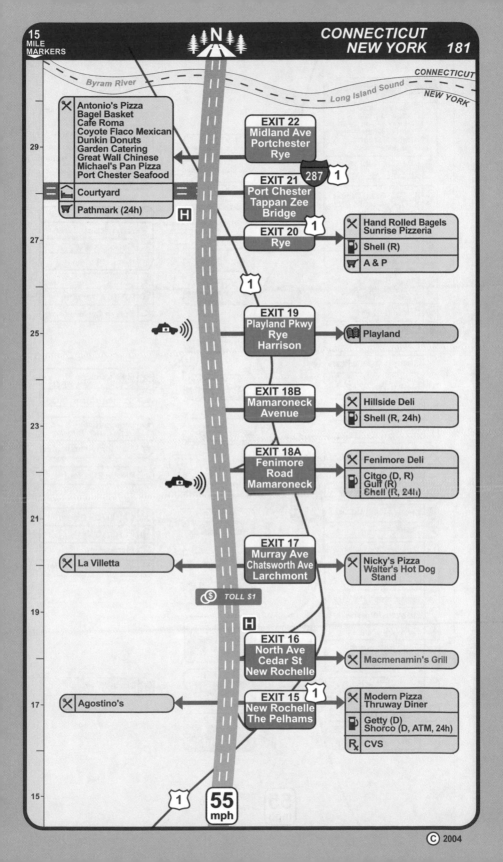

Byram River

CONNECTICUT
Long Island Sound
NEW YORK

Antonio's Pizza
Bagel Basket
Cafe Roma
Coyote Flaco Mexican
Dunkin Donuts
Garden Catering
Great Wall Chinese
Michael's Pan Pizza
Port Chester Seafood

Courtyard

Pathmark (24h)

EXIT 22
Midland Ave
Portchester
Rye

287 / 1

EXIT 21
Port Chester
Tappan Zee
Bridge

1

EXIT 20
Rye

1

Hand Rolled Bagels
Sunrise Pizzeria

Shell (R)

A & P

1

EXIT 19
Playland Pkwy
Rye
Harrison

Playland

EXIT 18B
Mamaroneck
Avenue

Hillside Deli

Shell (R, 24h)

EXIT 18A
Fenimore
Road
Mamaroneck

Fenimore Deli

Citgo (D, R)
Gulf (R)
Shell (R, 24h)

EXIT 17
Murray Ave
Chatsworth Ave
Larchmont

La Villetta

Nicky's Pizza
Walter's Hot Dog
Stand

TOLL $1

H

EXIT 16
North Ave
Cedar St
New Rochelle

Macmenamin's Grill

Agostino's

EXIT 15
New Rochelle
The Pelhams

1

Modern Pizza
Thruway Diner

Getty (D)
Shorco (D, ATM, 24h)

CVS

1

55 mph

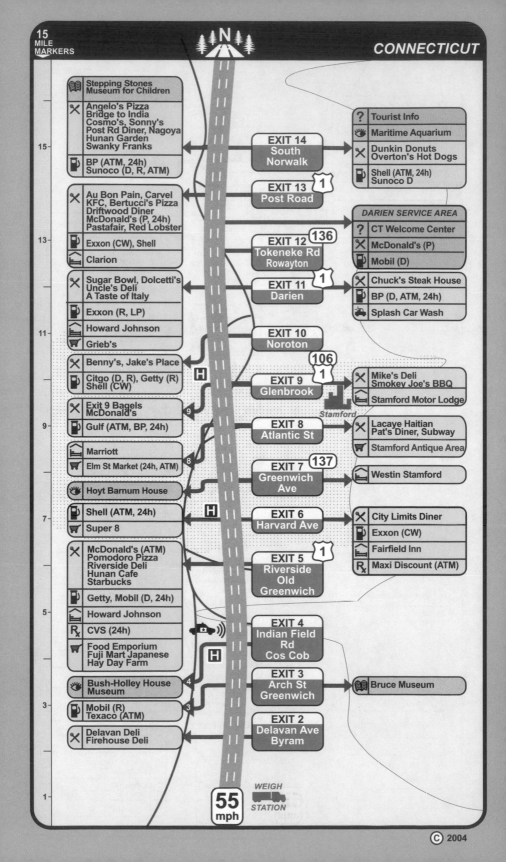

15

Stepping Stones Museum for Children

Angelo's Pizza
Bridge to India
Cosmo's, Sonny's
Post Rd Diner, Nagoya
Hunan Garden
Swanky Franks

BP (ATM, 24h)
Sunoco (D, R, ATM)

EXIT 14
South Norwalk

? Tourist Info
Maritime Aquarium
Dunkin Donuts
Overton's Hot Dogs
Shell (ATM, 24h)
Sunoco D

EXIT 13 **1**
Post Road

Au Bon Pain, Carvel
KFC, Bertucci's Pizza
Driftwood Diner
McDonald's (P, 24h)
Pastafair, Red Lobster

Exxon (CW), Shell

Clarion

DARIEN SERVICE AREA
? CT Welcome Center
McDonald's (P)
Mobil (D)

13

EXIT 12 **136**
Tokeneke Rd
Rowayton

Sugar Bowl, Dolcetti's
Uncle's Deli
A Taste of Italy

Exxon (R, LP)

Howard Johnson

Grieb's

EXIT 11 **1**
Darien

Chuck's Steak House
BP (D, ATM, 24h)
Splash Car Wash

11

EXIT 10
Noroton

Benny's, Jake's Place

Citgo (D, R), Getty (R)
Shell (CW)

H

106
EXIT 9 **1**
Glenbrook

Mike's Deli
Smokey Joe's BBQ
Stamford Motor Lodge

Exit 9 Bagels
McDonald's

Gulf (ATM, BP, 24h)

9

Stamford

9

Marriott

Elm St Market (24h, ATM)

8

EXIT 8
Atlantic St

Lacaye Haitian
Pat's Diner, Subway
Stamford Antique Area

Hoyt Barnum House

EXIT 7 **137**
Greenwich Ave

Westin Stamford

7

Shell (ATM, 24h)

Super 8

H

EXIT 6
Harvard Ave

City Limits Diner
Exxon (CW)
Fairfield Inn
Maxi Discount (ATM)

McDonald's (ATM)
Pomodoro Pizza
Riverside Deli
Hunan Cafe
Starbucks

Getty, Mobil (D, 24h)

Howard Johnson

CVS (24h)

Food Emporium
Fuji Mart Japanese
Hay Day Farm

EXIT 5 **1**
Riverside
Old
Greenwich

5

EXIT 4
Indian Field
Rd
Cos Cob

H

Bush-Holley House
Museum

4

EXIT 3
Arch St
Greenwich

Bruce Museum

3

Mobil (R)
Texaco (ATM)

3

Delavan Deli
Firehouse Deli

EXIT 2
Delavan Ave
Byram

1

55
mph

WEIGH
STATION

© 2004

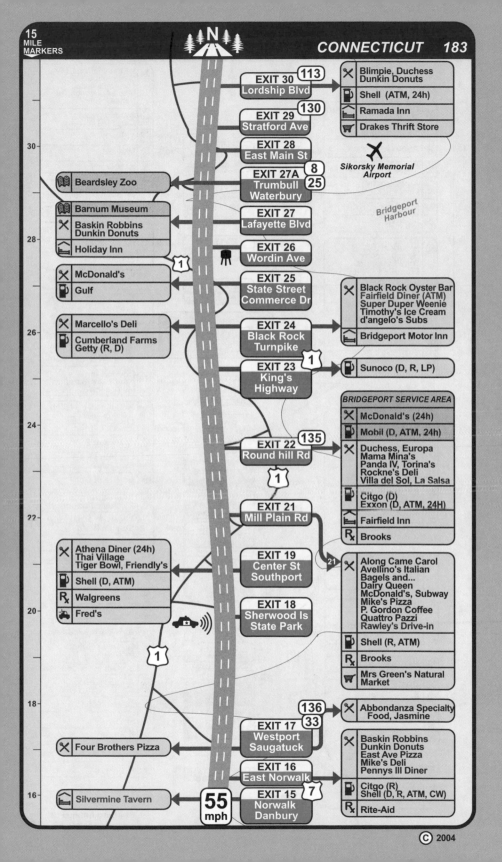

EXIT 30 113
Lordship Blvd

- Blimpie, Duchess Dunkin Donuts
- Shell (ATM, 24h)
- Ramada Inn
- Drakes Thrift Store

EXIT 29 130
Stratford Ave

EXIT 28
East Main St

Sikorsky Memorial Airport

EXIT 27A 8 25
Trumbull Waterbury

Beardsley Zoo

Bridgeport Harbour

Barnum Museum

Baskin Robbins Dunkin Donuts

Holiday Inn

EXIT 27
Lafayette Blvd

EXIT 26
Wordin Ave

McDonald's

Gulf

EXIT 25
State Street Commerce Dr

- Black Rock Oyster Bar Fairfield Diner (ATM) Super Duper Weenie Timothy's Ice Cream d'angelo's Subs
- Bridgeport Motor Inn

Marcello's Deli

Cumberland Farms Getty (R, D)

EXIT 24
Black Rock Turnpike

EXIT 23 1
King's Highway

- Sunoco (D, R, LP)

BRIDGEPORT SERVICE AREA
- McDonald's (24h)
- Mobil (D, ATM, 24h)
- Duchess, Europa Mama Mina's Panda IV, Torina's Rockne's Deli Villa del Sol, La Salsa
- Citgo (D) Exxon (D, ATM, 24H)
- Fairfield Inn
- Brooks

EXIT 22 135
Round hill Rd
1

EXIT 21
Mill Plain Rd

21
- Along Came Carol Avellino's Italian Bagels and... Dairy Queen McDonald's, Subway Mike's Pizza P. Gordon Coffee Quattro Pazzi Rawley's Drive-in
- Shell (R, ATM)
- Brooks
- Mrs Green's Natural Market

Athena Diner (24h) Thai Village Tiger Bowl, Friendly's

Shell (D, ATM)

Walgreens

Fred's

EXIT 19
Center St Southport

EXIT 18
Sherwood Is State Park

1

EXIT 17 136 33
Westport Saugatuck

- Abbondanza Specialty Food, Jasmine
- Baskin Robbins Dunkin Donuts East Ave Pizza Mike's Deli Pennys III Diner

Four Brothers Pizza

EXIT 16
East Norwalk

Silvermine Tavern

55 mph

EXIT 15 7
Norwalk Danbury

- Citgo (R) Shell (D, R, ATM, CW)
- Rite-Aid

© 2004

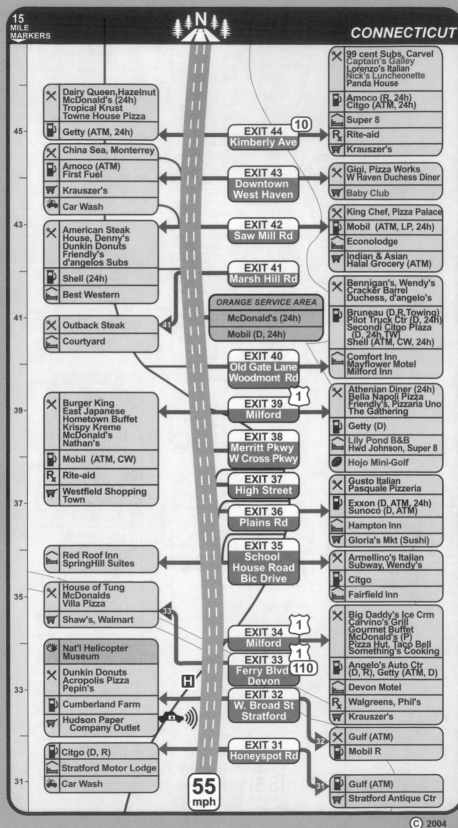

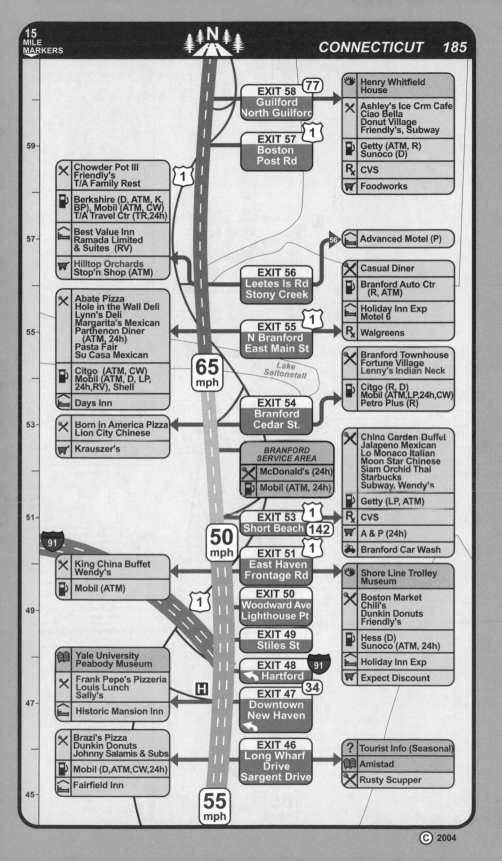

EXIT 58 77
Guilford
North Guilford

EXIT 57 1
Boston
Post Rd

1

Henry Whitfield House

Ashley's Ice Crm Cafe
Ciao Bella
Donut Village
Friendly's, Subway

Getty (ATM, R)
Sunoco (D)

CVS

Foodworks

Chowder Pot III
Friendly's
T/A Family Rest

Berkshire (D, ATM, K, BP), Mobil (ATM, CW)
T/A Travel Ctr (TR,24h)

Best Value Inn
Ramada Limited
& Suites (RV)

Hilltop Orchards
Stop'n Shop (ATM)

56 Advanced Motel (P)

EXIT 56
Leetes Is Rd
Stony Creek

Casual Diner

Branford Auto Ctr (R, ATM)

Holiday Inn Exp
Motel 6

EXIT 55 1
N Branford
East Main St

Walgreens

Abate Pizza
Hole in the Wall Deli
Lynn's Deli
Margarita's Mexican
Parthenon Diner (ATM, 24h)
Pasta Fair
Su Casa Mexican

Branford Townhouse
Fortune Village
Lenny's Indian Neck

Citgo (ATM, CW)
Mobil (ATM, D, LP, 24h,RV), Shell

Days Inn

Citgo (R, D)
Mobil (ATM,LP,24h,CW)
Petro Plus (R)

65 mph

Lake Saltonstall

EXIT 54
Branford
Cedar St.

Born in America Pizza
Lion City Chinese

Krauszer's

China Garden Buffet
Jalapeno Mexican
Lo Monaco Italian
Moon Star Chinese
Siam Orchid Thai
Starbucks
Subway, Wendy's

BRANFORD SERVICE AREA

McDonald's (24h)

Mobil (ATM, 24h)

Getty (LP, ATM)

CVS

A & P (24h)

Branford Car Wash

EXIT 53 1
Short Beach 142

50 mph

EXIT 51 1
East Haven
Frontage Rd

Shore Line Trolley Museum

91

King China Buffet
Wendy's

Mobil (ATM)

Boston Market
Chili's
Dunkin Donuts
Friendly's

Hess (D)
Sunoco (ATM, 24h)

Holiday Inn Exp

Expect Discount

1

EXIT 50
Woodward Ave
Lighthouse Pt

EXIT 49
Stiles St

Yale University
Peabody Museum

Frank Pepe's Pizzeria
Louis Lunch
Sally's

Historic Mansion Inn

EXIT 48 91
Hartford

H

EXIT 47 34
Downtown
New Haven

Brazi's Pizza
Dunkin Donuts
Johnny Salamis & Subs

Mobil (D,ATM,CW,24h)

Fairfield Inn

EXIT 46
Long Wharf
Drive
Sargent Drive

Tourist Info (Seasonal)

Amistad

Rusty Scupper

55 mph

59
57
55
53
51
49
47
45

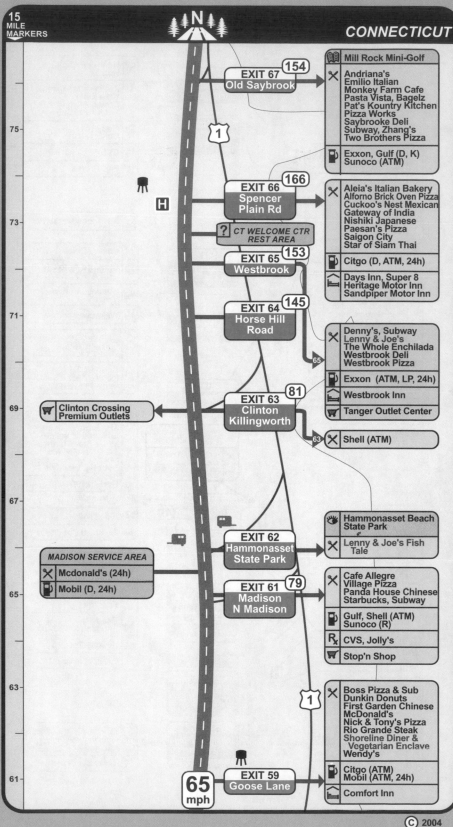

N

CONNECTICUT

Mill Rock Mini-Golf

EXIT 67 154
Old Saybrook

Andriana's
Emilio Italian
Monkey Farm Cafe
Pasta Vista, Bagelz
Pat's Kountry Kitchen
Pizza Works
Saybrooke Deli
Subway, Zhang's
Two Brothers Pizza

Exxon, Gulf (D, K)
Sunoco (ATM)

EXIT 66 166
Spencer
Plain Rd

Aleia's Italian Bakery
Alforno Brick Oven Pizza
Cuckoo's Nest Mexican
Gateway of India
Nishiki Japanese
Paesan's Pizza
Saigon City
Star of Siam Thai

? CT WELCOME CTR
REST AREA

Citgo (D, ATM, 24h)

EXIT 65 153
Westbrook

Days Inn, Super 8
Heritage Motor Inn
Sandpiper Motor Inn

EXIT 64 145
Horse Hill
Road

Denny's, Subway
Lenny & Joe's
The Whole Enchilada
Westbrook Deli
Westbrook Pizza

65 Exxon (ATM, LP, 24h)

Westbrook Inn

Tanger Outlet Center

Clinton Crossing
Premium Outlets

EXIT 63 81
Clinton
Killingworth

63 Shell (ATM)

Hammonasset Beach
State Park

EXIT 62
Hammonasset
State Park

Lenny & Joe's Fish
Tale

MADISON SERVICE AREA

Mcdonald's (24h)

Mobil (D, 24h)

EXIT 61 79
Madison
N Madison

Cafe Allegre
Village Pizza
Panda House Chinese
Starbucks, Subway

Gulf, Shell (ATM)
Sunoco (R)

Rx CVS, Jolly's

Stop'n Shop

1

Boss Pizza & Sub
Dunkin Donuts
First Garden Chinese
McDonald's
Nick & Tony's Pizza
Rio Grande Steak
Shoreline Diner &
  Vegetarian Enclave
Wendy's

65 mph

EXIT 59
Goose Lane

Citgo (ATM)
Mobil (ATM, 24h)

Comfort Inn

© 2004

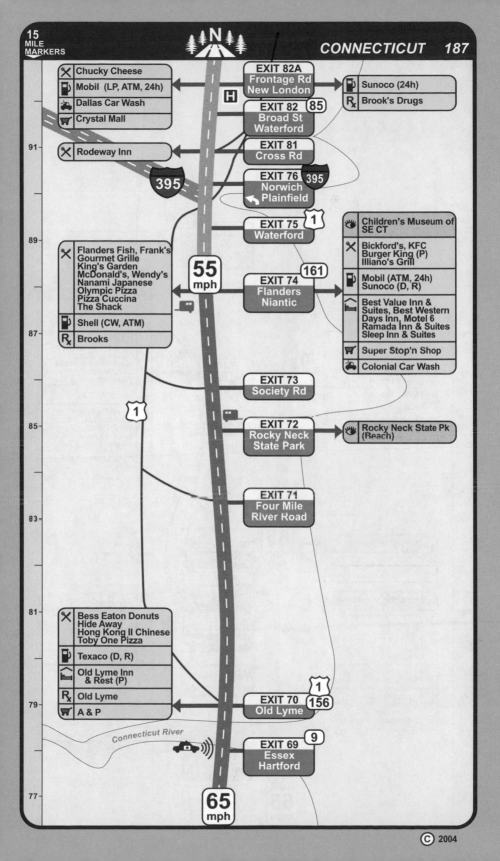

N

EXIT 82A
Frontage Rd
New London

H

EXIT 82 85
Broad St
Waterford

EXIT 81
Cross Rd

EXIT 76 395
Norwich
Plainfield

EXIT 75 1
Waterford

55 mph

EXIT 74 161
Flanders
Niantic

EXIT 73
Society Rd

1

EXIT 72
Rocky Neck
State Park

EXIT 71
Four Mile
River Road

EXIT 70 1 156
Old Lyme

EXIT 69 9
Essex
Hartford

65 mph

Left side (top to bottom):

✗ Chucky Cheese
⛽ Mobil (LP, ATM, 24h)
🚗 Dallas Car Wash
🛒 Crystal Mall

✗ Rodeway Inn

395

✗ Flanders Fish, Frank's
Gourmet Grille
King's Garden
McDonald's, Wendy's
Nanami Japanese
Olympic Pizza
Pizza Cuccina
The Shack
⛽ Shell (CW, ATM)
Rx Brooks

✗ Bess Eaton Donuts
Hide Away
Hong Kong II Chinese
Toby One Pizza
⛽ Texaco (D, R)
🛏 Old Lyme Inn
& Rest (P)
Rx Old Lyme
🛒 A & P

Connecticut River

Right side (top to bottom):

⛽ Sunoco (24h)
Rx Brook's Drugs

🖐 Children's Museum of
SE CT
✗ Bickford's, KFC
Burger King (P)
Illiano's Grill
⛽ Mobil (ATM, 24h)
Sunoco (D, R)
🛏 Best Value Inn &
Suites, Best Western
Days Inn, Motel 6
Ramada Inn & Suites
Sleep Inn & Suites
🛒 Super Stop'n Shop
🚗 Colonial Car Wash

🖐 Rocky Neck State Pk
(Beach)

Mile markers (left edge):
91
89
87
85
83
81
79
77

© 2004

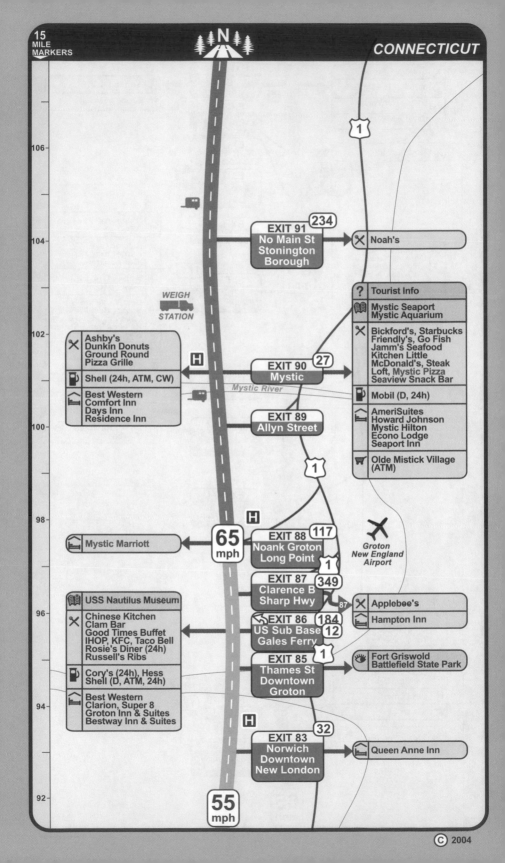

N

EXIT 91 (234)
No Main St
Stonington
Borough

Noah's

WEIGH STATION

? Tourist Info

Mystic Seaport
Mystic Aquarium

Bickford's, Starbucks
Friendly's, Go Fish
Jamm's Seafood
Kitchen Little
McDonald's, Steak
Loft, Mystic Pizza
Seaview Snack Bar

H

EXIT 90 (27)
Mystic

Ashby's
Dunkin Donuts
Ground Round
Pizza Grille

Shell (24h, ATM, CW)

Best Western
Comfort Inn
Days Inn
Residence Inn

Mystic River

Mobil (D, 24h)

AmeriSuites
Howard Johnson
Mystic Hilton
Econo Lodge
Seaport Inn

Olde Mistick Village
(ATM)

EXIT 89
Allyn Street

1

H

65 mph

EXIT 88 (117)
Noank Groton
Long Point

Mystic Marriott

Groton
New England
Airport

1

EXIT 87 (349)
Clarence B
Sharp Hwy

87

Applebee's

Hampton Inn

USS Nautilus Museum

Chinese Kitchen
Clam Bar
Good Times Buffet
IHOP, KFC, Taco Bell
Rosie's Diner (24h)
Russell's Ribs

Cory's (24h), Hess
Shell (D, ATM, 24h)

Best Western
Clarion, Super 8
Groton Inn & Suites
Bestway Inn & Suites

EXIT 86 (184)(12)
US Sub Base
Gales Ferry

EXIT 85
Thames St
Downtown
Groton

1

Fort Griswold
Battlefield State Park

H

EXIT 83 (32)
Norwich
Downtown
New London

Queen Anne Inn

55 mph

© 2004

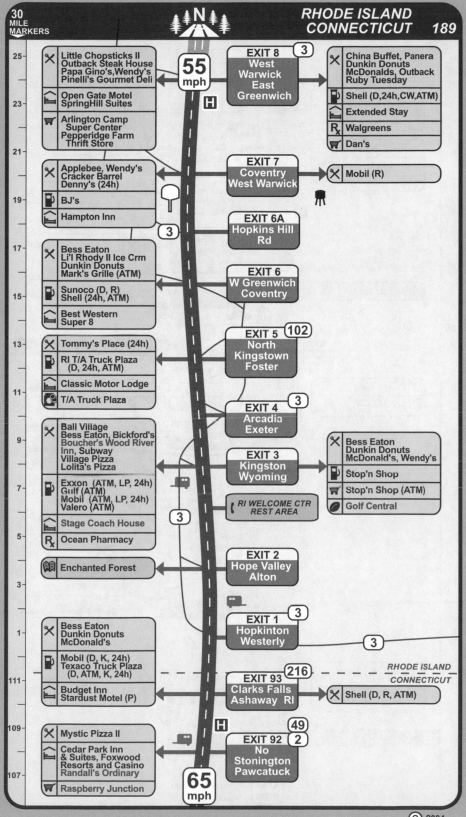

30 MILE MARKERS

N

55 mph

EXIT 8
West Warwick
East Greenwich — 3

- ✕ Little Chopsticks II, Outback Steak House, Papa Gino's, Wendy's, Pinelli's Gourmet Deli
- 🛏 Open Gate Motel, SpringHill Suites
- 🛒 Arlington Camp Super Center, Pepperidge Farm Thrift Store

EXIT 8 (right side):
- ✕ China Buffet, Panera, Dunkin Donuts, McDonalds, Outback, Ruby Tuesday
- ⛽ Shell (D, 24h, CW, ATM)
- 🛏 Extended Stay
- ℞ Walgreens
- 🛒 Dan's

EXIT 7
Coventry
West Warwick
- ✕ Applebee, Wendy's, Cracker Barrel, Denny's (24h)
- ⛽ BJ's
- 🛏 Hampton Inn
- (right) ✕ Mobil (R)

EXIT 6A
Hopkins Hill Rd

EXIT 6
W Greenwich
Coventry
- ✕ Bess Eaton, Li'l Rhody II Ice Crm, Dunkin Donuts, Mark's Grille (ATM)
- ⛽ Sunoco (D, R), Shell (24h, ATM)
- 🛏 Best Western, Super 8

EXIT 5 — 102
North Kingstown
Foster
- ✕ Tommy's Place (24h)
- ⛽ RI T/A Truck Plaza (D, 24h, ATM)
- 🛏 Classic Motor Lodge
- T/A Truck Plaza

EXIT 4 — 3
Arcadia
Exeter

EXIT 3
Kingston
Wyoming
- ✕ Ball Village, Bess Eaton, Bickford's, Boucher's Wood River Inn, Subway, Village Pizza, Lolita's Pizza
- ⛽ Exxon (ATM, LP, 24h), Gulf (ATM), Mobil (ATM, LP, 24h), Valero (ATM)
- 🛏 Stage Coach House
- ℞ Ocean Pharmacy

EXIT 3 (right side):
- ✕ Bess Eaton, Dunkin Donuts, McDonald's, Wendy's
- ⛽ Stop'n Shop
- 🛒 Stop'n Shop (ATM)
- Golf Central

RI WELCOME CTR REST AREA

EXIT 2
Hope Valley
Alton
- 📖 Enchanted Forest

EXIT 1 — 3
Hopkinton
Westerly
- ✕ Bess Eaton, Dunkin Donuts, McDonald's
- ⛽ Mobil (D, K, 24h), Texaco Truck Plaza (D, ATM, K, 24h)
- 🛏 Budget Inn, Stardust Motel (P)

RHODE ISLAND
CONNECTICUT

EXIT 93 — 216
Clarks Falls
Ashaway RI
- (right) ✕ Shell (D, R, ATM)

EXIT 92 — 49 / 2
No Stonington
Pawcatuck
- ✕ Mystic Pizza II
- 🛏 Cedar Park Inn & Suites, Foxwood Resorts and Casino, Randall's Ordinary
- 🛒 Raspberry Junction

65 mph

© 2004

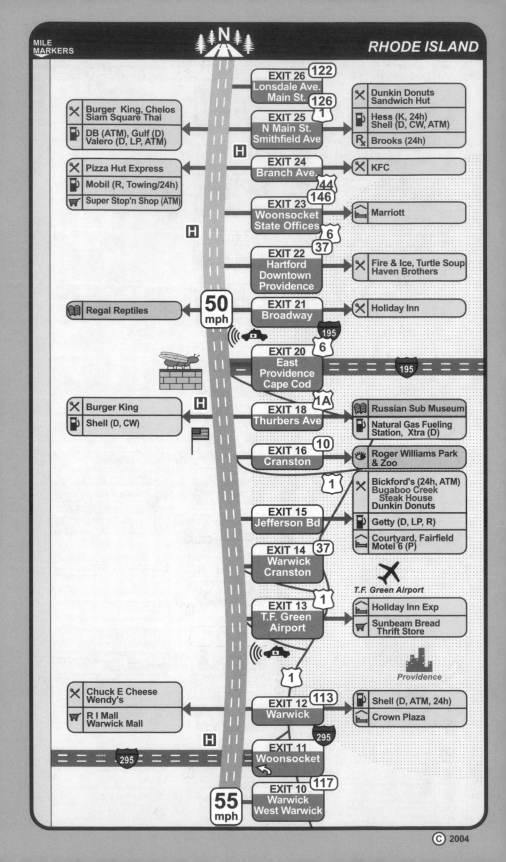

MILE MARKERS

N

RHODE ISLAND

EXIT 26 **122**
Lonsdale Ave.
Main St.

126
1

EXIT 25
N Main St.
Smithfield Ave

🍴 Dunkin Donuts
Sandwich Hut

⛽ Hess (K, 24h)
Shell (D, CW, ATM)

℞ Brooks (24h)

🍴 Burger King, Chelos
Siam Square Thai

⛽ DB (ATM), Gulf (D)
Valero (D, LP, ATM)

H

EXIT 24
Branch Ave.

🍴 KFC

🍴 Pizza Hut Express

⛽ Mobil (R, Towing/24h)

🛒 Super Stop'n Shop (ATM)

44
146

EXIT 23
Woonsocket
State Offices

🏨 Marriott

6
37

H

EXIT 22
Hartford
Downtown
Providence

🍴 Fire & Ice, Turtle Soup
Haven Brothers

50
mph

EXIT 21
Broadway

🍴 Holiday Inn

📖 Regal Reptiles

🚗 ((•

195
6

EXIT 20
East
Providence
Cape Cod

195

H

EXIT 18
Thurbers Ave

1A

📖 Russian Sub Museum

⛽ Natural Gas Fueling
Station, Xtra (D)

🍴 Burger King

⛽ Shell (D, CW)

EXIT 16
Cranston

10

👁 Roger Williams Park
& Zoo

1

🍴 Bickford's (24h, ATM)
Bugaboo Creek
Steak House
Dunkin Donuts

⛽ Getty (D, LP, R)

🏨 Courtyard, Fairfield
Motel 6 (P)

EXIT 15
Jefferson Bd

EXIT 14
Warwick
Cranston

37

✈
T.F. Green Airport

1

EXIT 13
T.F. Green
Airport

🏨 Holiday Inn Exp

🛒 Sunbeam Bread
Thrift Store

🚗 ((•

1

Providence

🍴 Chuck E Cheese
Wendy's

🛒 R I Mall
Warwick Mall

EXIT 12
Warwick

113

⛽ Shell (D, ATM, 24h)

🏨 Crown Plaza

H

295

295

EXIT 11
Woonsocket

EXIT 10
Warwick
West Warwick

117

55
mph

© 2004

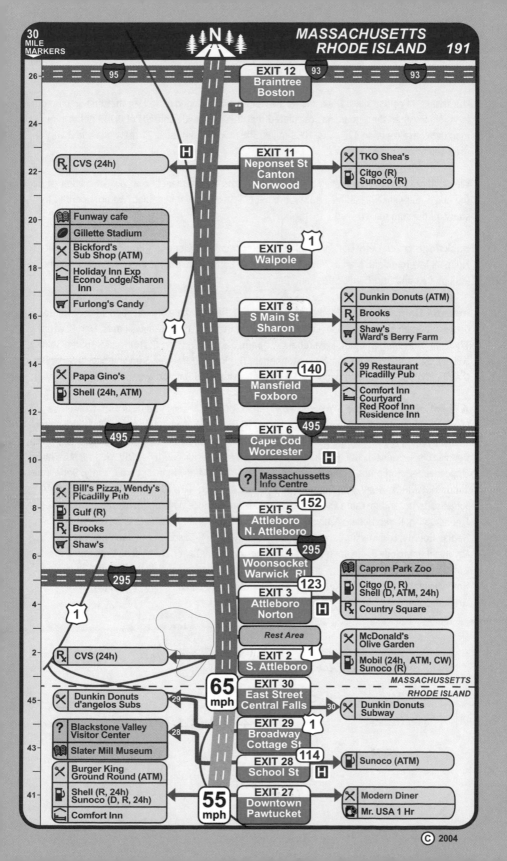

Acknowledgements

"The journey of a thousand miles begins with one step." Lao-Tze, the Simple Way No. 64

Our thanks, of course, go to Dave and Kathy Hunter, who nudged us to take that first step on our long journey. Stan the actuary has calculated that this info-guide consists of 6,743 items in our map data base covering 422 exits, 1089 miles, 301 stories, 54 photos, 51 drawings and 2 very tired authors.

We could not possible have taken all those figures and turned them into a book by ourselves. By the end of our year, we had help from more people then we ever imagined. We are honored to show off the sum of your work.

Backstage crew: Gerry Gatien, Caroline Taillefer, Sarah Bellefontaine, Brandon Posner, Stuart Nulman, Taketomo and Marcus families, Nancy and Eddie Chin, Ronnie and Ira Kaplan, Flo and Irv Phillips, Bea and Burt Dermer, Rose and Ben Wald

Industry Help: Publisher's Marketing Association, the incredible organization where we took courses to learn about the book publishing industry in the U.S.; SPAN newsletters; Dan Poynter The Self-Publishing Manual: Leila Albala, Illegally Easy Halloween Costumes; Margaret Goldick, AELAQ; Gail and Ilan Hofmann; Kelly Monaghan, The Intrepid Traveler; Sam Spiegel, Partners Book Distributing; Kate and Doug Bandos, KSB Promotions; Evelyn Hannon, www.journeywoman.com

A Tip of our Hats to the States: New England Tourism: Manny Witt, Lisa Witt; **RI** Melissa Divine; BlackstoneValley: Bob Billington, Angela Hyllestedok, Mary Harrington; **CT** Southeastern Conn. Mystic & more: Deborah Donovan; Coastal Fairfield: Mary Lukens, Pat Palombi; New Haven: Rennie Loisel; Connecticut East: Diana Ketner; **NY** Westchester County: Traci L. Suppa; **NJ** Phyllis Oppenheimer; Burlington County: Darlene A. Scocca; **MD** Mindy Bianca; Cecil County: Bob White, Sandy Maruchi-Turner; Prince George County: Matt Neitzey; Harford County: Diane Molner; **VA** Julia Scott; Alexandria: Laura Overstreet, Merrie Morris; Prince William County: Patti Bryant; Fredricksburg: Karen Hedelt; Ashland: George Edwards; Richmond: Janene Charbeneau; **NC** Halifax County: Lori Medlin; Johnston County: Donna Bailey-Taylor; Dunn: Dana Cochran; Fayetteville: Melody Foote, John Meroski; Lumberton: Mary Taylor; **SC** Melissa Williams; Santee-Cooper Country: Mary Shriner; Florence: Linda Jordan; Lowcountry: Lois Brady, Jim Wescott; Hardeeville: June Smith; **GA** Kitty Sikes; Kingsland: Tonya Rosado; McIntosh County: Shelly Grissett; Savannah: Erica Backus; **FL** Tom Flanigan.

Merci Beaucoup

Stan Sandra

Bring home a Taste of your Trip

SQUASH CASSEROLE

From the Summerton Diner, Exit 108, Summerton, SC

Catherine (Cat) Dingle, the cook who prepares this recipe, has been working here for 25 years, so she really knows her locals' tastebuds. The recipe actually comes from Lynelle Blackwell, the second generation owner who now runs the diner.

This is the only restaurant the we have ever eaten in where we prefer eating our vegetables first. We wouldn't leave unless they parted with this recipe, and our family and everyone else who has tasted it just loves it. It's real comfort food.

SQUASH CASSEROLE

3 lb. butternut squash - or any kind: yellow, crookneck, etc.

1 1/2 cups sour cream

2 1/2 cups (about 8 oz. in a block) shredded cheddar cheese
or more, to taste

1 pkg. dry onion soup mix (Lipton or any other)

Topping (optional): 1/2 cup crushed soda crackers mixed with
1 Tbsp melted butter, or crumbled biscuits with butter

- *Peel squash, cut in cubes and then boil until very soft (about 20 min.) so squash can be mashed easily*

- *Mix in shredded cheddar, sour cream and dry onion soup and put in a 10 x 10 casserole dish*

- *If desired, crumbled biscuits or soda crackers mixed with melted butter, sprinkle on top and bake for about 20 min. at 350 until lightly browned*

- *You can omit the topping and just serve it without baking, but then prepare it a few hours ahead or a day ahead, so the onion soup has a chance to blend in. Just re-heat it when you are ready to serve.*

Serves 8 as a side dish.

The recipe is very forgiving and you can add or subtract some of the sour cream, cheese or dried soup to suit your taste buds.

Campgrounds Near I-95 Exits

State	Exit	Campground Name	Phone	# of sites	Distance	Directions
MA	6B	Normandy Farm Camping	508-543-7600	400	5.4	I-495 N to exit 14A, 1 mi. up hwy 1 to Thurston St, turn right 1.5 mi.
MA	6A	Canoe River	508-339-6462	150	3.5	I-495 S to exit 10, E on Rte 123 ¾ mi., left on Newland/Mill St 2.4 mi.
RI	1	Frontier Family Camper Pk	401-377-4510	225	1	South on Rte 3, left on Frontier Rd to end, left on Maxson Hill Rd.
CT	93	Holly Tree Campground	401-596-2766	160	2	Take Rte 216 2mi. South from I-95
CT	92	Highland Orchards Resort	800-624-0829	275	0.25	N on Rte 49. Northbound: left on Rte 2 right on service rd, left on Rte 49, 1st right
CT	90	Seaport Campground	860-536-4044	130	2	1 ¼ mi. N on Rte 27 then ½ mi. East on Rte 184
CT	74	Aces High RV Park	860-739-8858	90	3.5	Rte 161 west on Chesterfield Rd.
CT	72	Camp Niantic by the Atlantic	860-739-9308	135	1	South to Rocky Neck Park, turn right at stop light. (Rte.156).
CT	62	Riverdale Farm Campsite	860-669-5388	222	2.5	N 1 block, right on Duck Hole Rd ¼ mi., cross cement bridge, left on River Rd 1 ¾ mi.
NJ	2	Timberlane Campground	856-423-6677	96	11	Rte 322 E to I-295, N to exit 18. Turn right on Timberlane Rd. for 1 mi.
MD	109	Woodlands Camp.Resort	410-398-4414	160	6	Rte 279 South, cross Rte 40 onto Rte 7. First left on Old Elk Neck Rd.
MD	80	Bar Harbor RV Park	410-679-0880	93	4	South 1 ¼ mi. to US 40, turn right 1.7 mi to Long Bar Harbor Rd.
MD	25	Cherry Hill Park	301-937-7116	380	1	Rte 1 S. First right on Cherry Hill Rd.
MD	11	Duncan's Family Camp.	410-741-9558	238	10.3	Rte 4 South 9.5 mi to Rte 408, left on Sands Rd.
VA	152	Prince William Travel Trailer Village	703-221-2474	75	2.5	2 ½ mi North on Rte 234 to campground on left
VA	143	Aquia Pines Camp Resrt	540-659-3447	125	0.5	½ mi N on Hwy 1
VA	98	King's Dominion	800-922-6710	225	0.5	Adjacent to Kings Dominion
VA	89	Kosmo Village Camp.	804-798-6689	17	2	West to US 1, turn South (right) 1 ¼ mi
VA	89	Americamps Richmond N.	804-798-5298	144	1	East on Rte 802 N Lewiston Rd. then 1 mi south on service road
VA	61	Roadrunner Campground	804-796-5160	67	1.5	East on Rte 10, make 1st left at Jefferson Davis Hwy for 1 mile
VA	41	The South Forty KOA	800-KOA-8545	114	0.5	East on Rte 35 Courtland Rd, turn right ¼ mi.
VA	17	Yogi Bear's Jellystone Park & Emporia	434-634-3115	90	1.5	1 ½ mi south on US 301
VA	4	Cattail Creek RV & Camp.	434-634-9935	60	2.75	Rte 629 West (Moore's Ferry Rd.)
NC	173	Interstate Inn	252-536-4111	28	200 Yds	E on Rte 158 behind motel
NC	173	Ponderosa Campground	252-536-4741	40	1	1 mi East on Hwy 158
NC	154	Enfield / Rocky Mount Kampground	252-445-5925	89	0.75	West on Rte 481 ¾ mi
NC	116	Rock Ridge	252-291-4477	67	1.9	West on Rt 42 (follow signs)

Campgrounds Near I-95 Exits

State	Exit	Campground Name	Phone	# of sites	Distance	Directions
NC	98	Selma/Smithfield RVacation	919-965-5923	60	0.5	S on Pine Level Selma Rd to N on-ramp, right on Campground Rd 0.4 mi
NC	90	Best Holiday Trav-L-Park	919-934-3181	104	300 yds	300 yards up US 701
NC	61	Fayetteville /Wade KOA	800-562-5350	86	0.25	East 1/4 mi
NC	44	Lazy Acres Campgrounds	910-425-7614	55	1.25	West on Claude Lee Rd (Rte 2341) 1 mi, right at Lazy Acres Drive
NC	41	Spring Valley	910-425-1505	38	2	3/4 mi N on Rte 59 (cross Hwy 301), then 1 mi N on service rd.
NC	14	Sleepy Bear's RV Park	910-739-4372	102	0.25	150 yards West on US 74, then 1/4 mi.north on Kenric Rd.
NC	1	Camp Pedro	843-774-2411	100	0.2	South on US 301 1/4 mi
SC	193	Bass Lake	843-774-2690	68	0.5	1 block N, right on Bass Lake Place for 1/5 mi
SC	169	Florence KOA	843-665-7007	132	1	1 block S on Rte 26, left turn on East Campground Rd. for 1 mi.
SC	157	Swamp Fox	843-665-9430	65	0.75	1/4 mi on southbound service rd., right turn on Meadors Rd.for 1/2 mi
SC	150	Lake Honey Dew Camping	843-346-0700	40	0.2	Northwest corner right off exit ramp
SC	119	Camper's Paradise	803-473-3550	60	0.4	1 block East on Rte 261 then 1 block South on Hwy 63
SC	102	Santee Lake Campground	803-478-2262	200	0.5	West 1 block to Rte 14, turn right to lakefront
SC	102	Cooper's Landing	803-478-2549	21	1	East on CR 400
SC	98	Lake Marion Resort	803-854-3083	87	2.5	East on Hwy 6
SC	77	Comfort Inn	843-563-4180	24	50 ft	I-95 & Rte 78
SC	68	Shuman's	888-533-8731	14	3	2 1/2 mi East on Rte 61, 1/4 mi. N on Hwy 15
SC	53	Green Acres RV Park	800-474-3560	106	0.5	Rte 63 West for 1 block, then right turn at Campground Rd. for 0.4 mi
SC	33	The Oaks at Point South	843-726-5728	39	3	N on Rte 17, E on Yamassee to stop sign then N on Campground Rd
SC	33	Point South KOA	800-726-5733	56	1	N on Rte 17, E on Yamassee to stop sign then right on Campground Rd
GA	94	Bellaire Woods	912-748-4000	142	2.5	2 1/2 mi West on Hwy 204
GA	90	Waterway	912-756-2296	36	3.5	1 mi East on Rte 144, turn North (left) on Hwy 17 2.5 mi to Kings Ferry Bridge
GA	87	KOA Savannah South	912-756-3396	125	0.25	1/4 mi South on 17
GA	76	Glebe Plantation	912-884-5218	42	0.5	West 1 block in US 84 / Rte 38. Turn right 1/2 mi on Glebe Plantation Rd.
GA	58	Lake Harmony RV Park	912-832-4338	50	0.5	West 1/2 mi.
GA	58	Mcintosh Lake RV Park	912-832-6215	38	0.75	3/4 mi. West on Rte 57
GA	49	Inland Harbor	912-437-6172	50	400 ft	400 ft East on Hwy 251
GA	49	Tall Pines	912-437-3966	45	0.5	East on Rte 251, left at Lakeshore
GA	29	Blythe Island Regional Camp	800-343-7855	97	4	1/2 mi West on Hwy 17 then 3 1/2 mi N on Blythe Island Hwy
GA	1	Country Oaks	912-729-6212	40	0.4	0.4 mi West on St.Mary's Rd.
GA	1	Koa Kingsland, Jacksonville N	912-729-3232	100	0.5	Exit 1 West to campground

Golf Courses Near I-95 Exits

State	Exit	City	Course Name	Address	Public or Semi-Pvt	Phone	Par	Directions
RI	8	East Greenwich	East Greenwich G & CC	1646 Divison Rd.	SP	401-884-5656	36	South on Rte.2, right on Division Rd. ½ mi
RI	6	Coventry	Coventry Pines	Harkney Hill Rd.	P	401-397-9482	9	North 1 ¼ mi on Rte 3, left at Harkney Hill Rd. 2mi.
RI	3	Richmond	Meadow Brook	163 Kingstown Rd.	P	401-539-8491	72	Exit 3A to Rte 138E 1 ½ mi.
CT	92	Pawcatuck	Elmridge	229 Elmridge Rd.	P	860-599-2248	72	East on Rte 2 for ¾ mi., right on Elmridge Rd.
CT	87	Groton	Shennecosset	Plant St.	P	860-445-0262	71	Clarence Sharp Hwy S, right on Rainville, left on Benham for 1 ½ mi.
CT	74	East Lyme	Cedar Ridge	34 Drabik Rd.	P	860-691-4568	54	1 mi N on Flanders Rd.
CT	39	Orange	Grassy Hill CC	441 Clark Lane	P	203-795-3100	70	US 1 South ¾ mi. to Rte 121 2 ½ mi
CT	37N	Milford	Great River	130 Coram Lane	P	203-876-8051	72	North on High St./Wheelers Farm Rd. 2 mi., left on Herbert to Coram lane
CT	13N/14S	Norwalk	Oak Hills	165 Fillow St.	P	203-838-0303	72	US 1 to Richards Ave. 1.6 mi. to end, right to course
CT	51/52	New Haven	Ailling Memorial	35 Eastern St.	P	203-946-8014	72	High St to Laurel St., North 1.6 mi
CT	6	Stamford	E.Gaynor Brennan	451 Stillwater Rd.	P	203-324-4185	71	North on West Ave. 3/4 mi., left on Stillwater ½ mi.
MD	100	North East	North East Course	1500 Chesapeake Club Dr.	P	410-287-0200	70	South on Rte 272 for 3.75 mi.
MD	100	Rising Sun	Rising Sun Course	128 Karen Dr.	P	410-658-4343	71	North on Rte 272, left on Rte 274 for 2 ¼ mi
MD	89	Havre de Grace	Bulle Rock	320 Blenheim Lane	P	410-939-8887	71	East on Rte 155 2.2 mi., right on 40 for 2 mi.
MD	85	Aberdeen	The Wetlands	740 Gilbert Rd.	P	410-273-7488	71	West on 22 to Gilbert Rd, right for 1 ½ mi.
MD	80	Aberdeen	Ruggles	Bldg 5600 Aberdeen Proving Grnd	P	410-278-4794	72	543 south, left on 7 to Hwy 40, left to 715, right thru gate
MD	74	Joppa	Mountain Branch	1827 Mountain Rd.	SP	410-836-9600	72	North on Mountain Rd. (Rte 152) for 2 mi.
MD	51	Baltimore	Carroll Park	2100 Washington Blvd.	P	410-685-8344	10	/39 N only; left turn off exit.
MD	33	Laurel	Gunpowder	14300 Old Gunpowder Rd.	P	301-725-4532	70	West on 198 to Old Gunpowder Rd., left 1mi.
MD	33	Laurel	Patuxent Greens CC	14415 Greenview Dr.	SP	301-776-5533	72	East on 198 for 2 ¾ mi., right on 197, second left
VA	176	Alexandria	Greendale	6700 Telegraph Rd.South	P	703-971-3788	70	Exit 2 Telegraph Rd. South 3 ½ mi. on right.
VA	170	Alexandria	Pinecrest	6600 Little River Turnpike	P	703-941-1061	35	I-495 exit 52B, E on Rte.236 (Little River Tpke) 3 mi. on left

Golf Courses Near I-95 Exits

State	Exit	City	Course Name	Address	Phone	Public or Semi-Pvt	Par	Directions
VA	160	Woodbridge	The Ospreys at Belmont Bay	13401 Potomac Path Dr.	703-497-1384	F	70	S on Gordon, Right on US 1 1/4 mi, left on Dawsons Bch 1/2 mi, left to Belmont Bay
VA	150	Triangle	Forest Greens	4500 Poa Annua	703-221-0123	F	72	Rte 619 west for 1/4 mi.
VA	84	Glen Allen	The Crossings	800 Virginia Center Pkwy.	804-266-2254	F	72	Exit 84B Rte 1 N 1 block, right on Virginia Center Pkwy.
VA	83	Richmond	Belmont	1600 Hillard Rd.	804-501-4653	P	71	W on E Parham Rd, 1 1/4 mi S on US 1
NC	101	Selma	Cardinal CC	363 Parish Memorial Rd.	919-284-3647	SP	72	Pittman Rd. 1/4 mi to stop, left 500 yds, on Batten Farm Rd 2 1/2 mi
NC	97	Clayton	The Neuse	918 Birkdale Dr.	919-550-0550	SP	72	Rte 70 W 12 mi, right on 42 to Glen Laurel Rd.
NC	81	Four Oaks	Reede Creek	585 Reedy creek rd.	919-934-75C2	P	72	I-40W to exit 319, right on 210 2.25 mi, right at Lassiter Rd onto Reedy Creek Rd.
SC	164	Darlington	Beaver Creek	1133 East Mciver	843-393-5441	SP	72	North on 52 2 1/4 mi. to Palmetto Rd, turn right to Mciver
SC	160	Florence	Traces	4322 Southborough Rd.	843-662-7775	SP	72	I-20 West 4 mi to exit 137, left on 340, 2nd left and left again
SC	135	Gable	Sumter's National GC	7305 Myrtle Beach Hwy.	803-495-3550	SP	72	West on 378 1/4 mi on right
SC	119	Manning	Clarendon's CC	Bloomville Hwy	800-504-00C4	P	72	East on Rte 261 3mi on right
SC	98	Santee	Santee National GC	Hwy6	800-448-0152	P	72	1mi W on Hwy 6
GA	102	Savannah	Southbridge	415 SouthBridge Blvd.	912-651-5455	SP	72	East 1 exit to Dean Forest Rd, turn right 200 yds
GA	94	Savannah	Henderson	1 AL Henderson Dr.	912-920-4653	P	71	East to 1st light (Gateway Blvd. East), left 1 mile
GA	87	Richmond Hill	Waterford Landing	731 Waterford Landing Rd.	912-727-48<8	SP	71	South on 17 for 2.7 mi, left on Belfast Siding, right after 5 mi.
GA	67	Shellman Bluff	Sapelo Hammock	500 Marshview Dr.	912-832-4653	SP	72	East on 17 2.8 mi, left on Minton Rd.
GA	42	Brunswick	Coastal Pines	1 Coastal Pines Circle	912-261-0503	P	72	Rte 99 3mi on the right
GA	6	Kingsland	Laurel Island Links	233 Marsh Harbour Pkwy.	912-729-7227	P	72	East on Colerain Rd 2.5mi, left on Laurel Island Pkwy
GA	1	St.Mary's	Osprey Cove	123 Osprey Dr.	912-882-5575	SP	72	East on St Marys Rd 2.5 mi

Auto Mechanics Along I-95 Exits

State	Exit	Listing on our Maps	E/W of I-95	Phone	Hours	Towing
MA	11	Sunoco R	E	781-828-9190	M-Sat.	
MA	11	Citgo R	E	781-321-1344	M-Sat.	
MA	5	Gulf R	W	508-599-7344	M-Fri.	
RI	27	Sunoco D R 24h	W	401-726-9272	M-Sat.	
RI	27	Shell F 24h	W	401-726-9345	M-Sat.	
RI	24	Mobil R 24hTowing	W	401-521-9792/8606	M-Sat.	24h
CT	93	Shell D ATM R	E	860-599-4581	M-Fri.	
CT	74	Sunoco D R	E	860-739-2180		
CT	70	Texacc D R	W	860-434-8250	M-Sat.	
CT	61	Sunoco R		203-245-7534	M-Sat.	
CT	58	Getty ATM R	E	203-453-1323	M-Sat.	
CT	56	T/A Travel Ctr 24h TR	W	203-481-0301		
CT	55	Branford Auto Ctr R ATM	E	203-481-6572		24h
CT	54	Citgo R D	E	203-488-0800/481-9769	M-Fri.	
CT	44	Amocc 24h	E	203-932-8426/6322	M-Sat.	
CT	40	Bruneau's D R Towing/24h	E	203-878-2157	M-Sat.	24h
CT	37	Texaco R	E	203-874-9926	M-Fri.	
CT	37	Gulf R	E	203-874-2893		
CT	34	Angelo's Auto Ctr D R	E	203-783-3964		
CT	33	Sunoco R	E	203-377-4753	M-Sat.	
NY	20	Shell R	E	914-967-1612	M-Sat.	Yes
NY	18	Shell R 24h	E	914-698-1118	M-Sat.	
NY	18	Gulf R	E	914-698-2544/5252t	M-Sat.	
NY	18	Citgo D R	E	914-698-6444	M-Sat.	
NY	13	Gulf D R 24h	E	718-547-6106		
NJ	72	Mobil D R	W	201-944-3662		
NJ	9	Gulf D R 24hTowing	E	732-846-0074 Towing: 732-251-4333/5888.		M-Sat.	24h
NJ	8	Exxon R D	E	609-448-2122 Towing: 609-448-2746	M-Sat.	24h
NJ	7	Mobil R	E	609-298-4001	7 days 8-7	
NJ	7	Bordentown Auto D R	W	609-291-7131	7days.	
DE	3	Getty F	W	302-738-0342		
DE	3	Exxon D R ATM BP	E	302-453-1244		

State	Exit	Listing on our Maps	E/W of I-95	Phone	Hours	Towing
MA	3	Citgo D R	E	508-222-6670	M-Sat.	
MA	2	Sunoco R	E	401-726-6260		
RI	15	Getty D LP R	E	401-461-7309	M-Sat.	
RI	6	Sunoco D R	W	401-397-7865		
CT	32	Mobil R	E	203-377-6370		
CT	31	Citgo D R	W	203-378-5147	M-Sat.	
CT	24	Getty R D	W	203-368-2277	M-Sat.	
CT	23	Sunoco D R LP		203-259-3895		
CT	22	Sunoco D R LP	E	203-259-3895		
CT	21	Shell R ATM	E	203-259-7558		
CT	16	Shell D R ATM CW	E	203-866-6238		
CT	16	Citgo R	E	203-838-5155	M-Sat.	
CT	14	Sunoco D R ATM	W	203-855-9141		
CT	11	Exxon R LP	W	203-656-6653	M-Sat.	
CT	10	Getty R	W	203-655-1971		
CT	10	Citgo D R	W	203-656-1639; 24h Towing: 203-327-4240	M-Sat.	24h
CT	3	Mobil R	W	203-622-9353	M-Sat.	
NY	11	Shell ATM R 24h.	W	718-320-8227.	M-Sat 7-7	
NY	11	Mobil ATM R	E	718-379-8737/8731 Towing: 718-925-0468	7 days 7-7	24h
NY	10	Gulf ATM R 24h	W	718-320-7400, 914-562-2693	M-Sat	
NY	5	Amoco R 24h	E	718-822-6327,866-0216		
NY	4	Getty D R 24h	E	718-863-1470		
NJ	4	Mobil D R 24h	E	856-235-4740	M-Sat.	
NJ	4	Getty D R 24h	E	718-863-1470, 828-4549		
NJ	3	Gulf D R 24h Trucks	E	856-931-8882		
NJ	1	Coastal D R	W	856-933-1404		
NJ	1	Exxon D R	E	856-851-1899		
DE	1	Shell 24h R.	W	302-368-4322		
DE	1	Gulf D R	W	302-733-0522		

State	Exit	Service	Dir	Phone
MD	100	Mobil R	W	410-287-5900
MD	98	Sunoco D 24h ATM R		410-287-2170
MD	85	Shell (D, R)	B	410-272-1530
MD	83	Sunoco (D,R)		410-272-2705
MD	83	Exxon (D,R,ATM)	B	410-272-2705
MD	77	Shell R ATM 24h		410-676-1060
MD	67	Exxon R LP D ATM 24h	E	410-931-6320
MD	58	Mobil D R ATM 24h	E	410-633-2312
MD	57	Wayne Trinks R no gas	E	410-633-6570
MD	41	Shell R 24h ATM	E	410-799-3533
VA	177	Texaco D R	E	703-329-1780
VA	177	Sunoco R ATM CW	E	703-329-1611
VA	177	Mobil D R 24h	E	703-329-1516
VA	177	Exxon 24h R (24h)	W	703-836-5136 ..24h
VA	176	Citgo R	E	703-960-2255
VA	176	Amoco R	W	703-960-2030
VA	169	Mobil R 24h	W	703-451-2911
VA	163	Shell R ATM 24h	E	703-690-1300
VA	160	Exxon D R LP 24	W	703-494-4284
VA	152	Shell R	W	703-221-2215
VA	152	Chevron R ATM		703-221-8473
VA	150	Shell D R LP ATM	E	703-221-4131/1100 ... Towing: 703-221-4184 ..24h
VA	140	Texaco D R Towing (24h)	E	540-659-4034
VA	140	Shell D BP R ATM	W	540-658-1400
VA	133	Servicetown PTP Travel Plaza D S 24h TR		
VA	130	Amoco R D LP	W	540-371-1166 ..M-Set
VA	126	Mobil R	W	540-370-0147
NC	106	Wilco Travel Plaza Hess S D TR 24h TW	W	919-284-6109
NC	106	T/A Travel Ctr Shell S D TR ATM 24h TW		919-284-5121
NC	105	Big Boys Travel Store D S 24h TR ATM	E	919-284-4046
NC	102	BP R	W	919-284-3285 ..7 days to 10:30 pm
NC	79	Coastal R D		919-207-2111
SC	169	Petro D TR TW 24h ATM	W	843-661-0730
SC	157	Amoco R LP Towing (24h)		843-679-9006 ..24h
SC	119	T/A Travel Ctr D TR TW RVD S 24h	E	803-473-2568
SC	119	Exxon R ATM 24h	W	803-473-7777 ..24h
SC	98	Shell ATM D R 24h	W	803-854-5506/5076 ..24h
GA	36	Sun Coast RV	W	912-265-7379
MD	33	Shell R 24h	W	301-776-6485
MD	33	Exxon D R ATM	W	301-498-0572
MD	25	Shell R 24h ATM LP CNG	E	301-474-0215
MD	20	Shell R ATM 24h		301-577-1011
MD	11	Sunoco R D ATM 24h	W	301-420-8322, 301-736-1450
MD	9	Shell R 24h	E	301-736-3782, 301-899-9836
MD	4	Shell R 24h		301-894-6565
MD	3	Shell R	E	301-839-3377
MD	3	Chevron R D 24h	W	301-839-1555
MD	3	BP R TR D 24h	W	301-839-5743
VA	126	BP D R	E	540-898-8907
VA	118	Shell R D	E	540-582-6188
VA	118	Citgo D BP R ATM K 24h	W	540-582-5628
VA	104	Petro D TR TW ATM 24h	E	804-448-2723
VA	98	Texaco R 24h	W	804-876-3916
VA	92	T/A Travel Ctr D 24h S TR	W	804-798-6011
VA	92	Mobil BP R	E	804-798-9463
VA	78	Texaco D LP K R ATM	W	804-355-3550
VA	64	Shell R ATM	W	804-275-7876
VA	61	Sunoco - R (NO gas)	W	804-748-0255
VA	45	Texaco D R	E	804-732-9202
VA	33	Davis Truck Stop - Chevron	W	434-246-4641
VA	33	Exxon D R TR LP Towing/24h		
VA	31	Texaco D ATM K R Towing/24h	W	434-246-2039
VA	11	Sadler Travel Plaza Shell S D TR 24h	W	434-634-4312
VA	8	Simmons Travel Plaza Amoco S D TR 24h ATM BP	E	434-634-9296
VA		Citgo R. BP	E	434-634-9646
NC	75	Sadler Travel Plaza S D TR 24h	W	919-892-0106
NC	61	61 Truck Stop Citgo D TR K		910-483-9528
NC	49	BP D K R ATM	E	910-483-9393
NC	17	Mobil R 24h D ATM	E	671-8776, night:738-8882 ..24h
SC	97	Sam Key Truck & Towing Service TR	W	803-854-3338 ..Yes
SC	68	Shell C K TR RVD S 24h	W	843-589-5443
SC	38	Simco Travel Plaza TR D LP	W	843-589-3400
SC	8	BP D S 24h ATM TR	W	843-726-3084
SC	5	Exxon D R	W	843-784-6226 ..24h
GA	29	T/A Travel D TR S 24h	W	912-264-5530

We have tried to collect as complete and accurate information as we could, but repair shops unfortunately magically turn into mini-marts without any notice, so please call first to confirm.

Independent Motels and Bed & Breakfasts Along I-95 Exits

State	Exit	Name	E/W of I-95	Phone	Pets	Trucks RVs
RI	8	Open Gate Motel	W	401-884-4490, 800-370-5700	No	
RI	5	Classic Motor Lodge	W	401-397-6280		
CT	93	Stardust	W	860-599-2261	Smoking Rms	
CT	93	Budget Inn	W	860-599-0835/0845		
CT	92	Randal's Ordinary	W	860-599-4540		Yes
CT	92	Cedar Park Inn & Suites	W	860-535-7829, 866-535-7829	Some	
CT	90	Seaport Inn	E	800-536-2621		
CT	86	Grotor Inn & Suites	E	860-445-9784 or 800-452-2191		
CT	83	Queen Anne Inn	E	800-347-8818 or 860-447-2600	Yes	
CT	70	Old Lyme Inn & Rest	W	860-434-2600		
CT	69	Griswold Inn	W	860-767-1776		
CT	68	Liberty Inn AAA	W	860-388-1777		
CT	66	Sandpiper Motor Inn	E	860-399-7973		
CT	66	Heritage Motor Inn (May 1 to Nov 1 ONLY)	E	860-388-3743		
NY	10	Pelham Garden Motel	W	718-379-2300		
NJ	72	Hilltop Motel (on Rte 4)	W	201-944-5500		
NJ	16	Palace Hotel	E	201-866-0400		
NJ	13	Budget Inn	E	908-289-8900		
NJ	8	Town House Motel	W	609-448-2400	Yes	
NJ	7	Imperial Inn	E	609-298-3355	$5	Yes
DE	14	Superlodge	W	302-654-5544		
MD	109	Elkton Lodge	E	410-398-9400		Yes
MD	109	Elk Forge B&B	W	410-392-9007		
VA	177	Travelers MotelAAA	E	703-329-13100 or 800-368-7378		
VA	166	Hunter Motel	E	703-339-5400	No	
VA	126	Royal Inn	E	540-891-2700	No	
VA	126	Heritage Inn	E	540-898-1000	No	
VA	92	Henry Clay Inn	W	804-798-3100		
VA	92	Budget Inn	W	804-798-9291	No	

State	Exit	Name	E/W of I-95	Phone	Pets	Trucks RVs
RI	3	The Old Stagecoach House Inn	W	401-539-9600, 888-814-9600		
CT	56	Advanced Motel	E	203-481-4528	Yes	Yes
CT	47	Historic Mansion Inn	W	203-865-8324, 888-512-6278		
CT	40	Milford Inn	E	203-878-0685	No	
CT	40	Mayflower Motel	E	203-878-6854, 888-880-6854	No	Yes
CT	39	Lily Pad B&B	E	203-876-9996		
CT	34	Devon Motel	E	203-874-6634	No	
CT	31	Stratford Motor Inn	W	203-375-9779	No	
CT	24	Bridgeport Motor Inn	E	203-367-4404		
CT	22	Fairfield Inn	E	203-255-0491, 800-347-0414		
CT	19	Pequot Motor Inn	W	203-259-7885		
CT	15	Silvermine Tavern	W	203-847-4558		
CT	9	Stamford Motor Lodge	E	203-325-2655		
NY	3	Cross Bronx Motel	W	718-731-0300		
NJ	4	McIntosh Motor Inn	E	856-234-7194	No	Yes
NJ	4	Laurel Inn	W	856-235-7400	No	Yes
NJ	3	Bellmawr Motor Inn	W	856-931-6300	No	
NJ	1	Friendship Motor Inn	W	856-299-3700		
MD	100	Tail Winds Farm B&B	W	410-658-8187	Yes, even horses	Yes
MD	100	Crystal Inn (Flying J in back)	E	410-287-7100		Yes
VA	58	Chester Inn	E	804-526-4611		
VA	52	Royal Inn	E	804-733-0055	No	
VA	52	King Motel	E	804-733-7411	No	
VA	52	Economy Inn	E	804-861-4680	No	
VA	50	Flagship Inns	E	860-405-1111		
VA	47	Lasalle Motel	W	804-732-5710	No	

State	Exit	Name	Dir	Phone	Pets
VA	92	Ashland Inn	W	804-752-7777 or 877-888-2466	No
VA	81	Town Motel	E	804-266-8781	No
VA	64	VIP Inn	W	804-271-6081	No
VA	58	Interstate Inns	W	804-526-4772	
NC	173	Orchard Inn	E	252-536-2131	No
NC	173	Interstate Inn	E	252-536-4111	Yes
NC	145	Red Carpet Inn	E	252-446-0771	$5
NC	145	Deluxe Inn	E	252-446-2411	Yes
NC	145	Budget	E	252-977-3505	$5
NC	107	Deluxe Inn	E	919-284-3655	Yes
NC	107	Budget Inn	E	919-237-1178	
NC	97	Royal Inn	W	919-965-3716 or 800-368-8442	
NC	97	Luxury Inn	W	919-202-2000	
NC	95	Village Motor Lodge	E	919-934-7126	
NC	95	Log Cabin Motel	E	919-934-1534	$5
NC	90	Travelers Inn	E	919-934-4194	
NC	90	Four Oaks Motel	W	919-963-3596	
SC	181	Abingdon Manor	E	888-752-5090	Yes
SC	164	Thunderbird Inn	W	843-669-1611	
SC	164	Suburban Extended Stay	E	843-665-2575	No
SC	157	Young's Plantation Inn	W	843-669-4171	
SC	157	Villager Lodge	W	843-673-0070	
SC	157	Tree Top Inn	W	843-662-7712 or 877-397-2561	$10
SC	157	Swampfox Inn	E	843-665-0803	
SC	150	Budget Inn	E	843-662-9478	
SC	115	Sunset Inn	W	803-473-2561	$5
SC	115	Carolina Inn	W	803-473-7565	Yes
SC	98	Santee State Park Cabins	W	803-854-2408	
SC	98	Mansion Park	W	803-854-2334	
SC	98	Clark's Inn	W	843-854-2141	
SC	98	Budget Motel	W	843-854-4864	
GA	87	Royal Inn	E	912-756-2778	No
GA	49	Open Gates B&B	E	912-437-6985	
GA	49	Jaysen Executive Inn	W	912-437-5373	

State	Exit	Name	Dir	Phone	Pets
VA	47	Heritage Motor Lodge	W	804-732-3444	No
VA	17	Reste Motel	E	434-535-9100	No
VA	13	Dixie Motel		434-634-4512	
VA	8	Red Carpet Inn	E	434-634-4181	$5.35
NC	79	Dutch Inn	E	919-894-7562	$5
NC	73	Divine St. B&B	W	910-891-1103	
NC	72	Royal Inn	E	910-892-5886	Yes
NC	72	Express Inn of Dunn	W	910-892-8711	$5
NC	72	Budget Inn	W	910-892-6181	$5
NC	70	Relax Inn	E	910-892-8898	
NC	49	Deluxe Inn	E	910-484-2666	
NC	20	Deluxe Inn	E	910-738-4261	
NC	19	Traveler's Inn	E	910-738-2441	
NC	17	Southern Inn	E	910-738-1502	
NC	17	Budget Inn	E	910-739-3254	
NC	1	South of the Border Motor Inn		800-845-6011	
NC	1	Budget Motel	E	843-774-7761	
SC	82	Peachtree Inn	E	843 636-9393	Yes
SC	77	Southern Inn	W	843-563-3775	Yes
SC	77	American Inn AAA	E	843-563-2360	Yes
SC	57	Southern Inn	W	843-538-2280	Yes
SC	57	Carolina Lodge	E	843-538-7708	$5
SC	57	Budget Inn	W	843-538-3948	$5-10
SC	53	Thunderbird Inn AAA	E	843-538-2503	Yes
SC	53	Rice Planter's Inn	E	843-538-8964, or 800-647-4831 (after 3 pm)	Yes
SC	53	Deluxe Inn	W	843-538-3233	$5
SC	38	Palmetto Lodge	W	843-589-2361	Yes
SC	21	Carolina Lodge	W	843-726-6050	Yes
SC	5	Economy Inn	E	843-784-2201	Yes
SC	5	Deluxe Inn	W	843-784-3155	Yes
GA	38	Guest Cottage & Suites	W	912-264-6767	No
GA	3	Kingsland Inn	W	912-729-5528	Yes

We have tried to determine which of these accepts pets, but some information may be missing and may change without notice, so please call first to confirm

Driving Memories

Here's some space to jot a few notes to remember places
or people you've met along the way.

EXPENSES — SOUTH

| DATE | MILEAGE | | GAS Gallons | DAILY COSTS | | | | | | | | STATE | EXIT | TOWN | MOTEL | | |
| | START OF DAY | END OF DAY | | | | | | | | | | | | | NAME | | CONF # |
					DAILY TOTAL	BR	LUNCH	DINNER	GAS	SLEEP	OTHER	TOTAL					

EXPENSES — NORTH

	MILEAGE				DAILY COSTS									MOTEL		
DATE	START OF DAY	END OF DAY	DAILY TOTAL	GAS Gallons	BR	LUNCH	DINNER	GAS	SLEEP	OTHER	TOTAL	STATE	EXIT	TOWN	NAME	CONF #

Help us plan our next I-95 journey

To ensure that this book stays up-to-date and responsive to your needs, it would help immensely if you could send us some feedback. If you live, work or drive on this road frequently, please let us in on your favorite eateries, local shops, local sights, kids' fun or historical trivia. Please feel free to let us know about any quirky, interesting tidbits up to 5 miles or so off an exit.

snail mail: Travelsmart, *Drive I-95*
P.O. Box 3,
Roxboro, Quebec, CANADA   H8Y3E8
e-mail: comments@drivei95.com
online: fill out the comments page on our web site: www.drivei95.com

☐   Please add my name to your mailing list or e-mail list so you can send me future newsletters or discount coupons. (NOTE: We do not share this list with others)

Your Name _____

Phone: (only used to if we need more info about your comments)_____

Address _____

City _____ State/Province _____ Zip or Postal Code _____

e-mail _____

Have any of your favorites been missed?

Name_____ Exit # _____

Address _____ State _____

Phone _____ Website _____

Comments_____
_____
_____
_____

Have any of the places mentioned disappointed you in any way?

Name _____

State _____ Exit # _____

Comments_____
_____
_____
_____

OVER ☞

Are there any changes that you have noticed - i.e. the gas station or motel changed its name or restaurant closed?

Name _____

State _____ Exit # _____

Address _____

Phone _____ Website _____

Comments _____

_____

_____

_____

What additional information would you like to see in a future edition?

_____

_____

_____

_____

_____

_____

_____

_____

_____

_____

_____

_____

_____

_____

_____

_____

_____

_____

_____

Thanks for the feedback. We appreciate it and so will all of the other travelers who Drive I-95.

Stan Sandra

Drive I-95 Mail Order Form for yourself or for a gift

Use this to order another copy or for next year's edition so you will be the first to have one (before the bookstores even receive them). You can also order online at www.drivei95.com or over the phone from BCH company at 888-GUIDE95 (all major credit cards accepted). Each new edition will be available in September. The book makes a **perfect gift** for a relative who will be traveling, a teacher, your secretary, a student attending college along I-95 (or their parents for visiting days), salesmen, campers and RVers, military personnel, truckers or anyone who enjoys reading about America.

If you want the gift book autographed and personalized, please fill in the lines provided below ($5 extra).

Your name _____

Address _____

City _____ State/Province _____ Zip or Postal Code _____

e-mail address _____ Phone _____

Please send _____ copies of Drive I-95 to the above address.

I have enclosed my check for $_____ Checks should be made out to Travelsmart.

Credit Card type _____

Card # _____ Expiry date_____

Name on Card _____

Your signature _____

Price for books **shipped to the U.S.**: $22.95 each plus $4.00 shipping and handling. There is no extra shipping charge if you order up to 3 books. Add $1.50 for each additional book. Checks payable in U.S. funds. Add $5 for the personalization.

Price for books **shipped to Canada.**: $29.95 plus $3.50 for shipping and handling. There is no extra shipping charge if you order up to 3 books. Add $1.50 for each additional book. Checks payable in Canadian funds. Add $5 for the personalization.

Personalized words _____

_____

_____

To contact us: Travelsmart
P.O. Box 3
Roxboro, Quebec, Canada   H8Y 3E8
Phone: 514-684-4020   Fax: 514-684-6938
e-mail: orders@drivei95.com

"I just wanted to tell you how useful your book Drive I-95 was on our recent trip to Florida. It was our first road trip, and I'm not sure it would have gone as smoothly as it did without your book. As the navigator, I can tell you I really missed it when we got onto I-75 in Florida"

A. R., PA

"thanks for the great I 95 book, info better than GPS. I loved the radio stations the best ..."

K.E.

"My husband, a map person at heart, was totally taken with the format of the book. I found it easy to read, fun and so different. Nice job"

R.L., CT

"...a highly valued travel companion... My wife is our navigator and copilot. Your publication will make her task of selecting a place to spend the night, or to grab a tasty lunch, a pleasure."
"I pick(ed) up a second copy... this evening for my brother. I am not about to let my copy leave my hands."

B.K., NJ